Women and the UN

This book provides a critical history of influential women in the United Nations and seeks to inspire empowerment with role models from bygone eras.

The women whose voices this book presents helped shape UN conventions, declarations, and policies with relevance to the international human rights of women throughout the world today. From the founding of the UN and the Latin American feminist movements that pushed for gender equality in the UN Charter, up until the Security Council Resolutions on the role of women in peace and conflict, the volume reflects on how women delegates from different parts of the world have negotiated and disagreed on human rights issues related to gender within the UN throughout time. In doing so it sheds new light on how these hidden historical narratives enrich theoretical studies in international relations and global agency today. In view of contemporary feminist and postmodern critiques of the origin of human rights, uncovering women's history of the United Nations from both Southern and Western perspectives allows us to consider questions of feminism and agency in international relations afresh.

With contributions from leading scholars and practitioners of law, diplomacy, history, and development studies, and brought together by a theoretical commentary by the Editors, *Women and the UN* will appeal to anyone whose research covers human rights, gender equality, international development, or the history of civil society.

Rebecca Adami is Associate Professor at the Department of Education, Stockholm University and Research Associate at the Centre for International Studies and Diplomacy, SOAS University of London (School of Oriental and African Studies). She specializes in critical human rights theory through counternarratives, and studies on intersectionality, cosmopolitanism and childism. Author of the book *Women and the Universal Declaration of Human Rights*. In 2018 a UN photo exhibit "Women Who Shaped the Universal Declaration" based on the book was exhibited at the United Nations in New York by Secretary General António Guterres and first Latin American female President of the General Assembly María Fernanda Espinosa Garcés, now available online.

Dan Plesch is Professor of Diplomacy and Strategy at SOAS University of London. His books include, The Beauty Queen's Guide to World Peace, Human Rights After Hitler and America, Hitler and the UN. His research focuses on strategies for preventing global war and emphasises a restorative archeology of knowledge of the effective peacemaking work in the 1940s.

Routledge Explorations in Development Studies

This Development Studies series features innovative and original research at the regional and global scale. It promotes interdisciplinary scholarly works drawing on a wide spectrum of subject areas, in particular politics, health, economics, rural and urban studies, sociology, environment, anthropology, and conflict studies.

Topics of particular interest are globalization; emerging powers; children and youth; cities; education; media and communication; technology development; and climate change.

In terms of theory and method, rather than basing itself on any orthodoxy, the series draws broadly on the tool kit of the social sciences in general, emphasizing comparison, the analysis of the structure and processes, and the application of qualitative and quantitative methods.

Critical Reflections on Public Private Partnerships
Edited by Jasmine Gideon and Elaine Unterhalter

Political Participation and Democratic Capability in Authoritarian States
Lien Pham and Ance Kaleja

The Global Architecture of Multilateral Development Banks
A System of Debt or Development?
Adrian Robert Bazbauers and Susan Engel

Philanthropic Foundations in International Development
Rockefeller, Ford, and Gates
Patrick Kilby

Foreign Aid and Development in South Korea and Africa
A Comparative Analysis of Economic Growth
Kelechi A. Kalu and Jiyoung Kim

Women and the UN
A New History of Women's International Human Rights
Edited by Rebecca Adami and Dan Plesch

Youth Civic Engagement and Local Peacebuilding in the Middle East and North Africa
Prospects and Challenges for Community Development
Edited by Ibrahim Natil

For more information about this series, please visit: www.routledge.com/Routledge-Explorations-in-Development-Studies/book-series/REDS

Women and the UN

A New History of Women's International
Human Rights

**Edited by Rebecca Adami
and Dan Plesch**

Routledge
Taylor & Francis Group

LONDON AND NEW YORK

First published 2022
by Routledge
2 Park Square, Milton Park, Abingdon, Oxon OX14 4RN

and by Routledge
605 Third Avenue, New York, NY 10158

Routledge is an imprint of the Taylor & Francis Group, an informa business

British Library Cataloguing-in-Publication Data
A catalogue record for this book is available from the British Library

Library of Congress Cataloging-in-Publication Data
Names: Adami, Rebecca, editor. | Plesch, Daniel, editor.
Title: Women and the UN : a new history of women's international human rights / edited by Rebecca Adami and Dan Plesch.
Description: Milton Park, Abingdon, Oxon ; New York, NY : Routledge, 2021. | Includes bibliographical references and index.
Identifiers: LCCN 2021005991 (print) | LCCN 2021005992 (ebook)
Subjects: LCSH: Women's rights--History. | United Nations--History.
Classification: LCC HQ1236 .W6375 2021 (print) | LCC HQ1236 (ebook) | DDC 323.3/4--dc23
LC record available at https://lccn.loc.gov/2021005991
LC ebook record available at https://lccn.loc.gov/2021005992

ISBN: 978-0-367-47823-0 (hbk)
ISBN: 978-1-032-04938-0 (pbk)
ISBN: 978-1-003-03670-8 (ebk)

DOI: 10.4324/9781003036708

Typeset in Times
by SPi Global, India

This volume is dedicated to Peg Snyder (1929-2021),
founding director of the UN Development Fund for Women
(today's UN Women).

Contents

Contributors   ix
Introductory note: Learning journey for a feminist:
Making women visible, recognizing women's
achievements and demanding power to women   xiii
TORILD SKARD

Preface: Women of the UN: Shifting the Narrative by
Revealing Forgotten Voices   xviii
FATIMA SATOR AND ELISE DIETRICHSON

1 **From women's rights to human rights: The influence of**
   Pan-American feminism on the United Nations   1
   KATHERINE M. MARINO

2 **The Latin American women: How they shaped**
   the UN Charter and why Southern agency is forgotten   17
   ELISE DIETRICHSON AND FATIMA SATOR

3 **Excavating hidden histories: Indian women in**
   the early history of the United Nations   39
   KHUSHI SINGH RATHORE

4 **International welfare feminism:**
   CSW navigating cold war tensions 1949   55
   REBECCA ADAMI

5 **Universal human rights for women:**
   UN engagement with traditional abuses, 1948–1965   71
   ROLAND BURKE

6   **Feminism, global inequality and the 1975 Mexico city conference**   88
    AOIFE O'DONOGHUE AND ADAM ROWE

7   **Who wrote CEDAW?**   104
    ELLEN CHESLER

8   **Were children's rights ever a feminist project?**   125
    LINDE LINDKVIST

9   **Creating UNSCR 1325: Women who served
    as initiators, drafters, and strategists**   139
    CORNELIA WEISS

10 **Commentary: The restorative archeology of knowledge
    about the role of women in the history of the
    UN – Theoretical implications for international relations**   161
    REBECCA ADAMI, DAN PLESCH AND AMITAV ACHARYA

    Index   169

Contributors

Amitav Acharya, Distinguished Professor, American University
Amitav Acharya is the UNESCO Chair in Transnational Challenges and Governance and Distinguished Professor at the School of International Service, American University, Washington, DC. He is the first non-Western scholar to be elected (for 2014-15) as the President of the International Studies Association (ISA), the largest and most influential global network in international studies. Previously he was a Professor at York University, Toronto, and the Chair in Global Governance at the University of Bristol.

Roland Burke, Senior Lecturer, History LaTrobe University
Roland Burke is author of *Decolonization and the Evolution of International Human Rights* (University of Pennsylvania Press). His current research examines the shifting accents of the human rights system, and the constellation of activists, across the 1980s and 1990s (*London Review of International Law*). Roland has examined memorialization processes around the Universal Declaration of Human Rights (*Journal of Global History, International History Review, History & Memory*), and the gulf between legal lexicons of rights diplomacy, and the power of emotion in rights and humanitarian campaigns (*Diplomacy & Statecraft*, and *Human Rights Quarterly*).

Ellen Chesler
Ellen Chesler is currently Senior Fellow at the Roosevelt Institute and Research Fellow at the Ralph Bunche Institute on International Affairs, City University of New York. She is author of *Woman of Valor: Margaret Sanger and the Birth Control Movement in America*, 1992, 2007; co-editor of *Where Human Rights Begin: Health, Sexuality and Women in the New Millennium*, 2005; co-editor of *Women and Girls Rising: Progress and resistance around the world*, 2015, and has written numerous essays, articles, and blogs. She worked for many years in philanthropy, most recently at the Open Society Foundations, and early in her career, in government. She holds a B.A. from Vassar College and a Ph.D. in history from Columbia University

Elise Dietrichson
Elise Dietrichson, is a Research Associate at the Centre for International Studies and Diplomacy, SOAS University of London (School of Oriental and African Studies), where she also completed her MA in International Studies and Diplomacy. Together with Fatima Sator, Elise has engaged in advocacy engagements, including TEDxPlaceDesNations 2018 and the HBO Documentary "Bertha Lutz" (2021). The chapter contributions to this book is written in the personal capacity of Elise Dietrichson and views expressed here are her personal views. These chapters should not be seen as a UN Women publication, research presented here was conducted prior to taking up her role as staff in UN Women April 2019.

Linde Lindkvist, Senior Lecturer at Stockholm University College
Linde Lindkvist is associate dean and senior lecturer in human rights studies at the University College Stockholm. He specializes in questions of human rights history, the right to religious freedom, and children's rights. He is the author of Religious Freedom and the Universal Declaration of Human Rights (2017). His current project concerns the origins of the UN Convention on the Rights of the Child.

Katherine M. Marino, Associate Professor, UCL
Katherine M. Marino is an associate professor of history at the University of California, Los Angeles. She is the author of *Feminism for the Americas: The Making of an International Human Rights Movement* (University of North Carolina Press, 2019) which received the Latin American Studies Association Luciano Tomassini Latin American International Relations Book Award and co-won the International Federation for Research on Women's History Ida Blom-Karen Offen Prize in Transnational Women's and Gender History, among other awards.

Aoife O'Donoghue, Professor of International Law and Global Governance, Durham University
Professor O'Donoghue's research centres on public international law, constitutionalism, and feminism with a particular interest in global governance and legal theory. Aoife's work examines constitutionalism, tyranny, utopias and feminism, legal theory and international legal history. Aoife works on theories of tyranny and tyrannicide with her monograph Tyranny and the Global Legal Order coming out in 2021. Aoife also works with collaborators on developing ideas around feminist utopias, manifestos, and global constitutionalism. With Máiréad Enright of Birmingham Law School and Julie McCandless of Kent Law School, Aoife is Co-Director of the Northern/Irish Feminist Judgments Project and is embarking on a new project with Máiréad Enright and Liam Thornton and Catherine O'Rourke to revisit Northern/Ireland constitutional texts.

Adam Rowe, Phd Candidate, Durham University
Adam is a Ph.D. candidate, part-time tutor, and a deputy-director of the Global Law and Justice research group, at Durham University. He obtained his LL.B at Newcastle University in 2016 and his LL.M (also from Newcastle University)

in 2017. Adam's research interests concern the theory of international law. He has written about the political nature of state sovereignty and its influence upon the legal nature of certain norms, and the problems of causation implicit within contemporary legal theories. His current research explores issues of international legal ontology. Specifically, it seeks to apply a Nietzschian framework to the concept of state sovereignty. Adam has published two pieces on the dilemma of causation in International Legal Theory in *Edinburgh Student Law Review* and on Soft Sovereignty and the Legality of Humanitarian Intervention in the *North East Law Review*.

Fatima Sator

Fatima Sator is a Research Associate at the Centre for International Studies and Diplomacy, SOAS University of London (School of Oriental and African Studies). She holds a BA in economics and a Master's in International Relations and Diplomacy, from SOAS and in journalism from University of Neuchâtel. Together with Elise Dietrichson, Fatima spoke at TEDxPlaceDesNations in 2018. Their work features in the HBO Documentary "Bertha Lutz" (2021) and in several mainstream media, including the New York Times, Washington Post, Associated Press, Daily Mail, and *Le Monde Diplomatique*.

Khushi Singh Rathore

Khushi Singh Rathore is a PhD candidate in International Politics at the Centre for International Politics, Organization and Disarmament (CIPOD), Jawaharlal Nehru University, India. Her doctoral research project is on the role of Vijaya Lakshmi Pandit, India's first woman diplomat, in the history of Indian foreign policy making. Her research interests are Gender and Diplomacy, Feminist IR, Diplomatic History & International History. Currently, she is also serving as a member-at large of the Feminist Theory and Gender Studies Executive Committee, *International Studies Association*; and is the Graduate Student Representative for the Gendering IR Working Group, *British International Studies Association*.

Torild Skard

Torild Skard is a Senior Researcher in the social sciences with special interest in women and children. A pioneer in the women's movement nationally and internationally, she was formerly a MP and became the first woman President in the Norwegian Parliament in 1973. She was then the first Director for the Status of Women in UNESCO, Paris, in 1984, the first woman Director General in the Norwegian Ministry of Foreign Affairs, in 1986, and the first woman Regional Director of UNICEF in West and Central Africa, in 1994. She has written numerous books, studies and articles, her most recent being "Women of Power – Half a century of female presidents and prime ministers worldwide".

Cornelia Weiss

Cornelia Weiss is a retired military colonel, having served in the Americas, Europe, and the Pacific. Honors received include the US Air Force Keenan Award for making the most notable contribution to the development of international law and medals from Colombia for human rights and military justice accomplishments. She holds a BA in Women's Studies from the University of Utah, an MA from Chile's national academy of strategy and policy studies, and a JD from Vanderbilt University School of Law. She first learned about UNSCR 1325 when attending the Inter-American Defense College in 2010-2011. Knowing that history is often used as an excuse to exclude women, she excavates forgotten history about women, peace, and power.

Introductory note

Learning journey for a feminist: Making women visible, recognizing women's achievements, and demanding power to women

Torild Skard

Senior Researcher, former President in the Norwegian Parliament and Director-General of the Ministry of Foreign Affairs, Director of UNESCO and UNICEF

When the United Nations was created after the Second World War, my mother Åse Gruda Skard was there as the only woman in the Norwegian delegation. The 50 states that met in San Francisco in 1945 to create a new international organization to maintain peace and security, all had male-dominated governments. Only 3 per cent of the representatives at the conference were women.

My mother was appointed, because there was an active Norwegian women's rights group in London, where the government of Norway was established in exile during the War. The group demanded that at least one woman should be included in the country's delegation to San Francisco in addition to the 15-20 men, and my mother was exceptionally well suited for the task. First and foremost, she lived in the US at the time and spoke English fluently. My family fled to America when the Germans attacked Norway in 1940, and we settled down in Washington DC with my mother's father, who was Norwegian Minister of Foreign Affairs from 1935 to 1941. In addition, my mother had distinguished herself by being the first woman in our country with a university degree in psychology. She was active in labor and women's rights groups and well connected with international organizations.

Feminist in male-dominated society

Mother's participation in San Francisco was very exciting, and she had to tell me about her experiences numerous times. I was particularly interested in the role of the women at the conference. Soon after the war my family went back to Norway, and I grew up in a society with widespread male domination. Practically all the important positions were held by men, and in school, I was harassed by boys in my class, because girls were not supposed to be clever and active.

Fortunately, my family supported me. Mother held a high position as associate professor at Oslo University, worked as a child psychologist, was active in the women's movement worldwide and participated in UNESCO's activities. At times, she took me and my sister with her and brought prominent women home. I got acquainted with people from different cultures and was inspired by women who asserted themselves in other parts of the world. In addition, my grandmother, who stayed in Norway during the war, became an important role model. Born in 1871 she was the first farmer's daughter in her part of the country who got higher education, and she fought for women's suffrage, which we got in 1913. At home she took time and explained our patriarchal traditions for me and how women struggled to change them. She said I must not give up, but qualify myself the best I could, never forget that I was a woman and claim my rights.

I joined the women's movement as soon as I could, and worked hard to qualify myself professionally in education, psychology, and sociology. I engaged in various organizational and political activities, learned French in addition to English and got involved in international cooperation. And during my working life I obtained high posts no woman had occupied earlier: as President in the Norwegian Parliament, Director for the status of women in UNESCO Headquarters, Director General for the Multilateral Department in the Norwegian Ministry of Foreign Affairs and Regional Director for UNICEF in West-and Central Africa.

Putting women's rights into practice was tougher than I expected. Both nationally and internationally progress was slow. Though all UN member states supported the equal rights for women and men in principle and confirmed this numerous times, men in power did not often walk the talk. Instead they used many different techniques to maintain their privileges. They denied that women were discriminated and concealed existing inequalities. Accounts of women's activities and achievements in the past as well as the present were extremely rare.

San Francisco 1945

The UN was our most important organization for international collaboration. Practically all the nation states were members. But there were few studies of how the system worked in practice, and gender perspectives were lacking, though the purpose of the UN was not only to maintain peace and security, but also promote human rights and fundamental freedoms.

After I retired from UNICEF, I started a research project in 2005 about women and the UN to gain better knowledge about how women's rights were promoted worldwide. I went back to the establishment of the UN in 1945, and my immersion in the San Francisco proceedings revealed that the official UN accounts were both incomplete and partly incorrect. They only had a brief statement about women's rights, noting that faith in the equal rights of men and women was inscribed in the Charter by four women delegates. This made me wonder. My mother told me that the women at the conference disagreed among themselves. I had to delve into the original documents.

There were not many women delegates and advisers at the United Nations Conference on International Organization (UNCIO). Only independent Allied states were included, and as the world war was not over, many states were unable to attend. Totally, there were 22 delegations from the Americas, 14 from Europe, 10 from Asia, and 4 from Africa. Only 12 of them had female members with functions other than ordinary secretarial assistance.

In addition to the official government delegations a great number of nongovernmental organizations were invited to send "consultants" to San Francisco to broaden the scope of the discussions and ensure a solid basis for the negotiations. These also included women's organizations, and gatherings were held during the conference so NGO representatives could meet with UNCIO participants.

Already on the first day of the conference my mother tried to get in touch with the other women delegates and advisers to unite them in a group. Nobody else seemed to think of this, so she invited them for tea with other prominent women, both journalists and others, as well as the Norwegian female secretaries. She established contact with 13 colleagues: 7 from Latin-America, 1 from Canada, 1 from the US, 2 from England, 1 from Australia, and 1 from China.

These women were far from "standardized," mother noted. The delegates from Latin-America were clearly the most active promoting women's rights. They were headed by Dr Bertha Lutz, a prominent scientist from Brazil, and both the President and Vice-President of the Inter-American Commission of Women, Minerva Bernardino from the Dominican Republic and Amalia C. de Castillo Ledón from Mexico attended the conference. They felt that they represented the women of the world and wanted to include references to "women" as often as possible in the Charter.

The female representatives from USA, Canada, and England had a different view. According to their opinion, they participated in the negotiations as "delegates", not women, and saw no reason to differentiate between women and men. Virginia Gildersleeve from the US, who was Dean of a women's college, even suggested deleting the word "women" from the phrase "the equal rights of men and women" in the preamble of the Charter, because she thought it was unnecessary and implied a segregation of women. But this was opposed by a man from the South: the head of the South African delegation, Field Marshall Smuts, who drafted the text, and the amendment was rejected.

The Chinese delegate Dr. Wu Yi-fang and my mother had what she described as an "intermediate" position. They supported women's rights, but not when they thought it was unreasonable. All in all, it was a very small group of women from Norway and China in addition to those from Latin-America who collaborated to make sure the founding documents of the new organization were satisfactory from women's point of view. But mother felt that they achieved more than they could hope for. And at the end of the conference, Bertha Lutz proposed on behalf of all the women that a special commission should be established to follow-up the status of women in different countries, and this was supported by a clear majority.

Getting UN history right

During my research, it was fascinating to find out how a nearly completely male-dominated assembly could proclaim the equal rights of men and women. The active lobbying of women's NGOs, the differing views of various female delegates, and the supportive action of leading male politicians were particularly worth noting. I published my study on "Getting Our History Right: How Were the Equal Rights of Women and Men Included in the Charter of the United Nations?"[1] and the events in such an international context led to further interest in the status of women in different countries, particularly in Latin-America, to understand the basis for the action of different representatives.

Inspired by my work, students and scholars at the School of Oriental and African Studies (SOAS) at the University of London followed-up with further research. This resulted in several scholarly publications, media coverage, and conferences at the UN in Geneva and New York.[2] In 2017, the International Studies Association (ISA) and SOAS established a Bertha Lutz Prize to honor her, and in 2019, the UN changed the official account of the negotiations in San Francisco in 1945, noting that two of the female representatives, Bertha Lutz from Brazil and Minerva Bernardino from Dominican Republic, proposed to add "women" to the Charter.[3]

Slow progress

Though women's rights were confirmed in the UN Charter in 1945 and again in the Universal Declaration of Human Rights in 1948 and a special UN commission dealt with the status of women, there was not much progress before the second feminist wave in the 1960-70s. Then approaches changed, and the International Women's Year in 1975 became a turning point in women's history with the world conference in Mexico, the UN Decade for Women and the Convention to eliminate discrimination against women. The large global women's conferences were driving forces in promotion of the status of women. The conferences were special not only because they focused on women's issues, but because they were dominated by women, and prominent female advocates for women's rights played key roles. In addition to the government meetings, simultaneous global meetings of women's NGOs were also held.

The world conferences were followed up by numerous initiatives of different kinds. But the recommendations required a rethinking and reorganization of work in the whole UN system. The commitment of both women and men, special knowledge, and competence as well as resources were required. And the follow-up encountered bureaucratic problems and resistance to change as well as to gender equality. Seven decades after the UN was established, only one of four top leaders in the system were women. But with enough political will and resources, progress could be made. In 2017, the newly elected UN Secretary-General António Guterres appointed 50/50 women and men in the UN Senior Management Group for the first time.

Being an intergovernmental organization, the development of the UN is to a great extent determined by the national leaders and representatives of member states. But the progress of women in politics has generally been very slow. By the end of 2020, women only constituted a minority of 1/4 of the members of parliament and 1/5 of the cabinet ministers worldwide, and only 27 women were appointed or elected presidents and prime ministers in independent states during the year. The number of prominent women varied from one continent to the other, as did their way to the top and the role they played in power. They generally inspired other women as role models, but they did not always promote women's interests. Resistance increased if they tried to be "feminist" in one way or the other. So, some avoided this completely. But most of the women top leaders in practice did something positive for women, to a greater or lesser degree, though it might not always be easy to discover.

Strengthening the position of women is more complex than is often realized. It requires sustained long-term action by various actors to change established traditions, social structures, and power hierarchies. A basic condition is the existence of active women working together, making women visible, approving their rights, recognizing their achievements, and demanding power to women. Though they are partly hidden in the history of the UN and member states, they have made a difference and are the reason for the progress that has been made despite the difficulties.

Notes

1 Torild Skard, "Getting Our History Right: How Were the Equal Rights of Women and Men Included in Charter of the United Nations?," *Forum for Development Studies* June, no. 1 (2008): 37–60.
2 See preface and chapter 2 in this anthology.
3 Carolyn Hannan, Aina liyambo, and Christine Brautigam, "A Short History of the Commission on the Status of Women" (New York: UN Women Headquarters, 2019).

Bibliography

Hannan, Carolyn, Aina liyambo, and Christine Brautigam. "*A Short History of the Commission on the Status of Women.*" New York: UN Women Headquarters, 2019.
Skard, Torild. "Getting Our History Right: How Were the Equal Rights of Women and Men Included in Charter of the United Nations?" *Forum for Development Studies* June, no. 1 (2008): 37–60.

Preface

Women of the UN: Shifting the Narrative by Revealing Forgotten Voices

Fatima Sator and Elise Dietrichson

It is difficult to claim the origins of ideas that have become universal, such as the idea of gender equality. Still, as ideas become accepted by a majority and become a norm, the particular life story of the individuals that first championed them, cannot be reduced to a singular collective narrative and should as such not be forgotten because "these unique life stories carry with them the potential to change."[1]

I—Fatima Sator—grew up wishing I was a man. Because to me, men were free. In Algeria, men went and came as they pleased, they saw and dated whoever they wanted, they had careers, they seemed important, their opinion mattered, they were entitled double heritage to that of their sisters, their words weighed twice as much as those of women's. I found it unfair that I would live with the restrictions of a woman. Then I realized, that this was not only my reality, but a shared one.

At 12 years old, I decided that I would contribute in creating equal rights and opportunities for men and women. I didn't know it then, because I didn't know that there was a word for it, but I had identified myself as a "feminist." I had an aunt who always declared herself as a feminist but she didn't have a good reputation, was portrayed as "angry" and I was told that if I acted like her "I would never find a husband." In my view, not "finding" a husband turned into a kind of compliment. When I insistently raised my voice on issues related to feminism, with the support of my parents, this wasn't well received by my friends and family. People told my parents that this was the result of a "Western" education. That I was choosing the wrong battle, that feminism wasn't "our" fight—that we had other issues to deal with, such as unemployment or economic insecurity. According to them, I should leave feminism to "the others"—referring to anyone beyond the Mediterranean Sea, not "us."

I was confused, were they right? Was I the only one feeling that feminists described the very injustice I was confronted with as a woman in Algeria? It took me several years before I could find the answer to this question. Years later, I studied a Masters in International Relations at the School of Oriental and African Studies (SOAS), in London and that is when I met Elise who was also studying women in diplomacy. Elise Dietrichson was from Norway and we engaged in hours of conversations around feminism, the United Nations and diplomacy. For me, she represented "the others" I had been told about.

Elise grew up being taught in school how the first UN Secretary General, Trygve Lie, was Norwegian. She visited with excitement the Security Council Chamber at the UN headquarters in New York furnished and decorated by Norway, understanding that Norway was an important supporter of the UN and its creation. She felt proud in knowing that Norway had a progressive female Prime Minister, Gro Harlem Brundtland, when she grew up. Women in leadership was typical Norwegian. I, on the other hand, had not been taught my Algerian roots and how they were connected to gender equality, nor to the values of the UN. The story of the Latin American women changed that for me: I saw brown women, not dictated by Western imperialists, speaking out for women's rights. There they were; my role models. What this all really shows, is that the way history is presented to us is crucial for what values we take ownership of. For Elise growing up, UN values were national values, and these values were her values.

Rediscovering women in history

Elise and I wanted to find the women champions in history in our quest for understanding where values in the UN come from. We asked ourselves "Who do we have to thank for having gender equality inscribed in international organizations today?" We looked to the UN Charter because it said to represent us all and called "the constitution of the world" when created more than 75 years ago.

It was when turning to the meeting protocols and minutes from 1945 in UN archives that we discovered Bertha Lutz, the delegate from Brazil, one of only four women to sign the UN Charter. Her memoirs with her machine and handwritten letters located in a paper box[2] right in the heart of London—just a short walk away from SOAS at the London School of Economics (LSE) Women's Library—was almost untraceable in history books. The archive of the UN and Lutz' notes were so fascinating! According to minutes from UNCIO and the journal of this Brazilian scientist, frog-lover and diplomat; Bertha Lutz was specifically sent by the Brazilian Government in 1945 as a Brazilian delegate to the UNICIO in San Francisco to advocate for the inclusion of gender equality in the UN Charter.[3] The Latin American delegates were termed "extremist"-feminists, wanting the word "women" everywhere. Seventy-five years later, we were amazed by the fight these women delegates put up for us to include women in the founding documents of the UN.[4] It was then we understood that this story was still important to unearth as it has significant implications for the future.

Explicit recognition of women's rights is not something we should take for granted. Remember that only 30 delegations out of 50 present at the San Francisco Conference[5] in 1945, represented countries where women had the right to vote. Remember that women diplomats were denied access to diplomatic posts in most countries. Remember that women were not mentioned in the original draft of the UN Charter.[6]

Taking for granted our rights, and how we got there was something Bertha Lutz critiqued already in 1945. She felt that women from countries where women's rights were more advanced had forgotten how these rights were given to them. In a tea meeting, the British women advisors told Bertha Lutz that as she was in the Kings Private council, this meant women in Britain had arrived at gender equality. Bertha Lutz was clear saying that, no, this meant only that a few individuals had been invited but they were not representative of all women. One of our favorite quotes by Bertha Lutz, that really made an impression on us, was when she said after meeting the American and British delegates that: "It is a strange psychological paradox that often those who are emancipated by the efforts of others are loath to acknowledge the source of their freedom."[7]

Why are women in history forgotten?

This volume is a collection of texts representing the journey of women before us, women like Bertha Lutz who grew up with ideas and questions that had global reach. These texts speak of the realization that individual ideas only have value if they are recognized by the collective, owned and validated by the majority.

Just as women's rights weren't included by accident in the founding documents of the UN, neither will we claim that forgetting the contribution of women diplomats like Berta Lutz is accidental. And neither will her legacy, nor the broader legacy of the other women acknowledged in this volume be recognized if we continue to overlook it.

During most of the press conferences or interviews on the topic of the Latin American women who fought for gender equality in the UN Charter, a question was often asked "how come this story has been forgotten?"

For us forgetting the contribution of Bertha Lutz is an example of how the main narrative of history, the domination of accepted beliefs, references of what is considered normal by dominant actors in society, sometimes overshadow other significant events.[8] The idea that women will always defend women's rights, and that women always speak with one voice, and that the most progressive feminist usually are from Western countries overshadows the diversity of women's voices, their agency, and actions.

The presentation of history is political. It is skewed and shaped in favor of the most powerful, often men, which means that some of what we believe to be truths should be challenged. "If good ideas are found outside the West, they are often dismissed as imitation."[9] This is explained by some as why the contributions of the global South have generally been ignored and neglected.

Neglecting the historical contributions of Bertha Lutz is also a part of a wider tendency neglecting the contributions of *women* in international relations, and particularly, neglecting the fundamental Southern contributions to global norms, such as human rights and gender equality. The lack of recognition of the Latin American women, not only meant silencing their voices but silencing all women's voices, particularly those from the South, the conscious identity as "non-Western" was something Bertha Lutz used to describe herself and the other Latin American women representing the "South."[10] These women will only be rediscovered if there is a deliberate will to see the gaps left in history books, redefine what is important and put new value to sources earlier dismissed. Women wrote letters, journals, they told anecdotes, men who were actors in the public sphere wrote their biographies, men wrote our history books. Women were only heard as a group, while a man could make his mark as a state leader with a notable name.

Advocating for change

Before finding a research article authored by Torild Skard[11] on the role of Women and the UN Charter, neither Elise nor I had ever heard about Bertha Lutz before. This was mind-blowing. How could it be that we had never heard of Bertha Lutz? We who were international relations' students, feminists, and former interns at the UN, with a particular interest in women in diplomacy. We started asking our former colleagues at the UN, professors in IR, diplomats who worked on women's rights "have you heard of the Brazilian Diplomat who got women's rights into the UN Charter, Bertha Lutz?" We asked professors at SOAS, Brazilian and UN diplomats, UN staff, ambassadors, we looked at the UN Women website, the UN Blue Book series[12] but there was not a single mention of her and her legacy.

Our journey began with the inspiration from Torild Skard's work and with Dan Plesch' visionary research on UN History for the Future, we started the project "Women and the UN Charter."[13] Through our advocacy work we came in contact with researchers who shared this passionate interest for the hidden women in the history of the UN but this was a counter-narrative not recognized widely.

For Elise and I, this remarkable period in history, where it was the Latin American women who bore the torch for women's rights at the birth of the UN, truly ignited a fire in us. For us, as feminists, this piece of forgotten history was not only important in itself to understand how we got the first reference to equal rights of men and women. The call for recognition of Bertha Lutz and the Southern contributions to gender equality was a fascinating game changer to prove the global ownership, not only to the UN as such, but specifically to the idea of equality between men and women. We wanted to use Bertha Lutz impact on history to create awareness of the true global ownership on feminism. And we insisted on the "global" part of it.

Discovering that women from non-western countries fought for gender equality in the United Nations 75 years ago, despite opposition from delegates from the United Kingdom and the United States, countered the idea of those who had told us that "gender equality was a concept from the "North." The Latin American women were forerunners in advocating women's rights, and with getting this history right, to paraphrase Torild, we could re-claim gender equality as Algerian, as Southern, as well as it had been claimed Norwegian. This is essential because *how* we present history has important and very political implications, ownership being the most obvious.

Our first meeting with Brazilian students showed why the recognition of women like Bertha Lutz was important. When we visited the University of Rio de Janeiro,[14] in a class of 20 students from a variety of backgrounds, we started a debate on feminism and women in history but without calling it "feminism." The students were very vocal, claiming that men and women should have equal rights. Then we asked: "who would call themselves feminist?" Silence. Nobody spoke, nobody raised their hands. Only one student said, condescendingly, "feminism - this is something for European people." We felt we needed to change this dominant narrative. Bertha Lutz was Brazilian, feminism was a Brazilian "thing" and the challenge was how they did not know about her.

This volume and our story show why academic research should and must focus on impact outside its academic journals and conferences. That historic research changes our understanding of where ideas come from when we learn *who* the drafters of key UN documents were. They were not just Western, white and male, they were women, and women from the South.

It was because of the existence of an "impact fund" at SOAS that Elise and I got funding as newly graduates to continue speaking about the research. In September 2016, we went to the heart of the UN in New York to present our findings to the UN, academics and journalists. Edith Lederer, Associated Press (AP) United Nations Correspondent was fascinated by what we had to share. She immediately organized a press conference at the United Nations Correspondent Association (UNCA).[15] Our findings were making the headlines of the most prominent newspapers: the Washington Post, the New York Times, AP, AFP, etc. Immediately, we were on TV and on the radio. Bertha Lutz was not unknown anymore. Writing women out of history is problematic because it contributes to women's subordination, as their agency is not taken seriously.

Two years later, in 2018, we were back to New York, to give a conference at the UN Trusteeship Council's room together with Rebecca Adami[16] from Stockholm University who spoke to the over 200 women delegates in the room of the legacy of female UN delegates from India and Pakistan amongst others to the wording of the Universal Declaration of Human Rights. This event was highly symbolic for us. First, it is known to be the first ever-organized conference honoring Southern legacy to Human Rights. And it was happening in a room full of history.[17] It was organized by Southern UN delegations in collaboration with SOAS and Stockholm University with Ambassadors from India, Pakistan, Ghana, Mexico, Colombia and South Africa presiding. Witnessing the woman Ambassador of India and the Ambassador of Pakistan honoring their own Human Rights legacy to the UN, through a feminist lens, was a strong message. At the end of the conference, our panel, made up of mostly women, left the room to let the next panel start, where mostly men entered the room to discuss disarmament.

In 2019, a new road sign in front the United Nations Office building in Geneva read "Bertha Lutz" which for us felt as a concrete proof that our advocacy work to recognize Bertha Lutz in the history of the UN had inspired others. Then, we saw more and more evidence that the legacy of Bertha Lutz was recognized. HBO produced a documentary on "Bertha Lutz,"[18] Elise and I gave TEDx talk at the UN in Geneva,[19] a painting by Leca Araujo honoring Bertha Lutz is on the walls of the UN in Geneva, Bertha Lutz is in children's books, International Studies Association (ISA) established the Bertha Lutz prize to promote research on women in diplomacy.[20] Bertha Lutz's legacy is now included into UN Junior Professional Officer training and updated in UN trainings and many large and small actions that proved that this story mattered today. The many women included in the chapters of this anthology deserve the same recognition for their role in international diplomacy and for inscribing women's rights in the history of main human rights documents of the UN.

Today, I would say to the 12-year-old me: no, they aren't right: feminism is not a "Western thing" or "the others" thing, it is as much Algerian, it is as much "us", as it is "theirs." There is no such thing as "us" and "them" when it comes to feminism, because it is a global, universal idea, that already 75 years ago was promoted by women from Latin America to South Asia and Africa. Women's human rights that should be owned by all who believe in a fair, equal, sustainable, and prosperous world for all.

This research changed our vision of the world. We hope that the historical narratives in this book will shift and deconstruct the existing narrative. If more women and men define themselves "feminists" we will continue the legacy of the women represented in this book.

Stories are powerful. In digging into history, we are looking for women who have been forgotten. This book reveals some of these forgotten names. We hope that it will inspire, empower, and light a fire in people who will read it.

Notes

1 Rebecca Adami, "On Subalternity and Representation: Female and Post Colonial Subjects Claiming Universal Human Rights in 1948," *Journal of Research on Women and Gender* 6 (2015): 64.

2 Lutz, B., 1945. Letter from Bertha Lutz to Corbett Ashby, New Rochelle (New York) in *Papers of Margery Irene Corbett Ashby*, 6B/106/7/MCA/C3. Women's Library, London;
Lutz, B., n.d.. Reminiscences of the San Francisco Conference that Founded the United Nations, Bertha Lutz Brazilian Plenipotentiary Delegate in *Papers of Margery Irene Corbett Ashby,* 6B/106/7/MCA/C2. Women's Library, London.

3 Lutz, n.d, 2.

4 The full Volumes from the United Nations Conference on International Organization is available at the British Library. United Nations, 1945. Special reference is made to the following volumes that address gender equality: *Documents of the United Nations Conference on International Organisation (UNCIO), Volume III, Dumbarton Oaks.* London and New York, United Nations Information Organization.;
United Nations, 1945. *Documents of the United Nations Conference on International Organisation (UNCIO), Volume VI Commission I, General Provisions.* London and New York, United Nations Information Organization.
United Nations, 1945. *Documents of the United Nations Conference on International Organisation (UNCIO), Volume VII Commission I, General Provisions.* London and New York, United Nations Information Organization.
United Nations, 1945. *Documents of the United Nations Conference on International Organisation (UNCIO), Volume X Commission II, General Assembly.* London and New York, United Nations Information Organization.

5 Ibid.

6 Steinstra, D., 1994. *Women's Movements and International Organizations.* New York: St. Martin's Press. 77.

7 Lutz, B., n.d.. Reminiscences of the San Francisco Conference that Founded the United Nations, Bertha Lutz Brazilian Plenipotentiary Delegate in *Papers of Margery Irene Corbett Ashby,* 6B/106/7/MCA/C2. Women's Library, London. pp. 5.

8 Adami, R. (2015). Counter Narratives as Political Contestations: Universality, Particularity and Uniqueness, *The Equal Rights Review,* No. 15, pp. 13–24.

9 'Amitav, Acharya. 2016. "Idea-shift': how ideas from the rest are reshaping global order." Third World Quarterly 37(7):1156–1170. doi: 10.1080/01436597.2016.1154433.

10 Dubois, Ellen and Derby, Lauren. 2009. "The strange case of Minerva Bernardino: Pan American and United Nations women's right activist" *Women's Studies International Forum: 43–50.*

11 Skard, T., 2008. Getting Our History Right: How Were the Equal Rights of Women and Men Included in the Charter of the United Nations?. *Forum for Development Studies*, June, Issue 1: 37–60.

12 Torild Skard, 2008, notes the lack of reference to Bertha Lutz in: The Blue Book Series - The United Nations and The Advancement of Women 1945–1996; The Short History of the Commission on the Status of Women, at the UN Women website; the CD-ROM, Women Go Global; and The United Nations Intellectual History Project Series.

13 Listed on SOAS website under "UN and the UN Charter" project's page. https://www.soas.ac.uk/cisd/research/women-in-diplomacy/women-in-the-un-charter/ Accessed 15 January 2021

14 *Universidade Federal do Rio de Janeiro 2017.*

15 Associated Press article from 2016: https://unca.com/unca-briefing-on-women-and-the-u-n-charter-a-southern-legacy/
SABC news clip "Research challenges role played by women in the UN Charter" https://www.youtube.com/watch?v=5sRWi8pz4R8

16 Adami, R. (2019). *Women and the Universal Declaration of Human Rights*. Routledge.

17 The Trusteeship mandate could be seen as serving both a continuation and critique of colonialism.

18 HBO "Bertha Lutz" https://www.producingpartners.com/berthalutz

19 Fatima Sator and Elise Dietrichson, TEDx "These Women Changes Your Life", TEDx presentation, presented December, 6, 2018 at Palais Des Nations, Geneva, Switzerland. Recording available: https://www.ted.com/talks/elise_luhr_dietrichson_fatima_sator_these_women_changed_your_life

20 ISA Bertha Lutz prize https://www.isanet.org/Programs/Awards/DPLST-Bertha-Lutz-Prize

Bibliography

Adami, Rebecca "On Subalternity and Representation: Female and Post Colonial Subjects Claiming Universal Human Rights in 1948," *Journal of Research on Women and Gender* 6 (2015): 64.

Adami, Rebecca (2015). "Counter Narratives as Political Contestations: Universality, Particularity and Uniqueness", *The Equal Rights Review*, 15, 13–24.

Acharya, Amitav. 2016. "Idea-shift': How Ideas from the Rest are Reshaping Global Order." *Third World Quarterly* 37(7):1156–1170. doi: 10.1080/01436597.2016.1154433.

Skard, T., 2008. Getting Our History Right: How Were the Equal Rights of Women and Men Included in the Charter of the United Nations?. *Forum for Development Studies*, June, Issue 1: 37–60.

Listed on SOAS website under "UN and the UN Charter" project's page. https://www.soas.ac.uk/cisd/research/women-in-diplomacy/women-in-the-un-charter/ Accessed January 15 2021.

Dubois, Ellen and Derby, Lauren. 2009. "The strange case of Minerva Bernardino: Pan American and United Nations Women's right activist" *Women's Studies International Forum*: 43–50.

Lutz, B., n.d.. *Reminiscences of the San Francisco Conference that Founded the United Nations, Bertha Lutz Brazilian Plenipotentiary Delegate* in *Papers of Margery Irene Corbett Ashby, 6B/106/7/MCA/C2*. London: Women's Library. p. 5.

Sator, Fatima and Dietrichson, Elise, TEDx "These Women Changes Your Life", TEDx presentation, presented December, 6, 2018 at Palais Des Nations, Geneva, Switzerland. Recording available: https://www.ted.com/talks/elise_luhr_dietrichson_fatima_sator_these_women_changed_your_life

Steinstra, D., 1994. *Women's Movements and International Organizations*. New York: St. Martin's Press.

Street, J., n.d. In *Papers of Margery Irene Corbett Ashby, in 6B/106/7/MCA/C3*. London: Women's Library.

United Nations, 1945. *Documents of the United Nations Conference on International Organisation (UNCIO), Volume III, Dumbarton Oaks*. London and New York: United Nations Information Organization.

United Nations, 1945. *Documents of the United Nations Conference on International Organisation (UNCIO), Volume VI Commission I, General Provisions*. London and New York: United Nations Information Organization.

United Nations, 1945. *Documents of the United Nations Conference on International Organisation (UNCIO), Volume VII Commission I, General Provisions*. London and New York: United Nations Information Organization.

United Nations, 1945. *Documents of the United Nations Conference on International Organisation (UNCIO), Volume X Commission II, General Assembly*. London and New York: United Nations Information Organization.

1 From women's rights to human rights

The influence of Pan-American feminism on the United Nations

Katherine M. Marino

Introduction

Soon after arriving at the United Nations Conference on International Organization (UNCIO) in San Francisco in 1945, Brazilian delegate Bertha Lutz wrote to
friends back home that "Latin American women" would be "the most helpful"
in advancing women's rights.[1] Although women from the U.S. and British delegations refused to promote women's rights in the Charter, the female representatives from the Dominican Republic, Mexico, and Uruguay were self-identified
feministas. For the past two decades, they had all been engaged, with Lutz, in a
Pan-American feminist movement that elevated women's rights to international
treaties. At the UNCIO, these Latin American women collaborated to achieve
a number of key goals: incorporating women's rights into the purposes of the
organization, asserting women's rights as human rights, and ensuring the representation of women in all UN bodies. Bertha Lutz also proposed what became
the UN's Commission on the Status of Women. They accomplished these objectives against the objections of U.S. and British women who believed women's
rights goals too divisive or not important enough to include in the Charter, and of
the U.S. and British delegations that opposed human rights demands more generally. Without the work of these Latin American women, the UN Charter would
likely have contained little to nothing about women's rights.

Their pivotal work represented a culmination of over two decades of Pan-
American feminism, a transnational movement that fuelled grassroots exchange
and inter-American diplomacy for women's rights. This essay explores how
and why this movement drove their UNCIO contributions. Since the mid-1920s
Pan-American feminism provided a critical forum for Latin American feminist
innovations in international law, starting with an international treaty they devised
to advance women's rights, the Equal Rights Treaty. The movement also pio-
neered the first inter-governmental organization in the world to promote women's
rights, the Inter-American Commission of Women, or *Comisión Interamericana
de Mujeres* (CIM) that for the next two decades, launched the Equal Rights Treaty
into Pan American Union and other international meetings. In the 1930s and 40s
inter-American feminists connected their international defense of women's rights
to what was becoming known as international "human rights," based on multiple
and inter-connected grassroots struggles against fascism, racism, and imperialist

DOI: 10.4324/9781003036708-1

capitalism. Latin American feminists' insistence that after the Second World War the United Nations must enshrine rights for all regardless of race, sex, or class, and must include women in the peace deliberations compelled both the presence and actions the Latin American feminists in San Francisco. Their work also shaped Latin American feminists' contributions to the 1948 UN's Universal Declaration of Human Rights. Pan-American feminism not only pushed women's rights into human rights but also helped formulate international human rights.

Pan-American feminism's equal rights treaty

Pan-American feminism emerged from a broader moment of Pan-Americanism ushered in by the First World War that shattered the notion of European cultural superiority and opened a space for the "new" Latin American nations on the world stage. The U.S. government sought stronger ties with Latin American countries to protect its economic and political interests following the 1914 completion of the Panama Canal and resulting dramatic rise in trade with Latin America. This period saw a flourishing of new Pan-American organizations, congresses, publications, and institutions around culture, hygiene and medicine, child welfare, and feminism. Changes in transportation, communications, and industrialization sped these collaborations. Though a thin cover for U.S. imperialism, this new Pan-Americanism represented an opportunity that many Latin-American diplomats and lawyers seized to advance a new inter-American system promoting multilateralism as well as their own countries' political sovereignty and cultural advancement.[2]

The Great War and the 1917 Mexican Revolution raised the stakes around national self-determination and women's rights in the Americas. Having organized in regional gatherings since the 1910 International Women's Congress in Buenos Aires, Latin American feminists found in new Pan-American collaborations with U.S. women ways to gain legitimacy for their demands for women's political, civil, social, and economic rights. After the First World War, when many European countries had passed women's suffrage legislation, a number of Latin American male political leaders equated women's rights with cultural and civilizational advancement. At the 1923 Pan-American conference in Santiago, Chile, male diplomats from Guatemala and Chile made such arguments when they passed resolutions to charge the Pan American Union with the study and promotion of women's rights, responding as well to feminist pressure.[3]

Although Latin American feminists looked with high expectations to the Pan-American realm, they were often dismayed by interactions with U.S. counterparts who deemed themselves and their approaches to feminism as superior. Anglo-American women took on the role of "teachers" at the 1922 Pan American Women's Congress in Baltimore, Maryland, organized by U.S. feminist Carrie Chapman Catt and the U.S. League of Women Voters. Latin American activists were even more disturbed by Catt's subsequent disparaging comments about Latin American women lagging "forty years behind" those in the U.S. and her doubts that they were ready for the franchise.[4] Catt and other U.S. feminist leaders also routinely failed to grasp that political and civil equality under the law did not represent the highest priority of many Latin American feminists who also sought women's economic and social welfare and anti-imperialism. At a time when U.S. military interventions in Central America and the Caribbean, and economic imperialism in the region were cresting, U.S. feminists' failure to condemn imperialism repelled many Latin American counterparts. While utilizing Pan-American institutions, Latin American feminists also mobilized their own south-south collaborations that almost always emphasized anti-imperialism and a regional feminism led by Latin American women.

These dynamics helped spur the innovation that would be critical over the next two decades: an international law to promote women's rights. Two anti-imperialist feminists, Clara González (Panama), and Ofelia Domínguez Navarro (Cuba), both young lawyers leading radical wings of the women's movements in their countries, announced the idea of an international law to promote women's rights at the 1926 Congreso Inter-Americano de Mujeres in Panama City. They were inspired by efforts of international feminists after the Great War who were utilizing the League of Nations to make new global demands.[5] But more direct inspiration came from Latin American multi-lateral institution building and advances in international law: the Latin American Scientific congresses that since the nineteenth century sought uniform codes in the Americas in hygiene, health, and sanitation; the work of diplomats at the 1923 Pan-American conference in Santiago who had elevated women's rights to a Pan-American concern; and inter-American feminist ferment they saw growing. González and Domínguez sought social and economic justice for working women, rights of "illegitimate" children and their often single mothers, as well as Latin American sovereignty in the face of U.S. empire.[6] They proposed a "uniform and extensive action in the effort to obtain…women's political rights," and "the removal from the legislation of all the American countries judicial discrimination against women."[7] They believed that such an international treaty committing all signatory nations to women's equal political and civil rights would exert a moral weight in the hemisphere and provide the linchpin to other rights.

The passage of González and Domínguez's 1926 resolution in Panama helped galvanize new feminist activism before the 1928 Pan-American Congress of diplomats in Havana, Cuba. Feminists hoped the Havana conference would make meaningful the 1923 women's rights resolutions from Santiago. They were even more optimistic when the 1927 International Commission of Jurists in Rio de Janeiro, Brazil, proposed uniform legislation to be submitted to the Havana conference including removal of all legal incapacities of women throughout the continent.[8]

When Cuban feminists learned that no Latin American country was sending female representatives to the Havana conference, several reached out to the U.S. National Woman's Party (NWP), a group they knew for its radicalism in the U.S. suffrage movement, to enlist their help. NWP president Alice Paul was immediately interested. Paul had just obtained a degree in international law which she believed could help advance the NWP's key goal: the Equal Rights Amendment (ERA) that she had co-authored. The ERA, a bold constitutional guarantee that "men and women shall have equal rights throughout the United States and every place subject to its jurisdiction," had languished in Congress since its introduction in 1923.

Grasping that an international treaty could pressure domestic change, Paul dispatched to the January, 1928 Havana conference a number of uninvited NWP members, including its chair of international affairs, the outspoken and canny organizer Doris Stevens, NWP. When Stevens wrote to Paul from Havana about Cuban feminist and male Latin American diplomatic enthusiasm for an international women's rights treaty, Paul sent her a draft text of what became the Equal Rights Treaty. Drawing on the ERA's language, it was also similar to the resolution that González and Domínguez had asserted in Panama in 1926. It read: "The Contracting States agree that upon the ratification of this Treaty, men and women shall have equal rights throughout the territory subject to their respective jurisdictions."[9] Stevens inserted this treaty into the debates in Havana, where Cuban feminists supported it with alacrity and enlisted the U.S. women to march with them in the streets. Although Stevens faced stiff resistance to the treaty from U.S. State Department representatives, she found the "Latin American men… captivated by our treaty idea."[10]

The delight of Latin American diplomats stemmed in large part from their own efforts to transform international law in the Americas at that moment. The conference took place amidst U.S. military assaults in Nicaragua, deemed by many as the greatest international crime of the day, and Latin American statesmen had come to the conference to defend Latin American sovereignty. They saw the Equal Rights Treaty as part of their fight against the U.S. government, especially when NWP representatives made known that they did not side with the U.S. State Department. Latin American support paved the way for Cuban and U.S. feminists to speak before the plenary, marking the first time any woman had spoken before a Pan-American conference. In her speech, Doris Stevens underscored that women's equality and sovereignty mutually reinforced Latin American goals for national equality and sovereignty. Although the Equal Rights Treaty was not enshrined in the conference in Havana in 1928, this activism resulted in the creation of the Inter-American Commission of Women (CIM), the first intergovernmental organization promoting women's rights in the world.[11]

CIM's remit was to take up the charge laid out in the 1923 Santiago conference—to study, report on, and help advance women's rights in the region. It would include one representative from each of the 21 Western Hemisphere republics that participated in the Pan American Union. Because of her leadership in Havana, Pan American Union representatives elected Stevens as its chair. Selecting several other countries by lottery, Pan American Union leaders also enlisted Panamanian feminist Clara González (author of the 1926 international women's rights resolution) as one of its first commissioners. González's appointment to CIM, whose offices were located in the Pan American Union headquarters in Washington, D.C., coincided with her studies in New York while on a fellowship from the Panamanian government. González devoted tremendous time and legal expertise to creating a large compendium of women's status under law in the hemisphere. This volume, the first of its size and international scope, would be essential to CIM's strategy at international conferences.[12] Over the next decade, when CIM launched the Equal Rights Treaty into Pan American Union, League of Nations, and International Labor Organization (ILO) conferences, they insisted the treaty was necessary to removing the many documented legal incapacities women faced.

Their work crested at the 1933 Seventh International Conference of American States in Montevideo, Uruguay, where four countries (Cuba, Ecuador, Paraguay, and Uruguay) signed the Equal Rights Treaty. The conference also unanimously passed CIM's Equal Nationality Treaty, a treaty requiring all signatory nations to grant independent nationality rights to married women. Many women in the U.S. and other parts of the world forfeited their nationality rights when they married. After Montevideo, even the United States, so opposed to treaty ratification that impeded states' rights, ratified the Equal Nationality Treaty in 1934 and, thanks to feminist pressure, passed a legislative act granting married women equal nationality rights.[13] Other countries in the Americas also passed women's nationality rights laws upon ratifying the Equal Nationality Treaty.[14]

One person who noted the importance of such treaties was Brazilian feminist Bertha Lutz who served as a technical advisor to her country's delegation at the Montevideo conference. Lutz had engaged in Pan-American feminism since she was a delegate to the 1922 Baltimore Pan American Women's Conference. Before CIM existed, she had formulated an idea for an equal nationality treaty. Anticipating arguments for universal human rights treaties, she wrote, "I see not advantage in putting the unjust tradition over the fairness to all citizens, regardless of sex or marital status, nor putting the sovereignty of nations over the rights of people."[15] After the 1933 consolidation of Hitler's power in Germany and 1937 rise of Getulio Vargas's Estado Novo, Lutz had even more reason to oppose national sovereignty in favor of supranational rights of people. Over the next decade, Lutz and other Pan-American feminists increasingly looked to the inter-American realm as a guarantor of rights and shield against dictatorships.

Popular front Pan-American Feminism: From equal rights to human rights

In the mid-to-late 1930s, CIM's international women's rights work grew in import and urgency following the Great Depression and rise of right-wing authoritarian regimes throughout Europe and the Americas that threatened women's rights. Throughout the Americas and world, "popular fronts" emerged uniting communists, socialists, workers, intellectuals, and feminists. Pan-American feminism entered a new stage, what I have called Popular-Front Pan-American Feminism. This inter-American movement upheld equal rights for women at the same time that it promoted working women's economic and social welfare and anti-fascism.

Between the mid-1930s and mid-1940s, Latin American and Caribbean countries saw a mushrooming of explicitly anti-fascist groups that demanded women's rights alongside a range of other causes: Puerto Rican nationalism, nationalization of Mexican oil, an inter-American workers' movement, freedom of Aprista political prisoners in Peru, the Republican cause in the Spanish Civil War, and rights for indigenous and African-descended people. These popular-front feminist groups were connected to each other and included robust national organizations like the Movimiento pro la Emancipación de la Mujer Chilena (MEMCh) in Chile and the Frente Único Pro Derechos de la Mujer (FUPDM) in Mexico. Both founded in 1935, these were mass organizations including several hundred thousand women.[16]

Popular-Front feminist groups saw CIM's Equal Rights Treaty as a useful tool in their anti-fascist fight. It gained the endorsement of socialist feminists around the world. The 1934 World Committee of Women against War and Fascism in Paris praised the treaty as a force against fascism, and the following year, Russian feminist and diplomat Alexandra Kollontai hailed it as "the first step in international action with regard to equality of the sexes."[17] In 1937, Latin American statesmen pushed the treaty into the League of Nations General Assembly.[18] These official measures as well as feminist grassroots mobilizations around the treaty helped block "fascist" legislation, such as a law that would have reduced women's minimum wages in Chile and one that would have made married women's legal status that of minors in Argentina.[19] At the regional ILO conferences in 1936 in Chile and 1939 in Cuba, popular-front feminists drew on the treaty to demand state-sponsored maternity leave and child care, including for rural and domestic workers.[20]

Because of the connections forged by the Popular Front between women's rights and the rights of racial and religious minorities, by the late 1930s, anti-fascist feminists utilized the term "human rights" to describe a broad array of rights "without distinction of sex nor of race, of fortune, of class, of beliefs."[21] African-descended Latin American feminists were central to this articulation of what was becoming known in these years as international "derechos humanos." Drawing on legacies of Pan-Africanism, and on the vitality of Black communist thought and activism, Black domestic workers in Uruguay, Brazil, Cuba, Panama, and elsewhere demanded that anti-racism be a fundamental part of the popular front feminist struggle. Afro-Cuban women articulated the concept of "triple aggression" against Black women that the popular front and feminism both must confront.[22]

These influences were felt in the 1938 Pan-American conference in Lima, where Mexican popular-front feminist and FUPDM leader Esperanza Balmaceda promoted a resolution for women's rights that encompassed maternity legislation, and also worked in support of the Cuban and Mexican delegations that ushered in new resolutions for "derechos humanos."[23] Because of their work, the Lima Declaration pronounced "respect for the rights of all nations and of all individuals regardless of race or religion."[24] Popular-front feminism's force was evident in this developing language of human rights that grew even stronger during the Second World War.

Towards the United Nations: Women's rights and human rights

During the war, popular-front Latin American feminists kept their demands for an inter-connected set of "human rights" that included "women's rights" at the forefront of the fight against Nazi-fascism. They paid close attention to the January,

1942 Pan-American conference in Rio de Janeiro that upheld the Declaration of the United Nations and committed Latin America to Allied war aims. This Declaration reaffirmed the connections between individual and international security enshrined in Franklin D. Roosevelt's Atlantic Charter and Four Freedoms—freedom of speech, freedom of worship, freedom from want, and freedom from fear. These four freedoms, and especially the social rights implied in "freedom from want," became central to growing articulations of "human rights" throughout the Americas and the world. Recognizing the pivotal role that women were playing to work for the Allied cause, inter-American feminists hoped that women's and human rights would be enshrined in new global order to emerge after the war.[25]

Latin American popular-front feminists and diplomats were thus disappointed by the 1944 Bretton Woods and Dumbarton Oaks conferences that charted postwar plans for the United Nations. Both conferences presaged a global order dominated by the United States, Great Britain, China, and the Soviet Union, overlooking decades of Pan-American multi-lateral institution-setting. The Dumbarton Oaks agreements also gave cursory mention to "human rights" and neglected women's rights entirely. Popular-front feminists pushed CIM representatives to bring these concerns to the February, 1945 Inter-American Conference on Problems of War and Peace, at Chapultepec Castle in Mexico City.[26]

At this Chapultepec conference where Latin American delegates aired grievances with the Dumbarton Oaks resolutions, Minerva Bernardino from the Dominican Republic, and Amalia de Castillo Ledón from Mexico, now CIM president and vice president, conveyed popular-front feminist demands. Bernardino and Castillo Ledón were not popular-front feminists. They were liberal feminists who emphasized legal equality, social and economic rights for working women, and cooperation with their nation states, which in Bernardino's case was the Trujillo dictatorship.[27] Castillo Ledón, appointed as the new Mexican CIM commissioner in the government of Manuel Ávila Camacho, represented what historian Gabriela Cano has called "state feminism."[28]

Nevertheless, both women shared some women's rights goals with popular front feminists, and the latter viewed them as allies on whom to apply pressure. One list of demands addressed to Castillo Ledón before Chapultepec urged her to promote resolutions for international women's political, civil, social, and economic rights; a "Charter for Women and Children" that specifically recognized the social function of maternity; measures against imperialism, racism, fascism; and a resolution for all Allied countries to include female delegates in their delegations that would chart the postwar peace.[29]

Although Bernardino (Dominican Republic) and Castillo Ledón (Mexico) did not incorporate all of these goals, they did insist upon women's civil and political rights as well as social and economic rights, a Women's and Children's Charter that stipulated maternity legislation, and anti-racism.[30] Emphasizing women's work during the Second World War, they anticipated the "chaotic avalanche of unemployment" for women that would follow the war and urged proactive study of and measures to address this problem.[31] They underscored that anti-racism was central to their women's rights agenda, emphasizing that specific attention must be paid to the social, economic, and political rights of "Latin American women, black women, and women of different indigenous races." Drawing on the language of many Latin American diplomats at that conference, they asserted that "rights of all nations" were inter-dependent with women's and human rights.[32] Their resolutions particularly resonated with those of Cuban and Mexican Delegations that defined human rights as "social and economic rights" for both individuals and nations, and for "equality in sovereignty of the States and of the individual liberty [of all peoples] without religious or racial prejudices."[33] As one U.S. State Department bulletin noted, commitments to individual rights under international law "were more positively defined" at Chapultepec "than at previous inter-American meetings" that had over the "past half-century" been "leading toward the establishment of the ideal of social justice as a cardinal objective of international relations." It explained how women's rights resolutions represented the most meaningful manifestation of individual rights and social justice under international law.[34]

Also important, at Chapultepec, Bernardino and Castillo de Ledón inserted a resolution insisting that Latin American countries must send women in their delegations to the conference that would form the United Nations several months later in San Francisco.[35] Latin American governments responded to this resolution, sending a number of women, including Castillo Ledón and Bernardino themselves. Their Chapultepec resolutions primed them for their activism in San Francisco in 1945.

Pan-American feminism shapes the United Nations

At the largest diplomatic conference in history in San Francisco that began in April, 1945, Latin American women represented a proportionately high number of the delegates and technical advisors. Of the only six female full delegates, three were from Latin America: Bertha Lutz from Brazil, Minerva Bernardino from the Dominican Republic; and Isabel Pinto de Vidal, a senator and longtime feminist from Uruguay. The other three were Virginia Gildersleeve, dean of Barnard College, from the U.S.; Wu Yi-Fang, president of Ginling College, a Christian women's college, from China; and Cora Casselman, a member of Parliament from Canada. Amalia de Castillo Ledón was an advisor to her country's delegation, as were Adela Formoso de Obregón Santacilia from Mexico, Isabel Sánchez de Urdaneta from Venezuela, and María Piedad Castillo de Leví from Ecuador. All of these Latin American women were Pan-American feminists.[36]

Bertha Lutz emerged as a key leader of this Latin American feminist bloc. Having played a central role in Pan-American feminism since attending the 1922 Pan-American Women's Congress in Baltimore and the 1933 Montevideo conference, Lutz had also promoted working women's rights globally at the 1944 ILO conference in Philadelphia. Before the Chapultepec conference, she convened a large gathering of feminists in Rio de Janeiro that supported Bernardino and Castillo Ledón's work there.[37]

However, like Bernardino and Castillo Ledón, Lutz was not a popular-front feminist. Appointed to the conference by Getulio Vargas, Lutz identified proudly as an "Anglo-Brazilian," due to her mother's British ancestry and her own connections with English-speaking feminists whom she had long deemed more capable than Spanish-speaking feminists. Her global feminism was inextricably bound up in her admiration for British and Anglo-American "liberalism" and in colonialist and white supremacist politics. Although a decided opponent of Nazi-fascism, she also decried the growth of Brazilian Communism in the mid 1940s, in part because of what she described as its "race and colour feeling."[38]

However, Lutz's work in San Francisco was only possible because of the mobilizations of popular-front Pan-American feminists who understood women's rights as connected with rights for all regardless of race, class, or religion. Before the conference, Popular-Front feminists applied pressure on Latin American women going to the conference, insisting they include in the UN Charter an array of "human rights" and explicit anti-fascist commitments.[39] Lutz realized, as the conference went on, that the most influential voices for women's and human rights were not the U.S. or Great Britain delegations, but rather representatives from a host of U.S. non-governmental organizations like the National Association for the Advancement of Colored People (NAACP), League of United Latin American Citizens (LULAC), and representatives from smaller countries—those from Latin America, as well as Ethiopia, India, and elsewhere. She collaborated with these representatives around human rights resolutions for all regardless of race, class, and sex.[40]

Lutz also quickly realized that Virginia Gildersleeve from the US and British advisers and MPs Ellen Wilkinson and Frances Hosbrugh objected to including women's rights in the Charter, believing women's rights were either too controversial or not important enough to include. She was more disappointed to learn that most "unofficial observers" from U.S. women's groups that gathered at the UN with "consultant" status as believed the same.[41] The internecine debates around U.S. feminism that had divided groups for over two decades around the Equal Rights Amendment that many feared would eliminate protective labor legislation, hamstrung U.S. women's ability to form a united front. A representative from the NWP, one of the few U.S. groups that supported feminist resolutions in San Francisco, noted the "surprising situation" that the most organized and avid supporters of women's "civil, political, and economic equality" were "from South America" and Australian feminist and adviser Jessie Street. Meanwhile, "women of the United States are so divided among themselves that there is no effective demand at this moment."[42]

This Latin American feminist vitality would not have been not surprising to anyone paying attention to Pan-American feminism for the past two decades. Drawing on decades of experience at Pan-American conferences, the Latin American women worked expeditiously to form a drafting committee with Street and several U.S. women. They drew up a number of proposed amendments to the Dumbarton Oaks agreement to insert women's and human rights into as many parts of the UN Charter as possible.[43]

Their plodding work in committee meetings and lobbying of delegates outside them also drew on skills they had honed in Pan-American conferences, and they enabled signal victories that Elise Luhr Dietrichson and Fatima Sator provide more detailed descriptions of in their chapter in this volume. On May 5, 1945,

Lutz, Bernardino, and Castillo Ledón were the first to propose that "Chapter 1, Purposes," of the UN Charter should include the following sentence: "To ensure respect for human rights and fundamental freedoms, without discrimination against race, sex, condition, or creed." Their proposal influenced the human rights wording incorporated into the Charter in Chapter 1 and in Chapter 9.[44] Later, based on the amendment Isabel Pinto Vidal drafted, and a long, uphill battle, they were responsible for the wording in Article 8 of the Charter, that the UN "shall place no restrictions on the eligibility of men and women to participate in any capacity and under conditions of equality in the principal and subsidiary organs."[45]

Finally, with the help of Indian delegate Arcot Ramaswami Mudaliar who chaired the commission tasked with organizing the Economic and Social Council (ECOSOC), Lutz proposed what became the UN's Commission on the Status of Women. Known as the "Brazilian Declaration," this resolution declared ECOSOC's promotion of "human rights and fundamental freedoms for all without distinction of sex," necessitated a commission devoted to women's rights. This Commission would "study and prepare reports on the political, civil, and economic status and opportunity of women with special reference to discrimination and limitations placed upon them on account of their sex."[46] In spite of U.S. opposition, a large majority, including many Latin American diplomats, supported it. The Mexican delegate commended Lutz on "a grand slam."[47]

A number of historical factors facilitated these achievements. Antifascist promotion of women's rights connected with a broader human rights agenda, and for many, women's contributions to the war effort justified their full citizenship. But another key factor was the alliance the "smaller and medium powers," including the Latin American bloc, forged around women's and human rights proposals, especially when delegations from "the Great Powers," such as the United States and Great Britain, worked against them. The U.S. delegation actively opposed human rights because it would be held accountable for Jim Crow and other human rights violations against African Americans in the South.[48] When the Great Powers held UN veto power, smaller and medium powers saw ECOSOC and other UN subsidiary organs that promoted human rights as one way to expand their power within the UN. Because of Latin American and other nations' lobbying, ECOSOC grew from a tangential to a "principal" organ of the UN.

By the end of the conference, UNCIO attendees and the press recognized how instrumental Latin American feminists were to the Charter's human rights and women's rights resolutions. In her report afterward to Brazil's foreign minister, Lutz urged him to ensure the UN Commission on the Status of Women was in fact created, and that its leadership be "in Latin American hands since our republics… are currently in the vanguard of feminist demands."[49]

In spite of Lutz's hopes, when the UN formally created the Commission on the Status of Women in June 1946, U.S. women led it. Some of these U.S. women had in fact opposed its creation as a separate body from the newly-created Commission on Human Rights. US women's continuing internal debates shaped the perceived viability of the UN and its Commission on the Status of Women in the aftermath of their creation, although Latin American feminists like Bernardino would also play critical roles in it.[50]

As Rebecca Adami has demonstrated, Latin American feminists and other women from the Global South continued to make their mark on the UN, and most notably on the UN Universal Declaration of Human Rights. Eleanor Roosevelt, chairing the committee, opposed explicit inclusion of women's rights, asserting that women were tacitly included "human rights" and "rights of man." Hansa Mehta (India), the other female delegate on the drafting committee, worked closely with Bernardino, Castillo Ledón, and Jessie Street, to revise the Declaration's statements of equality for "all men" to "all human beings" and to insert women's rights.[51] As a representative at the Lake Success meeting that finalized the Declaration, Amalia Castillo Ledón drew on these collaborations to advance a firmer assertion that men and women had "equal rights" under marriage in Article 16. She also expanded the definition of "family" in that Article so it was not defined by marriage only. The original statement, "The family deriving from marriage is the natural and fundamental group unit of society" (that went on to aver rights for men and women), excluded illegitimate children. The committee accepted Castillo Ledón's suggested alternative—"the family is the natural and fundamental group unit of society and shall be entitled to protection." Her work reflected long-standing Latin American feminist efforts for the rights of children born out of wedlock and those of working women seeking maternity support.[52] Castillo Ledón had just come from the 1948 Ninth Pan-American Conference in Bogota, Colombia, where seven Latin American countries ratified CIM's Inter-American Convention to Grant Political Rights to Women, and nine its Inter-American Convention to Grant Civil Rights to Women.

All of these international treaties were critical to women's rights throughout the region. In the 1940s, amidst a wave of democratization, Latin American countries passed women's suffrage: in Guatemala and Panama in 1945; Argentina and Venezuela in 1947; in Chile and Costa Rica in 1949; Haiti in 1950; Bolivia in 1952; Mexico in 1953; Honduras, Nicaragua, and Peru in 1955; Colombia in 1957; and Paraguay in 1961.[53] As historian Eugenia Rodríguez Sáenz explains, democratization was not primarily responsible for women's suffrage legislation which transformed "Latin American women's political and citizenship-based identities." Rather, "the international mobilization and organization of women and the international conventions on political rights of women," and resulting "growing international pressure," were critical for their approval.[54]

Pan-American feminist legacies in the UN and human rights

Soon after these conferences, the Cold War and militarization of the hemisphere diminished the viability of interlinked fights for women's and human rights. Sharp distinctions emerged between "civil and political rights" associated with capitalist democracy versus "social and economic rights," associated with communism. A number of CIM representatives in the 1950s and 60s who promoted women's civil and political rights supported dictatorships in the hemisphere. Government repression against leftists and outlawing of communist parties throughout the

Americas tremendously limited formerly broad and socialist-inspired feminist movements.

The Cold War also contributed to a broader historical amnesia around Pan-American feminism. Such amnesia was facilitated by accounts by U.S. figures like Virginia Gildersleeve who not only downplayed but erased critical work of Latin American feminists at the UN San Francisco conference in her memoir *Many a Good Crusade*. Her memoir pokes fun at Lutz and other Latin American feminists there, and even asserts fallaciously that Lutz's resolution for the Commission on the Status of Women was rejected. This misrepresentation infuriated Lutz who wrote in the margins of her copy of Gildersleeve's pages "much wrong and biased information" and "liar!"[55] Later in her life, Lutz believed that her work instilling women's and human rights into the UN Charter was one of the greatest accomplishments of her life, and bemoaned that she received "no credit for it."[56]

Decades later, Lutz did receive credit at the 1975 UN International Women's Year Conference in Mexico City that formally acknowledged her work in the founding charter. More broadly, the critical groundwork that she and other Pan-American feminists laid from the 1920s through the 40s would be taken up again by social movement mobilizations in the 1970s and 80s when Latin American feminists emerged en masse to oppose violence of dictatorships and U.S. imperialism, and to demand social justice and women's rights. Latin American groups were again critical to shaping the array of global feminisms that emerged from the 1975 UN Conference in Mexico City that launched the UN Decade of Women.[57] In regional gatherings called *Encuentros feministas Latinoamericanos y del Caribe*, Latin American feminists continued developing the idea of "women's rights as human rights" years before the concept became a cause célebre at the 1995 UN Beijing conference for women. The first encuentro in Bogotá, Colombia, in 1981 instituted an "International Day against Violence against Women" in honor of the Maribal sisters assassinated by the dictatorship of Rafael Trujillo in the Dominican Republic.[58] In 1988, CIM, which revived around this time after having suffered budget cuts, drafted the first international convention that defined gender-based violence as a violation of human rights in the Convention of Belém do Para. When the Organization of American States adopted it in 1994, it became the first legally binding international treaty on violence against women. CIM acknowledged this accomplishment as a direct legacy of its work dating back to the 1920s and 30s Equal Rights Treaty and of its human rights work with the 1945 UN Charter. In the years since, feminists' use of this treaty has intersected with grassroots mobilizations and drawn on the understandings of personal, private violence, and state violence as interconnected phenomenon.[59]

Feminists who draw on these inter-American and UN treaties recognize that they are not perfect instruments, nor do they represent the sum total of their demands. International agreements can become empty promises in pursuit of legitimacy, especially when countries refuse to hold themselves accountable to international human rights law. Yet, throughout Latin America, UN, Inter-American, and ILO treaties have shaped constitutions, legislative reform, policy development, and judicial decisions in ways that meaningfully affect people's lives.[60] Activists who defend a broad array of human rights deem them important levers in political climates that are otherwise unresponsive or hostile to their goals. The history of Pan-American feminism and its influence on the United Nations demonstrates the long history of these movements, and of the global power of Latin American feminism.

Notes

1 Bertha Lutz to "Amigas," April 30, 1945, Q0.ADM, EVE.CNF, TXT.27, VOL 6, Fundo Federação Braziliera pelo Progresso Femenino, Arquivo Nacional, Rio de Janeiro, Brazil (AFBPF).
2 Katherine M. Marino, *Feminism for the Americas: The Making of an International Human Rights Movement* (Chapel Hill: UNC Press, 2019), 18–21; Juan Pablo Scarfi, *The Hidden History of International Law in the Americas: Empire and Legal Networks* (New York: Oxford University Press, 2017); Greg Grandin, "The Liberal Traditions in the Americas: Rights, Sovereignty, and the Origins of Liberal Multilateralism," *American Historical Review* 117, no. 1 (February 2012): 68–91.
3 Marino, *Feminism for the Americas*, 35–36.
4 Ibid. 29–35.
5 Mona Siegel, *Peace on Our Terms: The Global Battle for Women's Rights after the First World War* (New York: Oxford University Press, 2020).
6 Marino, *Feminism for the Americas*, 42–52.
7 Clara González, "La mujer latin-americana ante la conquista de sus derechos políticos," *La Ley* 2, nos. 16–18 (1926), 892–93.
8 Ofelia Domínguez Navarro, *50 años de una vida* (Havana: Instituto Cubano del Libro, 1971), 80–81; Jane Norman Smith, "For the Equal Rights Treaty," *Equal Rights*, February 25, 1928, 21.
9 Marino, *Feminism for the Americas*, 53–58; Alice Paul to Doris Stevens and Jane Norman Smith, January 27, 1928, box 70, folder 15, Doris Stevens Papers (DSP).
10 Marino, *Feminism for the Americas*, 61. Paul recognized that using an international treaty for women's rights would be "revolutionary" in the U.S. where states' rights prevailed, but she found legal precedent in the 1920 Supreme Court case, *Missouri v. Holland* that protected migratory birds in the United States and Canada that concluded "a treaty applied against the interests of an individual state did not constitute a violation of the Tenth Amendment."
11 Marino, *Feminism for the Americas*, 64–66.
12 Ibid, 70.
13 Beatrice McKenzie, "The Power of International Positioning: The National Woman's Party, International Law, and Diplomacy, 1928–34," *Gender and History* 23, no. 1 (April 2011): 130–46.
14 Marino, *Feminism for the Americas*, 118.
15 Ibid., 99; Untitled notes from Lutz, "Tese a nacionalidade de mulher casada," Q0.ADM, CPA.NMC.3, AFBPF. Lutz fiercely opposed Doris Stevens's leadership of CIM in spite of her support for international women's rights treaties. See Marino, *Feminism for the Americas*, Chapter 3.
16 Jocelyn Olcott, *Revolutionary Women in Postrevolutionary Mexico* (Durham: Duke University Press, 2005), Karin Rosemblatt, *Gendered Compromises: Political Culture and the State in Chile, 1920–1950* (Chapel Hill: UNC Press, 2000.
17 Marino, *Feminism for the Americas*, 128.
18 "Letters from Geneva," and "Debate at League of Nations," *Equal Rights*, October 15, 1935, 1–3; "Move to Save Feminism from Dictatorships Pushed," *Washington Post*, September 26, 1935, 10.
19 Marino, *Feminism for the Americas*, 142, 147.
20 Ibid., 130–34, 184.

21 Paulina Luisi, Comité Femenina Paz y Libertad, Congreso Mundial de Mujeres, October 1939, caja 252, carpeta 5, Archivo Paulina Luisi, Archivo General de la Nación, Montevideo, Uruguay (PL-AGN).

22 Takkara Keosha Brunson, "Constructing Afro-Cuban Womanhood: Race, Gender, and Citizenship in Republican-Era Cuba, 1902–1958," (Ph.D. dissertation, University of Texas at Austin, 2011), 209–10; 221–23; Marino, *Feminism for the Americas*, 166–67.

23 Marino, *Feminism for the Americas*, 162–66.

24 *Diario de sesiones [de la] octava Conferencia Internacional Americana, Lima, diciembre de 1938* (Lima: Imp. Torres Aguirre, 1939), 562; "A Program for All," *New Orleans Times Picayune*, January 11, 1939.

25 Marino, *Feminism for the Americas*, 178–90.

26 Ibid., 190–92

27 Bernardino later wrote that achieving women's political rights under dictatorships in fact helped preserve those rights after such regimes fell (though she did not comment on human rights violations committed by the dictatorship itself). Minerva Bernardino, *Lucha, agonía y esperanza: trayectoria triunfal de mi vida* (Santo Domingo: República Dominicana, Editoria Corripio, 1993), xxviii. Ellen DuBois and Lauren Derby, "The Strange Case of Minerva Bernardino: Pan American and United Nations Women's Rights Activist," *Women's Studies International Forum* 32 (2003): 43–50.

28 Gabriela Cano, "El 'feminismo de estado' e Amalia de Castillo Ledón durante los gobiernos de Emilio Portes Gil y Lázaro Cárdenas." *Relaciones Estudios de Historia y Sociedad* 149 (Winter 2017): 39–69.

29 Untitled list of demands, 1945, caja 7, exp. 130, Archivo Particular Amalia González Caballero de Castillo Ledón, Secretaría de Relaciones Exteriores, Mexico City, Mexico (AGC-SRE).

30 Marino, *Feminism for the Americas*, 193–95.

31 *Diario de la Conferencia Interamericana sobre Problemas de la Guerra y de la Paz* (Mexico, 1945), 92.

32 Ibid., 84.

33 *Diario de la Conferencia Interamericana*, 43, 46.

34 Marion Parks, "That Women May Share," *Bulletin of the Department of State* Vol XIII, no. 317, July 22, 1945, p. 112.

35 *Diario de la Conferencia Interamericana*, 232.

36 Marino, *Feminism for the Americas*, 200.

37 Eileen Boris, *Making the Woman Worker: Precarious Labor and the Fight for Global Standards* (New York: Oxford University Press, 2019), Chapter 2; Marino, *Feminism for the Americas*, 202.

38 Lutz, "Reactions to Events in Brazil," March 1–15, 1945, QO.ADM, p. 1, AFBPF. For more on Lutz's racism, see Marino, *Feminism for the Americas*, 201, 205–206, 211.

39 Marino, *Feminism for the Americas*, 211.

40 Ibid., 207–211, 213–220.

41 Ibid., 202–206.

42 Edith Goode to Laura E.W. Kendall, May 23, 1945, series 7, reel 174, National Woman's Party Records microfilm.

43 Marino, *Feminism for the Americas*, 207.

44 Ibid. 209.

45 Ibid. 212–14.

46 Ibid. 216–220.

47 Quote from Ibid., 220.

48 Carol Anderson, *Eyes Off the Prize: The United Nations and the African American Struggle for Human Rights, 1944-1955* (Cambridge: Cambridge University Press, 2003), 8 and Chapter 1.

49 Quoted in Marino, *Feminism for the Americas*, 221.

50 Ibid.; see Rebecca Adami's essay in this collection.

51 Rebecca Adami, *Women and the Universal Declaration of Human Rights* (New York: Routledge, 2018).
52 Speech by Amalia Castillo Ledón, proceedings of 1948 Lake Success meeting, caja 9, esp. 150, Archivo Particular Amalia González Caballero de Castillo Ledón, Secretaría de Relaciones Exteriores, Mexico City, Mexico.
53 Francesca Miller, *Latin American Women and the Search for Social Justice* (Hanover: University Press of New England, 1991) 96.
54 Eugenia Rodríguez Sáenz, *La Guerra Fría y la transformación de las identidades políticas y ciudadanas de las mujeres en Guatemala, Costa Rica y Chile (1945-1973)* (San José: Universidad de Costa Rica, 2018), 3–4.
55 Lutz's notes on pages of Gildersleeve's book, Q0.PIT.96/100, AFBPF; Virginia Gildersleeve, *Many a Good Crusade* (New York: Macmillan, 1954).
56 Marino, *Feminism for the Americas*, 233.
57 Jocelyn Olcott, *International Women's Year: The Greatest Consciousness-Raising Event in History* (New York: Oxford University Press, 2017).
58 Nancy Saporta Sternbach, Marysa Navarro, Patricia Chuchryk, and Sonia E. Alvarez, "Feminisms in Latin America: From Bogotá to San Bernardo," *Signs* 17, no. 2 (1992): 393–434; Elizabeth S. Manley, "Revitalizing Feminism in the Dominican Republic," *NACLA Report*, November 17, 2018.
59 Mariana Prandini Assis, "Violence against Women as a Translocal Category in the Jursiprudence of the Inter-American Court of Human Rights," *Rev. Direito e Práx., Rio de Janeiro* 8, no. 2 (2017): 1507–1544.
60 Elisabeth Freidman, "Regionalizing Women's Human Rights in Latin America," *Politics & Gender* 5 (2009), 349–375.

Bibliography

Adami, Rebecca. *Women and the Universal Declaration of Human Rights*. New York: Routledge, 2018.
Anderson, Carol. *Eyes Off the Prize: The United Nations and the African American Struggle for Human Rights, 1944–1955*. Cambridge: Cambridge University Press, 2003.
Assis, Mariana Prandini. "Violence against Women as a Translocal Category in the Jursiprudence of the Inter-American Court of Human Rights." *Rev. Direito e Práx., Rio de Janeiro* 8, no. 2 (2017): 1507–1544.
Bernardino, Minerva. *Lucha, Agonía y Esperanza: Trayectoria Triunfal de mi vida*. Santo Domingo: República Dominicana, Editoria Corripio, 1993.
Boris, Eileen. *Making the Woman Worker: Precarious Labor and the Fight for Global Standards*. New York: Oxford University Press, 2019.
Brunson, Takkara Keosha. "Constructing Afro-Cuban Womanhood: Race, Gender, and Citizenship in Republican-Era Cuba, 1902-1958" Ph.D. diss., University of Texas at Austin, 2011.
Cano, Gabriela. "El 'feminismo de estado' e Amalia de Castillo Ledón durante los gobiernos de Emilio Portes Gil y Lázaro Cárdenas." *Relaciones Estudios de Historia y Sociedad* 149 (Winter 2017): 39–69.
Domínguez Navarro, Ofelia. *50 años de una vida*. Havana: Instituto Cubano del Libro, 1971.
Freidman, Elisabeth. "Regionalizing Women's Human Rights in Latin America." *Politics & Gender* 5 (2009), 349–375.
Gildersleeve, Virginia. *Many a Good Crusade*. New York: Macmillan, 1954.
González, Clara. "La mujer latin-americana ante la conquista de sus derechos políticos," *La Ley* 2, nos. 16–18 (1926), 865–893.

Grandin, Greg. "The Liberal Traditions in the Americas: Rights, Sovereignty, and the Origins of Liberal Multilateralism." *American Historical Review* 117, no. 1 (February 2012): 68–91.

Manley, Elizabeth S. "Revitalizing Feminism in the Dominican Republic," *NACLA Report*, November 17, 2018.

Marino, Katherine M. *Feminism for the Americas: The Making of an International Human Rights Movement*. Chapel Hill: UNC Press, 2019.

McKenzie, Beatrice. "The Power of International Positioning: The National Woman's Party, International Law, and Diplomacy, 1928–34." *Gender and History* 23, no. 1 (April 2011): 130–146.

Miller, Francesca. *Latin American Women and the Search for Social Justice*. Hanover: University Press of New England, 1991.

Olcott, Jocelyn. *International Women's Year: The Greatest Consciousness-Raising Event in History*. New York: Oxford University Press, 2017.

Olcott, Jocelyn. *Revolutionary Women in Postrevolutionary Mexico*. Durham: Duke University Press, 2005.

Rodríguez, Sáenz Eugenia. *La Guerra Fría y la transformación de las identidades políticas y ciudadanas de las mujeres en Guatemala, Costa Rica y Chile (1945–1973)*. San José: Universidad de Costa Rica, 2018.

Rosemblatt, Karin, *Gendered Compromises: Political Culture and the State in Chile, 1920–1950*. Chapel Hill: UNC Press, 2000.

Sternbach, Nancy Saporta, Marysa Navarro, Patricia Chuchryk, and Sonia E. Alvarez, "Feminisms in Latin America: From Bogotá to San Bernardo." *Signs* 17, no. 2 (1992): 393–434.

Scarfi, Juan Pablo. *The Hidden History of International Law in the Americas: Empire and Legal Networks*. New York: Oxford University Press, 2017.

Siegel, Mona. *Peace on Our Terms: The Global Battle for Women's Rights after the First World War*. New York: Oxford University Press, 2020.

2 The Latin American women

How they shaped the UN Charter and why Southern agency is forgotten

Elise Dietrichson and Fatima Sator

Introduction

The mantle is falling off the shoulders of the Anglo-Saxons and (...) we [the Latin American Women] shall have to do the next stage of battle for women. — Bertha Lutz, delegate for Brazil to the UNCIO.[1]

Considering the Latin American contributions to gender equality in the United Nations (UN) Charter, is the established narrative of global gender equality valid, if not, why not? To answer this question, this chapter will first present the origins of the hegemonic orthodoxy of global gender equality. This section will be followed by historical presentations from Latin America which will showcase how Southern contributions to gender equality have not been recognized. The core argument is based on recent consideration of empirical material that sheds light on the role of the Latin American contributions to women's rights in the UN Charter from 1945. The last section looks to third world feminism and ask why Latin American contributions to women's rights are unknown. Overall, it is claimed that the Latin American women delegates exercised decisive agency on behalf of women's rights and gender equality to the UN Charter in 1945 and that this fact challenges the modern narrative of global gender equality.

The Brazilian delegate Bertha Lutz was one of four women to sign the UN Charter in 1945 after the United Nations Conference on International Organization (UNCIO) in San Francisco, where the UN was established through the drafting of its Charter. Bertha Lutz, a leader of the feminists at the conference,[2] stated that women at the conference "were forerunners on women's contributions to world affairs."[3] And indeed they were. The most progressive women delegates represented the Latin American countries. Their vocal feminist claims were instrumental in establishing the first international agreement to declare women's rights as a part of fundamental human rights.[4] Western delegates, such as the American and British women delegates and advisors directly opposed several of the amendments that would ensure the rights of women in the Charter.[5] Despite the resistance, Latin American countries were able to get several amendments on gender equality included in the Charter and had "their share in international affairs."[6]

Advocates of a global view of international relations argue that contributions of delegates from the South in the founding of the UN have generally been neglected.[7] Few in the UN and diplomatic missions to the UN would today know

DOI: 10.4324/9781003036708-2

about the contributions to the UN Charter by Bertha Lutz and the other Latin American participants at the UNCIO.[8] In 2008, a reading of available literature showed that the UN's own accounts of UNCIO did not credit Latin American women delegates for the inclusion of women's rights in the Charter.[9]

After an introduction to the methodological choices made, this article will introduce the discussion of the global hegemonic orthodoxy. Amitav Acharya first coined the theory of Global International Relations (IR) to better understand the impact of the Western hegemonic orthodoxy in the presentation of history in IR.[10] This chapter will build on Global IR to understand the neglect of the Latin American contributions to women's rights in the UN Charter. Acharya notes that the tendency in IR to underplay the importance of Southern agency in the development of global norms is caused by the dominance of the global orthodoxy.[11]

The global hegemonic orthodoxy and its Eurocentric character often gives the impression that global norms originate in the West, leaving non-Western countries as passive recipients of these norms.[12] The origins of the UN are often subject to this narrative, a narrative used to delegitimize the global mandate of the UN. Consequently, the UN is argued by some as a product of a Western liberal order, a narrative that challenge multilateral cooperation today.[13] The notion of feminism is also subject to the same accusations of being a product of Western thought, an argument used by opponents of feminism to reject its relevance.[14] This chapter aims to challenge this latter claim by examining the Southern origins of global gender equality by presenting the contributions of Latin American women at the UNCIO in 1945, and the role of Bertha Lutz in particular.

The primary research used in this presentation entails a study of the minutes from the UNCIO and correspondence between feminists at the time of the UNCIO in 1945 and secondary research by Acharya that highlights how non-Western countries have been crucial in the development of the "foundational ideas of the postwar system."[15] The normative departure of this chapter is to make what has been invisible in history books, visible again, and consequently challenge the global hegemonic orthodoxy. The last section of this chapter discusses why the women delegates from Latin America and their contributions to gender equality have not been given proper recognition. Keeping in mind the story of Bertha Lutz at the UNCIO, the chapter will address to what extent third world feminism fails to contribute to the narrative of the South as a producer of global norms. It will be argued, with the research presented as a case study, that the narrative of third world feminism contributes to the silencing of Southern agency in the development of global norm. This latter claim is based on third world feminism's lack of engagement with Southern agency in the development of global norms. It is argued that the narrative of the marginalized South, in which third world feminist critique is based, does not account for positive agency played out by Southern actors. Thus, Southern actors, such as Bertha Lutz, who did indeed act to influence global norms, are not recognized by their own scholars.

This chapter presents findings from archival research and from the original minutes of the United Nations Conference on International Organization (UNCIO) in 1945, to complement existing research. The minutes from the UNCIO make up the legislative history of the UN and 22 volumes were published between 1945 and 1955.[16] A second set of primary sources are based on correspondence found in the archives belonging to Dame Margery Corbett Ashby who served as President of the International Alliance of Women, between 1923–1946. This was one of three major international women's movements at the time of the UNCIO.[17] The memoirs and biographies of the female delegates at the UNCIO: American delegate Virginia Gildersleeve, Australian advisor Jessie Street, Norwegian representative Åse Gruda Skard and the Brazilian delegate, Bertha Lutz, have also shaped the narrative of this article.

When presenting the "Southern" Latin American contributions to the UN Charter, it is often asked to what extent Latin America represents the South and the non-Western. Firstly, there is a general perception that Latin America is located in the global South[18] and represent third world countries.[19] This notion is also used by third world feminists.[20] Recent scholarly contributions on the UN and the global South refer to the 19 Latin American states that had delegations at the UNCIO as belonging to the South.[21] However, most importantly, women delegates from Latin America at the UNCIO themselves used these definitions stating they represented the "backward" South, and not the "advanced" West.[22]

Contesting the global hegemonic orthodoxy: Global IR and feminist critique

An explanation for the ignorance of Southern contributions to global norms can be found in how norms have been defined and researched.[23] Norms are generally created by several actors and based on a set of ideas. A widely accepted description of a norm is a "standard of appropriate behavior for actors with a given identity."[24] Norms are a sense of behavioral rules where what is seen as appropriate is judged by a community, and similarly, norm-breaking behavior is recognized as these actions are sanctioned or penalized by that community.[25]

It is argued that typically more powerful states introduce global norms, and that ideas diffuse from the North to the South.[26] Consequently, the West is generally seen as the producer of norms. An unfortunate consequence of this narrative has been a sidelining of non-Western contributions to norms, where ideas found outside the West are simply ignored or presented as imitation.[27] Further theorizing that build on this critique of norm diffusion is coined by Amitav Acharya`s Global IR which argues that traditional IR is rooted in Western history and as such represent a global hegemonic orthodoxy, where history outside the Western sphere is marginalized.[28] Consequently, there is no non-Western IR theory and Southern contributions to global norms are downplayed. There are two explanatory factors for the dominance of Western thought in IR theory: the conception of agency and norms.

This explains why Latin American contributions to human rights and feminism have wrongfully been described by historians as not *sui generis*.[29] Academic research recently began to challenge the privileging of Western norm-entrepreneurs and their contributions to universal norms over those of the global South. In this way norm creation is not limited only to materially powerful states.[30]

Agency is a central concept in the discussion on norms, as Acharya argues, a part of the explanation for the neglect of non-Western voices in IR has to do with the narrow definition of norm-makers. Western IR has tended to downplay the agency of non-Western countries because of a narrow definition of agency that rests on a standard of "civilization." Agency was viewed only in terms of states ability to wage war, to defend their sovereignty, dominate treaties, and enforce a certain behavior of states through compulsory power.[31] This definition of agency is a historical and self-serving formulation that has ignored advanced forms of non-Western agency. Acharya therefore calls for a broader understanding of agency and of who can be seen as a norm-entrepreneur. Agency should not be limited to material power, it should also include the ability to build norms and institutions based on ideational capabilities, such as resistance and normative action, that challenge the dominance of strong actors in establishing a global order. "Viewed as such, agency is not the prerogative of the strong. It can manifest as the weapon of the weak."[32] Overall, Global IR aims to open up a space where a broader range of agency can be recognized.

There are six main dimensions that describe a Global IR approach; it: (1) aims to recognize diversity, and is built on a pluralistic universalism, (2) draws its empirics from world history, (3) aims to add to existing IR, not replace it, (4) acknowledges regionalism as central in its study, (5) diverts from exceptionalism, and (6) recognizes multiple forms of agency.[33]

As a part of their project to counter the Western influence on IR theory, Acharya and Buzan (2007) put forward possible useful non-Western sources that to a large extent have been silenced. Historical patterns in the non-Western world should be acknowledged as a source of IR. The following sections will present the Latin American contributions to human rights in the UN Charter and feminism in the spirit of the dimensions of Global IR and, in this way, challenge Western IR.

The Latin American contribution to women's rights at the UNCIO

As explained by Marino in this volume, the transnational arena was an important steppingstone for Latin American feminists[34] and Latin American women are described as pioneers on women's rights.[35] This is often accredited to the fact that Latin American feminists were instrumental in establishing the first regional intergovernmental body, the Inter-American Commission of Women (CIM), tasked with specifically addressing issues related to the status of women. As such, the contributions of Latin American representatives at the UNCIO were a rather natural continuation of debates on human rights that had been present in the Latin American context for decades and not simply some imitation of Western ideas.

The United Nations Conference on International Organization (UNCIO) that resulted in the creation of the UN Charter, took place between 25 April 1945 and 26 June 1945 in San Francisco. Fifty countries were represented.[36] Only three percent of the representatives at the UNCIO were women, and at the time women only had voting rights in only 30 of the 50 countries present.[37] Despite the low representation of women, the UN Charter ended up being the first international agreement declaring women's rights as a part of international human rights. One of the key factors that would explain why human rights and women's rights in particular, was included in the UN Charter, was the presence of the Latin American delegation.

Women delegates at the UNCIO

Bertha Lutz (1894–1976) was described as a "complex figure of exceptional energy and talent"[38] and the "brains of the Brazilian woman's movement."[39] Lutz developed a remarkable career for a woman living in her time. She was a respected scientist and was the second woman in the history of Brazil to be appointed a public job.[40] Lutz was also the leading figure for the women's suffrage movement in Brazil[41] and established Brazil's first suffragist society, the *Federação Brasileira pelo Progresso Feminino* (FBPF), that worked towards women's right to vote, legislative protection for working women, and access to education.[42] The Brazilian Government was "proud of its brilliant young feminist"[43] as she became an experienced diplomat representing Brazil in a number of international conferences. Lutz was also elected to Parliament in 1934 where she successfully advocated for women's rights and social welfare in the drafting of Brazil's constitution.[44]

Minerva Bernardino (1907–1998) of the Dominican Republic was another prominent delegate from Latin America. Bernardino is described as a feminist diplomat and was said to have been "one of the most influential women at the United Nations."[45] Bernardino developed a flourishing international career and was president of the CIM during the UNCIO, and later chair of the Commission on the Status of Women (CSW) in 1954.[46] Senator Isabel P. de Vidal representing Uruguay, was the third official women delegate. Amelia C. de Castillo Ledón was vice chair of the CIM and participated as advisor for the Mexican delegation together with the founder of the women's university in Mexico, Adela Formoso de Obregón Santacilia. Venezuela had two female counsellors: Isabel Sánchez de Urdaneta, active in the Pan-American Union and Lucila L. de Pérez Diaz.[47] All together there were seven women in the Latin American delegations.

Weiss and Roy point out that 65 percent of the delegations to the UNCIO represented the global South, in which 19 independent Latin American countries made up the largest group of delegates.[48] The similar world view of many of these delegations meant that Latin American countries represented the most powerful voting block at the UNCIO.[49]

How women's rights were included in the UN charter

The four global powers, China, the UK, the US and the Soviet Union, met in 1944 in Dumbarton Oaks in the US where they agreed on a draft that served as the main text for discussion at the UNCIO. This first draft made no mention of women, and no women were present when it was drafted.[50]

This section will present the four different sections of the Charter where women's rights were discussed at the UNCIO: The Preamble, The working principles of the organization; the participation in the organs of the United Nations; and, the establishment of commissions under the Economic and Social Council.[51] These discussions on women's rights were initiated exclusively by female delegates at the conference.[52] The views of the female delegates and the contributions of Latin American delegates will be presented in the following sections. Overall, this material will contribute to the discussion on the South as a source of global norms.

The equal rights of men and women

The Preamble reaffirms the faith in human rights, and the equal rights of men and women.[53] The wording with the specific mentioning of women in the Preamble is seen as one of the first footholds of women's rights in the UN.[54] The mention of women is understood to have crucial importance as the UN, from its conception, then legitimized demands for equality between men and women.[55]

Lutz, Bernardino, Ledón, and Street are described as instrumental in the movement that demanded the specific mentioning of "equal rights of men and *women*"[56] (emphasis added). Bernardino was later given the credit for the specific mentioning of women in the Universal Declaration of Human Rights (UDHR) from 1948.[57] Field Marshall Jan Smuts from the South African delegation originally drafted the text mentioning women in which the Preamble was based. Smuts' draft was based on the Covenant of the League of Nations which Smuts had also drafted.[58]

In her memoirs, Virginia Gildersleeve describes how she removed the word 'women' from Smuts' draft in her own proposal for the Preamble. A decision she writes was based on a concern for better English[59] as she objected at the UNCIO that the resulting text was "complicated and difficult."[60] Adami notes how Gildersleeve seemed to lack a strategic vision compared to her Latin American counterparts in her understanding for the wording in the Charter, as could be determined by her rejection of any feminist coalition or lobby for women`s rights during the conference.[61] Gildersleeve is said to have received 65,500 letters during her time at the UNCIO, mainly from women advocating for their rights and the mentioning of women in the Charter.[62] It is therefore reasonable to believe, knowing the content of the letters she received, that she would be aware of the advocacy campaign for the specific mention of women. Lutz' agitation for the mentioning of women in the Charter was also supported by Jessie Street.[63]

Nondiscrimination based on sex

Chapter 1 in the UN Charter first mentions the promotion of human rights without distinction for race, sex, language, or religion. The inclusion of the word "sex" as part of this antidiscrimination phrase was another important point for the feminists at the UNCIO, this principle is repeated in four Articles in the Charter.[64]

As the first woman to address the constitutional assembly, Bertha Lutz was proud to announce that the inclusion of "sex" was an amendment suggested by Brazil, Uruguay, Mexico, and the Dominican Republic "at the request of the women on the delegations of these republics."[65] India also submitted a similar amendment.[66] The sponsoring powers and Gildersleeve fully supported this amendment presented by the Latin American states.[67]

However, according to the President of the International Alliance of Women, the British delegation was "typically not in favour of the addition of sex which it deemed unnecessary."[68] Moreover, it was only after Lutz held a "passionate plea for sex to be added,"[69] where her justification was based on the "magnificent war work done by women of the UK"[70] that the British delegation had "reluctantly accepted the compliment to agree to the word sex being added."[71] The war effort of women remained a central argument for the claim to women's rights at the UNCIO.[72] Jessie Street had also worked energetically for the inclusion of the wording and sent out letters before the UNCIO asking for support for amendments eliminating all discrimination based on sex.[73]

Article 8—Equal participation in the United Nations

Article 8 ensures that women can hold the same positions as men in the UN-system[74] Bertha Lutz spoke at the UNCIO stating that Article 8 is "a Latin American contribution to the constitution of the world."[75] In her visionary speech, Lutz continued to present the impact by women delegates in the drafting as an example of how "women at this conference are the forerunners on women's contributions to world affairs."[76] This was due to the women being considered as full-fledged citizens in their own countries.[77] Article 8 was written by the women delegates of Uruguay, Brazil, the Dominican Republic, and Mexico[78] and was presented by Vidal from Uruguay,[79] it was also supported by Australia. The Prime Minister and delegate of New Zealand continued the visionary notion of Lutz. He said that the women delegates:

> [D]eserve not only the congratulations but the thanks of the Conference and of democrats everywhere. It is owing to their efforts, and particularly to the efforts of the women delegates from Latin America, that this clause will find its way into the Charter.[80]

The passion expressed in Lutz' speech and the delegate from New Zealand might be a reaction to the hard fought battle as the Article "cause[d] a tremendous amount of discussion and debate related to gender."[81] The main opponents were the American and the British delegates[82] who stated that there was no need for the Article as "women were not to be excluded" from participating in the organization anyway.[83] However, Street, from the Australian delegation, noted that "There was nothing specific in the law which excluded women from voting and yet in practically every country the women had to carry on a long agitation before they were given the vote."[84] Lutz also used the same arguments in her speech at the conference noting "you would find that men have never found it unnecessary to make a statement of their rights. Why, then, should it be unnecessary to make a statement of the rights of women?"[85] With the aid of the Australian women's organization, Street made a noticeable impact in San Francisco.[86] The delegate from New Zealand made a similar warning to the delegates who did not think it was necessary to include sex equality as he noted: "They thought it was inherent in all our discussions and in all our decisions; but experience has not lent itself to that interpretation,"[87] and the women would feel that they were "helped by the sense that their work is recognized as the equal with that of men."[88] In the end however, the wording was not as inclusive as Jessie Street and the feminist delegates had wished for.[89]

The origins of a separate commission on the status of women

The Commission on the Status of Women (CSW), formally established in 1946, is also seen as one of the first formal recognitions of women's rights in the UN.[90] Even though it was not formally established at the UNCIO, its origins can be traced to the work of the Latin American female delegates before and at the UNCIO. The dispute at the UNCIO was mainly in regards to concerns that programmes on women's rights would not be given sufficient protection under the structure of a commission on human rights.[91] In hindsight, it is argued by researchers that women's issues would not have received adequate attention under the Commission on Human Rights.[92]

Lutz argued that the rights of women need to improve radically, and the part women have played in the recent war urge a consideration of their status, and that the UN should therefore set up a special commission on women. Such a commission was necessary as Lutz stated that there were "nowhere in the world where women had complete equality with men."[93] Lutz, Bernardino and Ledón's proposal for a commission on women was inspired by their work and experience from the Inter-American Commission of Women (CIM) which they also used as a precedent for the UN to follow.[94]

As suggested by the Indian delegate, Bertha Lutz moved to secure the support of Latin American women before she proposed the amendment, a text that was drafted by the Uruguayan delegation.[95] Lutz further described how there was a great interest in the proposal and that it gained wide support.[96]

Even though Bertha Lutz obtained wide support for the amendment, a women's commission was not established until 1946 as it was not within decision-making power of the UNCIO to create such a sub-commission.[97] The commission was later upgraded from a sub-commission to the Commission on the Status of Women (CSW) due to the lobbying of Street, Bergtrup and Latin American feminists.[98] Several women at the UNCIO later joined the CSW: Street became its first vice-chair and Bernadino (Dominican Republic), Ledón (Mexico), and Urdaneta (Venezuela) also held central positions. Even though Lutz can be credited for inspiring the creation of the CSW,[99] it is also said that without Bernardino, the CSW might not have been established.[100]

Southern women delegates and Western resistance

The opinions of the Latin American women at the UNCIO differed from many of the Western representatives, this supports the claim that Latin American delegates represented a non-Western perspective. Secondly, the distinctive contributions of Latin American feminists in the early 20th century have been "shrouded in historiographic assumptions."[101] Which supports Acharya's point that "if good ideas are found outside the West, they are often dismissed as imitation."[102] This section therefore serves to strengthen the claim that Latin American feminists at UNICO presented distinctive contributions that fundamentally departed from most Western delegates present at the UNCIO. There was a clear division based on a notion of backward versus advanced and Western versus non-Western. Finally, a careful reading of Southern contributions reveals how the skepticism of Latin American feminists towards the genuine inclusiveness of the term human rights might have been crucial in securing the strong language on gender equality in the UN Charter.

Lutz and Bernardino were conscious of how they, as Latin American delegates, were representing more "backward" countries in opposition to the "advanced" Western representatives. Lutz notes that after describing how the League of Women Voters and the American and British delegates were in opposition to Lutz that "It is a strange psychological paradox that often those who are emancipated by the efforts of others are loth [*sic*] to acknowledge the source of their freedom."[103]

This frustration can also be read from her statement on the International Alliance of Women as they first opposed a special commission on women, a view Lutz termed "too European"[104] and not representative.[105]

At the UNCIO, Latin American women clearly saw themselves as representatives of women in particular, a view that seemed to depart from the Western delegates. The female advisor to the Norwegian Delegation, Åse Gruda Skard, complained how the Latin American women "practically wanted the word women in every paragraph in 'the Charter' and perceived themselves very much *as* representatives of the women in the world."[106] The British women advisor, Florence Horsbrugh, thought "feminism rather unladylike" according to Lutz. Gildersleeve confronted Lutz saying that she hoped Lutz was not "going to ask for anything for women in the Charter since that would be a very vulgar thing to do"[107] whereby Lutz replied that "the need to defend rights of women was the main reason why the Brazilian Government [*sic*] had put me on the delegation."[108]

In a letter to the President of the International Alliance of Women, written only a couple of months after the conference, Lutz was clearly frustrated by Gildersleeve whom she describes as "by nature and vocation an extreme conservative."[109]

It can be argued that Gildersleeve, the British women delegates and later Eleanor Roosevelt's belief in the universality of human rights were informed by an Anglo-American political philosophy where the individual was placed in the centre, as the free, rational actor.[110] However, particularly at the time of the UNCIO, the rational actor, represented by the individual, was very much associated with masculinity, in the same way as the feminine represented the irrational.[111] Their view was an articulation of the frustration over protective legislation for women resulting in political subordination.[112]

Lutz, on the other hand, was a prominent advocate for citing the particular needs of women[113] as can be seen in her emphasis on the "explicit inclusion of women in positions of political power."[114] Therefore, without the presence of Latin American delegates such as Lutz and Bernardino, the British and American Western delegates would not have met the same objections to their masculine notion of human rights of man, where the rights of man would predominantly refer to men. This Western view also made it difficult to acknowledge the specific discrimination of women, and thus might explain why both Gildersleeve and organizations such as the International Alliance of Women first opposed a special Sub-Commission on women.[115] And so the paradox noted by Lutz and Bernardino plays out. Acknowledging the Western opposition to women's rights, Lutz writes in a letter, that it is now the responsibility of Latin American women to ensure that women's rights are recognized as a part of international human rights.[116]

Human rights and the UN Charter

Sikkink claims that it is unlikely that the UN Charter would have *any* references to human rights if the Latin American countries had not advocated for them at the UNCIO,[117] as such, the proposition that human rights originates in a Western political project is only partially right and should be scrutinized.[118] The UK and Soviet Union opposed human rights in the first draft of the UN Charter, called the Dumbarton Oaks Proposals. This draft, prepared by the UK, the US, China, and the Soviet Union, had only one reference to human rights.[119] The US did not reference human rights in their own draft of the UN Charter. More powerful states were concerned with other issues than human rights, such as securing sovereignty, hegemony, and the reorientation of their economy in the postwar era.[120] Still, some literature presents the human rights agenda of Latin American delegations at the UNCIO as a result of pressure from the United States.[121]

Locating agency in the South

In 2016, the presentation of women and the UN Charter in UN historic accounts[122] did not mention the contributions of Latin American women to language on gender equality in the UN Charter.[123] Instead, *all* women at the UNCIO, which would include the British and American representatives, are in these accounts repeatedly given the credit for women's rights in the Charter.[124] Furthermore, this representation of women at the UNCIO as a coherent group speaking with one voice contributes to women's subordination as their agency is not taken seriously, they remain defined by their gender and not their actions.[125] This presentation also implies that the non-Western, who are not a part of the global hegemonic orthodoxy of international relations, are not looked for by researchers, and are consequently not noted in history books. The data presented is thus an important corrective to the global hegemonic orthodoxy attributing feminism with a Western origin.[126] Rebecca Adami [127] also identifies the Western hegemonic orthodoxy to explain the silencing of non-Western contributions from women delegates from India and Pakistan in the drafting of the Universal Declaration of Human Rights (UDHR) in 1948.

An explanation for the ignorance of Southern contributions to global norms can be found in how norms have been defined and researched.[128] Norms are generally created by several actors and based on a set of ideas. A widely accepted description of a norm is a "standard of appropriate behavior for actors with a given identity."[129] It is argued that typically more powerful states introduce global norms, and that ideas diffuse from the North to the South.[130] Consequently, the West is generally seen as the producer of norms. An unfortunate consequence of this narrative has been a sidelining and ignorance of non-Western contributions to norms. [131] Further theorizing that build on this idea of norm diffusion is coined by Amitav Acharya`s Global IR which argues that traditional IR is rooted in Western history and as such represent a global hegemonic orthodoxy, where history outside the Western sphere is marginalized.[132] Global IR provides a useful framework to explain why Latin American contributions to human rights and feminism have wrongfully been described by historians as not *sui generis*.[133] The studies in this volume challenge the privileging of Western norm-entrepreneurs and their contributions to human rights over those of the global South. Women's international human rights are not norms created by materially powerful states.[134]

Agency can be found in women from the Global South, the neglect of their voices in the historical norm-setting of universal human rights in IR has to do with the narrow definition of norm-makers. Western IR continues to overlook the vital role of non-western countries because of a narrow definition of agency in international norm-setting. Thus, agency was viewed only in terms of state actors and not assigned women who officially represented governments but acted in their individual capacity for gender equality.[135] In human rights history, we need to question a self-serving formulation that has ignored advanced forms of non-Western agency.[136] Along with Acharya we call for a broader understanding of agency that include Bertha Lutz as a norm-entrepreneur. Agency should not be limited to material power, and as we have seen by re-visiting the founding of the UN with a Global IR lens, the forgotten women delegates sought to challenge the dominance of strong actors in establishing a global order.[137] Again: "Viewed as such, agency is not the prerogative of the strong. It can manifest as the weapon of the weak."[138] Overall, Global IR aims to open up a space where a broader range of agency can be recognized as this is central to the recognized Southern contributions to global norms accordingly.[139]

The limitations of third world feminism in locating positive agency from the South

Global IR aims at including world history and a diversity of voices to contest the Western centric hegemonic orthodoxy. This aim is very much aligned with that of postcolonial theory and third world feminism. So why have these theories not been able to recognize the positive agency put forward in Global IR? Lutz and the Latin American women at the UNCIO had agency as they could define women's rights for the UN Charter that spoke to their feminist views. They even succeeded in playing a more positive and proactive role in relation to women's rights than the Western powers did. However, when voices such as Lutz's, that clearly depart from the global hegemonic orthodoxy, are still able to influence the development of global norms, this might not be recognized by third world feminists' definition of agency.

It is not suggested here that third world feminism is the *cause* of the neglected contributions of Southern agency as academic research is predominantly influenced by Western liberal theory.[140] However, third world feminism conceptualization of agency is based on their lack of recognition of *positive* agency, defined as making active contributions to the development of norms using ideational capabilities.[141] Positive agency is neglected because third world feminism builds on the claim that the global South has been marginalized and excluded.[142] Even though these observations have served as an important critique of the global hegemonic orthodoxy, a consequence has been the lack of recognition of the positive contributions of the South to global norms, since acknowledging this would undermine their central claim of marginalization.[143] Thus, it can be said that the narrative of postcolonial theory "thrive[s] on this presumed marginality."[144]

Critical scholar Robert Cox (1981) focus on how social forces shape theory. According to Cox, "theory is always *for* someone and *for* some purpose."[145] In other words, theory will always have a perspective that is informed by its position in time and space and theory is inevitably a political project. Theories are used to see the world from a particular standpoint defined in terms such as "nation or social class, of dominance or subordination, of rising or declining power."[146] Although these perspectives do not solely define a theory, its initial perspective is an important factor as it would taint its explication. Each perspective uncovers reality and locates in it different kinds of issues that should be defined or solved.[147]

There is a common cause that unites third world feminism, namely political struggle and opposition against forms of dominance.[148] Third world feminist analysis includes a critique of Western feminism for a dominance through an 'othering' of third world women, as they are defined as powerless and/or victims by the Western humanist discourse, and seen as monolithic subjects.[149] The political project of Gayatri C. Spivak, one of the first contributors to third world feminism together with Chandra T. Mohanty, was therefore to engage with the knowledge and experience of disempowered groups and in this way challenge dominant narratives about them.[150] Overall, third world feminism recognizes agency through a logic of opposition which stems from the notion that where there is dominance there will always be resistance. This agency is "anchored in the history of specific struggles."[151] So, it could be argued that the theory of third world feminism is initially informed by a perspective that looks at dominance and subordination.[152] This explains how agency is present in the ability to resist and oppose[153] a negative form of agency according to Acharya.[154]

Furthermore, an example of the third world feminist narrative that is influenced by a perspective of domination and subordination can be read from Spivak's description of the UN conference on women as a "broad repressive ideological apparatus."[155] According to Spivak, the UN is based on "the notion that the rest of the world is unable to govern itself."[156] In her critique of the UN fourth world

conference on women in Beijing in 1995, Spivak asserts that these UN conferences are just a theatre for the North to seemingly embrace the South, when the
fact is that "the North organizes the South."[157] Spivak`s assumption builds on
the accusation that human rights as a concept is used by the "West" to "Civilize"
the non-Western.[158] Sikkink points out the paradox that plays out when postcolonial writers are not able to recognize alternative Southern voices. Their critique
of how the West imposes global norms on the South is often based on existing
research largely produced and conducted in the West. The paradox then is that
the design of postcolonial research in this way "reproduces the very situation
they wish to critique."[159] "In their efforts to stress how the countries of the global
North have silenced voices in the developing world and imposed Northern values
on them, they too have silenced the past by not carefully investigating sources
from the developing world itself."[160] Adami gives the example of how non-Western delegates are dismissed in critiquing the universal nature of human rights,
and as such "erodes the political force of individual women" who were amongst
the key advocates for equal rights in marriage in the UDHR from a non-Western
vantage point.[161] Similarly, the positive agency played out by Lutz and the Latin
American women at the UNCIO is not a part of the research agenda of postcolonial writers such as the third world feminists.

To summarize the points above, it can be argued that the agency of Latin
American women at the UNCIO is not found by third world feminists as they
do not represent the typical "victimized" women in Western literature. The
act of finding agency is also informed by these scholars' initial perspective as
defined by Cox, which focus on structures of dominance and subordination. As
an implicit function of the argument for the value and relevance of their work
presented by this perspective, it could be said that third world feminists make
general statements about agency in a narrative that present agency as resistance against exploitation. Stereotypes that could be equated with the Orientalist
"stereotypes they are marshalled against."[162] It is here that Acharya claims that
postcolonial writers thrive on a presumed marginality, and as a result the Latin
American women delegates at the UNCIO might be invisible to the analytical
lens of third world feminism.

Another aspect that might shed some light on where third world feminism
misses out on the positive agency of the South is the focus on the local and rejection of the "ethnocentric universal."[163] Mohanty and third world feminism are
critical of universal theories, simply put, as they are seen as Western values in
disguise that marginalize women from the South. Third world feminism's focus
is on the particular and the local as an authentic source of agency.[164] Although this
approach has served as important critique of the Western construct of third world
women, it could also indicate that third world feminism looks at the local to challenge the universal instead of embarking on research that could reveal Southern
origins and influence of universal norms. Consequently, the Western narrative as
the builders of global norms remain unchallenged and not scrutinized as they are
rejected all together as Western. "Thinking small is not enough; agency is not to
be had so predictably."[165] In other words, agency of Southern actors can also be
seen taking a hold in big units such as shaping global norms, as was shown with

the Latin American women at the UNCIO. By taking an empirical route when assessing universal norms[166] one could avoid binary representation of universal (North) vs. the particular (South). This empirical focus would recognize that Latin America had their share of influence in international relations, as noted by Lutz,[167] and should as such not be regarded as marginal to international politics.[168]

Conclusion

This chapter has aimed to present compelling evidence to underscore the crucial contributions of Latin American women delegates at the UNCIO and consequently challenge UN's presentation of this history. It systematically presented the four different sections of the Charter where women's rights and gender equality were discussed. Namely in the Preamble, the Articles mentioning nondiscrimination based on sex, Article 8 on equal participation in the UN, and the origins of the Commission on the Status of Women. Bertha Lutz, on behalf of the Brazilian delegation, presented amendments suggesting the addition of "sex" and a special sub-commission on women and Article 8. These references to women were hard fought battles, as the American delegate followed by the British often opposed these amendments.

Bertha Lutz stated that "there will never be an unbreakable peace in the world until the women help to make it."[169] Lutz' speeches were not only visionary, her passionate pleas for women's rights, supported by other Latin American women delegates, have also been crucial for how gender equality is understood by the UN today. These findings reveal that the foundations of the norm on gender equality which is central for global governance today can be traced back to the pioneering visions that Latin American women had for the UN Charter.

The instrumental role of Latin American women at the UNCIO demonstrates the significance of Southern agency in the development of global norms. These contributions consequently challenge the global hegemonic orthodoxy, the notion of feminism as a norm imposed on countries in the South[170] and the narrative of the West as the only builders of global norms. It is therefore claimed that the narrative of global gender equality, as presented in current UN accounts,[171] is not valid.

It was argued that despite the project of third world feminism to uncover Southern agency, the contributions of the Latin American women at the UNCIO have not been recognized by these scholars. The Latin American women at the UNCIO did indeed influence global norms; however, this is invisible to the analytical lens of third world feminism as it does not support their narrative of the marginalized South.

On a final note, an important motivation in conducting research that challenges the global hegemonic orthodoxy of gender equality is to inspire a more global ownership to gender equality. It is hoped that by challenging the Eurocentric narrative of gender equality, academics can open up a more productive space for multilateral cooperation on such matters. This again could allow diplomats and researchers to move beyond the dichotomized conversation defined in terms of the North and the South, the universal versus the particular.[172]

Notes

1   Marino, K. M., 2014. Transnational Pan-American Feminism: The Friendship of Bertha Lutz and Mary Williams, 1926–1944. *Journal of Women's History*, 26 (2): 79.
2   Gildersleeve, V., 1954. *Many a Good Crusade*. New York: The Macmillan Co.
3   United Nations, 1945. *Documents of the United Nations Conference on International Organisation (UNCIO), Volume VI Commission I, General Provisions*. London and New York, United Nations Information Organization, 172.
4   Skard, 10.
5   Skard,38; Pietilä, 10.
6   Lutz, B., 1945. Letter from Bertha Lutz to Corbett Ashby, New Rochelle (New York) in *Papers of Margery Irene Corbett Ashby*, 6B/106/7/MCA/C3. Women's Library, London; UNCIO, 1945, Vol. VI: 178.
7   Weiss, T. G. & Roy, P., 2016. The UN and the Global South, 1945 and 2015: past as prelude? *Third World Quarterly*, April, 37 (7): 1147–1155.
8   Implied through conversations between the authors and UN staff at the UN Headquarter in New York and Geneva (UN Women and UNOG) throughout 2016–2017.
9   Skard, 37–60.
10 Acharya, A., 2016. 'Idea-shift': How ideas from the rest are reshaping global order. *Third World Quarterly*, 37 (7): 1156–1170, 1157; Weiss and Roy, 1148.
11 Acharya, 2016, 1157.
12 Acharya, 2016, 1157; Sikkink, K., 2014. Latin American Countries as Norm Protagonists of the Idea of International Human Rights. *Global Governance*, 20: 389–404, 38; Rebecca Adami, "On Subalternity and Representation: Female and Post Colonial Subjects Claiming Universal Human Rights in 1948," *Journal of Research on Women and Gender* 6 (2015): 56–66.
13 Weiss and Roy, 1147; Acharya, 2016, 1157.
14 Haan, F. d., Allen, M., Purvis, J. & Daskalova, K., 2013. Introduction. In: F. d. Haan, M. Allen, J. Purvis & K. Daskalova, eds. *Women's Activism*. London: Routledge: 1–10, 6.
15 Acharya, 2016, 1160.
16 Skard, 41.
17 Rupp, L. J., 1997. *Worlds of Women: The Making of an International Women's Movement*. New Jersey: Princeton University Press, 4.
18 Sikkink, 390.
19 Jain, D., 2005. *Women, Development and the UN, A Sixty-Year Quest for Equality and Justice*. Bloomington and Indianapolis: Indiana University Press, 12.
20 Mohanty, C. T., 1991. Cartographies of Struggle: Third World Women and the Politics of Feminism. In: C. T. Mohanty, A. Russo & L. Torres, eds. *Third World Women and the Politics of Feminism*. Bloomington: Indiana University Press: 1–47, 5.
21 Weiss and Roy, 1148; Helleiner, E., 2014. Principles from the Periphery: The Neglected Southern Sources of Global Norms. *Global Governance*, 20: 359–360, 359.

Fawcett, L., 2012. Between West and non-West: Latin American Contributions to International Thought. *The International History Review*, December, 34 (4): 679–704.

22 Lutz, B., n.d. Reminiscences of the San Francisco Conference that Founded the United Nations, Bertha Lutz Brazilian Plenipotentiary Delegate in *Papers of Margery Irene Corbett Ashby,* 6B/106/7/MCA/C2. Women's Library, London; Bernardino 1947 in DuBois, E. & Derby, L., 2009. The Strange Case of Minerva Bernardino: Pan American and United Nations women's right activist. *Women's Studies International Forum,* (32): 43–50.

23 Acharya, A. & Buzan, B., 2007. Why is there no non-Western international relations theory? An Introduction. *International Relations of the Asia-Pacific,* 7 (3): 287–312.

24 Finnemore, M. & Sikkink, K., 1998. International Norm Dynamics and Political Change. *International Organization,* 4 (52): 887–917.

25 Finnemore, M. & Sikkink, K, 892.

26 Sikkink, 389.

27 Acharya, A., 2014a. Who Are the Norm Makers? The Asian-African Conference in Bandung and the Evolution of Norms. *Global Governance,* 20: 405–417, 407; Haan et. Al, 6.

28 Acharya and Buzan, 293.

29 Sikkink, 389–404; Miller, F., 2010. Chapter 14 Latin American Feminism and the Transnational Arena. In: K. Offen, ed. *Globalizing Feminisms.* New York: Routledge, 1789–1945.

30 Sikkink, 389–404.; Glendon, M. A., 2003. Idea, The Forgotten Crucible: The Latin American Influence on the Universal Human Rights. *Harvard Human Rights Journal,* (16): 27–39, 27.; Acharya, 2016, 1158.

31 Acharya, A., 2014b. Global International Relations (IR) and Regional Worlds. *International Studies Quarterly,* 58: 647–659, 405.; Acharya, 2014b, 651.

32 Acharya, 2014b, 651.

33 Acharya, 2014b, 652, 649.

34 Miller, 193; Marino, K. M., 2021. From Equal Rights to Human Rights: The Influence of Pan-American Feminism on the United Nations Charter and Universal Declaration of Human Rights. In *Women and the UN,* London: *Routledge.*

35 Skard, 8; Miller, 1789–1945.

36 Skard, 45.

37 Ibid., 37–38.

38 Sluga, G., 2013. Chapter 3. Spectacular Feminism- The international history of women, world citizenship and human rights. In: F. d. Haan, M. Allen, J. Purvis & K. Daskalova, eds. *Women's Activism.* London: Routledge, 47.

39 Marino, 68.

40 Marino, 71.

41 Sluga, 47.

42 Abdenur, A. E., 2016. Emerging powers and the creation of the UN: three ships of Theseus. *Third World Quarterly* 37 (7): 1171–1186, 1177, 1185.

43 Peck, M. G., 1944. *Carrie Chapman Catt. A Biography.* New York: H.W. Wilson, 360.

44 Sluga, 47.

45 DuBois and Derby, 47.

46 Ibid, Skard, 43.

47 Skard, 44.

48 Weiss and Roy, 1148.

49 Sikkink, 394.

50 Steinstra, D., 1994. *Women's Movements and International Organizations.* New York: St. Martin's Press. 77.

51 Skard, 47; Steinstra, 78.

52 Ibid.

53 United Nations, 1945. *Documents of the United Nations Conference on International Organisation (UNCIO), Volume III, Dumbarton Oaks.* London and New York, United Nations Information Organization, 467.

54 DuBois and Derby, 47.

55 Pietilä, 10; Offen, K., 2001. Women's Rights or Human Rights? International Feminism between the wars. In: P. Grimshaw, K. Holmes & M. Lake, eds. *Women's Rights and Human Rights: International Historical Perspectives.* New York: Palgrave. 243–252, 249–250.

56 Pietilä, 10; Lake, M., 2001. From Self-Determination via Protection to Equality via Non-Discrimination: Defining Women's Rights at the League of Nations and the United. In: P. Grimshaw, K. Holmes & M. Lake, eds. *Women's Rights and Human Rights: International Historical Perspectives.* New York: Palgrave: 254–271, 265.

57 Glendon, M. A., 2003. Idea, The Forgotten Crucible: The Latin American Influence on the Universal Human Rights. *Harvard Human Rights Journal*, (16): 27–39, 38; Waltz, S., 2002. Reclaiming and rebuilding the history of the Universal Declaration of Human Rights. *Third World Quarterly*, 3 (22): 437–448, 444

58 Sluga, 44; UNCIO, Vol. VI, 277.

59 Gildersleeve, 344: 346–347.

60 UNCIO, Vol. VI, 19.

61 Rebecca Adami *Women and the Universal Declaration of Human Rights.* New York & London: Routledge, 2019, 28.

62 Sluga, 44–45.

63 Ibid, 135.

64 Skard, 37–60.

65 United Nations, 1945. *Documents of the United Nations Conference on International Organisation (UNCIO), Volume X Commission II, General Assembly.* London and New York, United Nations Information Organization, 602; Galey, M. E., 1995. Chapter 1. Forerunners in Women's Quest for Partnership. In: A. Winslow, ed. *Women, Politics, and the United Nations .* London: Greenwood Press, 1–10, 7.

66 Galey, 7.

67 Gildersleeve, 351–352; UNCIO, Vol. X: 58.

68 Ashby, M. I. C., 1946. *United Nations - meeting in San Francisco in* Papers of Margery Irene Corbet Ashby, 6B/106/7/MCA/C3. Women's Library, London.

69 Ibid.

70 Ibid.

71 Ibid.

72 Sluga, 48.

73 Ashby; Street, J., n.d. In *Papers of Margery Irene Corbett Ashby,* in 6B/106/7/MCA/C3. Women's Library, London; Sekuless.

74 United Nations, 1945. *Documents of the United Nations Conference on International Organisation (UNCIO), Volume VII Commission I, General Provisions.* London and New York, United Nations Information Organization, 57.

75 UNCIO, Vol. VI: 172.

76 Ibid.

77 Ibid.

78 Ibid.

79 UNCIO, Vol. VII, 31.

80 UNCIO, Vol. VI, 171.

81 Steinstra, 78.

82 Sekuless, 134.

83 UNCIO, Vol. VII, 31, 64.

84 Sekuless, 135.

85 Street, *Truth or Repose*, 182 in Adami, 2019, 30.

86 Pietilä, 11.

87 UNCIO, Vol. VI: 171–172.

88   Ibid.
89   Sekuless, 135.
90   DuBois, 47.
91   Gaer, 60.
92   Pietilä, H. & Vickers, J., 1996. *Making Women Matter: The Role of the United Nations.* 3 ed. London: Zed Books, 118.
93   UNCIO, Vol. X, 213.
94   Miller, 202; DuBois and Derby, 47.
95   Lutz, n.d, 4.
96   UNCIO, Vol. X, 214; Lutz, n.d,4.
97   Steinstra, 81.
98   Rupp, 250.
99   Marino, 66.
100 DuBois and Derby, 48.
101 Miller, 194.
102 Acharya, 1157.
103 Lutz, n.d., 5.
104 Rupp, 1997, 224.
105 Ibid.
106 Skard, 1986, 95–95.
107 Lutz, n.d, 2.
108 Ibid.
109 Lutz, 1945.
110 Lake, 254–271; Meyers, D. T., 2004. *Stanford Library.* [Online] Available at: http://stanford.library.sydney.edu.au/archives/sum2007/entries/feminism-self/ [Accessed 5 July 2016].
111 Meyer, 20–66.
112 Lake, 269.
113 Freedman, E. B., 2003. *No Turning Back - The History of Feminism and the Future of Women.* New York: Ballantine Books, 68.
114 Marino, 69, 73.
115 Lake, 269
116 Marino, 79.
117 Sikkink, 394.
118 Waltz, S., 2002. Reclaiming and rebuilding the history of the Universal Declaration of Human Rights. *Third World Quarterly*, 3 (22): 437–448, 440.
119 Sikkink, 392–393; Waltz, 441.
120 Ibid.
121 An example of this presentation can be read in Galey's historical accounts of women and the UN where it is stated that representatives from the US went to Mexico to enlist Latin American support for the US proposals on human rights in the preparations for the UNCIO (Galey, 7).
122 The Blue Book Series-The United Nations and The Advancement of Women 1945–1996; The Short History of the Commission on the Status of Women, at the UN Women website; the CD-ROM, Women Go Global; and The United Nations Intellectual History Project Series
123 Skard, 41.
124 Ibid.
125 Rebecca Adami, also notes that other specific characteristics such as class, race, language, ethnicity and age creates structures of exclusion and inclusion that binds groups together, these are ignored when women are described as a homogenous group in Adami, Rebecca. "Counter Narratives as Political Contestation: Universality, Particularity and Uniqueness." *The Equal Rights Review* 15 (2015): 13–24, 17.
126 Haan et al., 6.

127 Adami, Rebecca "On Subalternity and Representation: Female and Post Colonial Subjects Claiming Universal Human Rights in 1948." *Journal of Research on Women and Gender* 6 (2015): 56–66.
128 Acharya and Buzan, 2007.
129 Finnemore and Sikkink, 891.
130 Sikkink, 389.
131 Acharya, 2014a, 407; Haan et al., 6.
132 Acharya and Buzan, 293.
133 Sikkink, 389–404; Miller, 1789–1945.
134 Sikkink, Glendon, 27; Acharya, 2016, 1158.
135 Acharya, 2014a, 405; Acharya, 2014b, 651.
136 Ibid.
137 Ibid.
138 Acharya, 2014b, 651.
139 Acharya, 2014a, 647–659.
140 Acharya, 2014b, 657.
141 Acharya, 2014a, 405; Acharya, 2014b, 651.
142 Amitav Acharya 26th July, 2016, in private email correspondence with the author.
143 Ibid.
144 Acharya, 2014b, 651.
145 Cox, R. W., 1981. Social Forces, States and World Orders: Beyond International Relations. *Millennium: Journal of International Studies*, 10(2): 126–155, 128.
146 Ibid.
147 Ibid.
148 Mohanty, 1991, 4.
149 Mohanty, C. T., 1984. Under Western eyes: Feminist Scholarship and Colonial Discourse. *Boundary 2*, Spring-Autumn, 3(13): 333, 335, 338.
150 Morton, S., 2003. *Gayatri Chakrovarty Spivak.* London: Routledge, 45–46.
151 Mohanty, 1991, 38.
152 Cox, 126–155.
153 Maggio, J., 2007. "Can the Subaltern Be Heard?": Political Theory, Translation, Representation, and Gayatri Chakravorty Spivak. *Alternatives: Global, Local, Political*, 32(4): 419–443, 422.
154 Acharya, 2014b, 647–659.
155 Spivak, G. C., 1996. Woman' as Theatre: United Nation's Conference on Women, Beijing 1995. *Radical Philosophy*, January-February, Volume 75, pp. 2–4, 2.
156 Ibid.
157 Ibid.
158 Ignatieff, M., and Gutmann, A. (2003). *Human rights as politics and idolatry.* University Center for Human Values Series. Princeton, NJ: Princeton University Press.
159 Sikkink, 400.
160 Ibid.
161 Adami. 59.
162 Robbins, B., 1992. Comparative Cosmopolitanism. *Social Text*, Issue 31/32, pp. 169–186, 175, 178.
163 Mohanty, 1984, 336.
164 Ibid. 345.
165 Robbins, 176.
166 Ibid, 182.
167 Lutz, 1945; UNCIO, Vol. VI,178.
168 Acharya, 2014b, 651.
169 UNCIO, Vol. VI, 171.
170 Haan et al., 5–6.
171 Skard, 37–60.

172 See Adami, R. 2012. "Reconciling Universality and Particularity through a Cosmopolitan Outlook on Human Rights", *Cosmopolitan Civil Societies*, 4(2): 22–37.

Bibliography

Abdenur, A. E., 2016. Emerging powers and the creation of the UN: Three ships of Theseus. *Third World Quarterly* 37(7): 1171–1186. doi:10.1080/01436597.2016.1154432

Acharya, A., 2014a. Who are the norm makers? The Asian-African conference in Bandung and the evolution of norms. *Global Governance* 20: 405–417. doi:10.1163/19426720-02003006

Acharya, A., 2014b. Global international relations (IR) and regional worlds. *International Studies Quarterly* 58: 647–659. doi:10.1111/isqu.12171

Acharya, A., 2016. 'Idea-shift': How ideas from the rest are reshaping global order. *Third World Quarterly* 37(7): 1156–1170. doi:10.1080/01436597.2016.1154433

Acharya, A. & Buzan, B., 2007. Why is there no non-Western international relations theory? An Introduction. *International Relations of the Asia-Pacific* 7(3): 287–312. doi:10.1093/irap/km012

Adami, R. "Counter narratives as political contestation: Universality, particularity and uniqueness." *The Equal Rights Review* 15(2015a): 13–24.

Adami, R. "On subalternity and representation: Female and post colonial subjects claiming universal human rights in 1948." *Journal of Research on Women and Gender* 6 (2015b): 56–66.

Adami, R. 2012. "Reconciling universality and particularity through a cosmopolitan outlook on human rights". *Cosmopolitan Civil Societies* 4(2): 22–37.

Adami, R. *Women and the Universal Declaration of Human Rights*. New York & London: Routledge, 2019.

Amrith, S. & Sluga, G., 2008. New histories of the United Nations. *Journal of World History* 47: 379–398.

Ashby, M. I. C., 1946. *United Nations - Meeting in San Francisco in Papers of Margery Irene Corbet Ashby, 6B/106/7/MCA/C3*. London: Women's Library

Cox, R. W., 1981. Social forces, states and world orders: Beyond international relations. *Millennium: Journal of International Studies* 10(2): 126–155. doi:10.1177/03058298810100020501

DuBois, E. & Derby, L., 2009. The strange case of Minerva Bernardino: Pan American and United Nations women's right activist. *Women's Studies International Forum* (32): 43–50. doi.org/10.1016/j.wsif.2009.01.005

Fawcett, L., 2012. Between West and non-West: Latin American contributions to international thought. *The International History Review*, December, 34(4): 679–704. doi:10.1080/07075332.2012.707980

Finnemore, M. & Sikkink, K., 1998. International norm dynamics and political change. *International Organization* 4(52): 887–917: doi:10.1162/002081898550789

Freedman, E. B., 2003. *No Turning Back-The History of Feminism and the Future of Women*. New York: Ballantine Books.

Gaer, F., 2009. Women, international law and international institutions: The case of the United Nations. *Women's Studies International Forum* 32: 60–66. doi:10.1016/j.wsif.2009.01.006

Galey, M. E., 1995. Chapter 1. Forerunners in women's quest for partnership. In: A. Winslow, ed. *Women, Politics, and the United Nations*. London: Greenwood Press, 1–10.

Gildersleeve, V., 1954. *Many a Good Crusade*. New York: The Macmillan Co.

Glendon, M. A., 2003. Idea, the forgotten crucible: The latin American influence on the universal human rights. *Harvard Human Rights Journal* 16(16): 27–39.

Haan, F. d., Allen, M., Purvis, J. & Daskalova, K., 2013. Introduction. In: F. D. Haan, M. Allen, J. Purvis & K. Daskalova, eds. *Women's Activism*. London: Routledge: 1–10.

Helleiner, E., 2014. Principles from the periphery: The neglected Southern sources of global norms. *Global Governance* 20: 359–360.

Ignatieff, M., & Gutmann, A. (2003). *Human Rights as Politics and Idolatry*. University Center for Human Values Series. Princeton, NJ: Princeton University Press.

Jain, D., 2005. *Women, Development and the UN, A Sixty-Year Quest for Equality and Justice*. Bloomington and Indianapolis: Indiana University Press.

Jolly, R., Emmerji, L. & Thomas, W. G., 2005. *The Power of UN Ideas: Lessons from the First 60 Years*. New York: United Nations Intellectual History Project.

Lake, M., 2001. From self-determination via protection to equality via non-discrimination: Defining women's rights at the league of nations and the United. In: P. Grimshaw, K. Holmes & M. Lake, eds. *Women's Rights and Human Rights: International Historical Perspectives*. New York: Palgrave: 254–271.

Lutz, B., 1945. *Letter from Bertha Lutz to Corbett Ashby, New Rochelle (New York)* in *Papers of Margery Irene Corbett Ashby, 6B/106/7/MCA/C3*. London: Women's Library.

Lutz, B., n.d.. *Reminiscences of the San Francisco Conference that Founded the United Nations, Bertha Lutz Brazilian Plenipotentiary Delegate* in *Papers of Margery Irene Corbett Ashby, 6B/106/7/MCA/C2*. London: Women's Library

Maggio, J., 2007. "Can the subaltern be heard?": Political theory, translation, representation, and gayatri Chakravorty Spivak. *Alternatives: Global, Local, Political* 32(4): 419–443. doi:10.1177/030437540703200403

Marino, K. M., 2014. Transnational Pan-American feminism: The friendship of Bertha Lutz and Mary Williams, 1926–1944. *Journal of Women's History* 26(2): 63–87. doi:10.1353/jowh.2014.0034.

Meyers, D. T., 2004. *Stanford Library*. [Online] Available at: http://stanford.library.sydney.edu.au/archives/sum2007/entries/feminism-self/ [Accessed July 5 2016].

Miller, F., 2010. Chapter 14 latin American Feminism and the transnational arena. In: K. Offen, ed. *Globalizing Feminisms*. New York: Routledge, 1789–1945.

Mohanty, C. T., 1984. Under Western eyes: Feminist scholarship and colonial discourse. *Boundary 2*, Spring-Autumn, 3(13), 333–358. https://www.jstor.org/stable/302821

Mohanty, C. T., 1988. Under Western eyes: Feminist scholarship and colonial discourse. *Feminist Review* 30: 61–88.

Mohanty, C. T., 1991. Cartographies of struggle: Third world women and the politics of feminism. In: C. T. Mohanty, A. Russo & L. Torres, eds. *Third World Women and the Politics of Feminism*. Bloomington: Indiana University Press: 1–47. doi:10.2307/302821

Morton, S., 2003. *Gayatri Chakravorty Spivak*. London: Routledge.

Offen, K., 2001. Women's rights or human rights? international feminism between the wars. In: P. Grimshaw, K. Holmes & M. Lake, eds. *Women's Rights and Human Rights: International Historical Perspectives*. New York: Palgrave. 243–252.

Peck, M. G., 1944. *Carrie Chapman Catt. A Biography*. New York: H.W. Wilson.

Pietilä, H., 2007. *The Unfinished Story of Women and the United Nations*. New York: Geneva: UN Non-Governmental Liaison Service (NGLS).

Pietilä, H. & Vickers, J., 1996. *Making Women Matter: The Role of the United Nations*. 3 ed. London: Zed Books.

Robbins, B., 1992. Comparative cosmopolitanism. *Social Text* 31/32: 169–186.

Rupp, L. J., 1997. *Worlds of Women: The Making of an International Women's Movement*. New Jersey: Princeton University Press.

Sekuless, P., 1978. *Jessie Street, A Rewarding but Unrewarded Life*. Queensland (St. Lucia): University of Queensland Press.

Sikkink, K., 2014. Latin American countries as norm protagonists of the idea of international human rights. *Global Governance* 20: 389–404. doi:10.1163/19426720-02003005.

Skard, Å. G., 1986. *Fulle hender (Full Hands)*. Oslo: Gyldendal.

Skard, T., 2008. Getting our history right: How were the equal rights of women and men included in the charter of the United Nations? June, 1: 37–60. doi:10.1080/08039410.2008.9666394

Sluga, G., 2013. Chapter 3. Spectacular Feminism-The international history of women, world citizenship and human rights. In: F. D. Haan, M. Allen, J. Purvis & K. Daskalova, eds. *Women's Activism*. London: Routledge.

Snider, C. J., 2007. Planning for peace: Virginia gildersleeve at the United Nations conference on international organization. *Peace and Change* 32(2): 168–185. doi:10.1111/j.1468-0130.2007.00425.x

Spivak, G. C., 1996. Woman'as theatre: United Nation's conference on women, Beijing 1995. *Radical Philosophy* 75: 2–4.

Steinstra, D., 1994. *Women's Movements and International Organizations*. New York: St. Martin's Press.

Street, J., n.d. In *Papers of Margery Irene Corbett Ashby,* in 6B/106/7/MCA/C3. London: Women's Library,

United Nations, 1945a. *Documents of the United Nations Conference on International Organisation (UNCIO), Volume III, Dumbarton Oaks*. London and New York: United Nations Information Organization.

United Nations, 1945b. *Documents of the United Nations Conference on International Organisation (UNCIO), Volume VI Commission I, General Provisions*. London and New York: United Nations Information Organization.

United Nations, 1945c. *Documents of the United Nations Conference on International Organisation (UNCIO), Volume VII Commission I, General Provisions*. London and New York: United Nations Information Organization.

United Nations, 1945d. *Documents of the United Nations Conference on International Organisation (UNCIO), Volume X Commission II, General Assembly*. London and New York: United Nations Information Organization.

Waltz, S., 2002. Reclaiming and rebuilding the history of the universal declaration of human rights. *Third World Quarterly* 3(22): 437–448. doi.org/10.1080/01436590220138378

Weiss, T. G. & Roy, Ps., 2016. The UN and the global South, 1945 and 2015: Past as prelude?. *Third World Quarterly* 37 (7): 1147–1155. doi:10.1080/01436597.2016.1154436

3 Excavating hidden histories

Indian women in the early history of the United Nations

Khushi Singh Rathore

Introduction

As part of my ongoing doctoral research, I have often encountered instances where I have had to justify the need to study the life and experiences of Vijaya Laksmi Pandit as the first woman diplomat of independent India. The one question that is repeatedly asked of my work is, "why study Nehru's sister?" Questions like this have made me realize that if a woman as powerful and prominent as Pandit could be sidelined in historical accounts of Indian foreign policy then who else has been forgotten? It is with this thought that I embarked upon the search for hidden histories of women envoys of India.

While there have been recent writings that have covered the history of women in international politics, the attention to the intellectual thoughts of women in international relations remains a new and relatively under-explored field of study.[1] These lacunae get further deepened when we shift the focus to the intellectual thought of women of colour in the making of world politics. This erasure is witnessed in the herculean task of locating women of colour in international history. Most historical accounts of the field are written to celebrate outcomes of deliberations and the end results. It is only when we turn our attention to the processes that entail the making of resolutions and the declarations that we find a clear picture of those who have been marginalized in the writings of international history. Hence, this chapter studies the deliberations in the first few years of the UN, where women representatives from India were amongst the main actors, to locate the contributions of Indian women in the early history of the UN.

Patricia Owens, writing on the history of women in international thought, succinctly argues against the usual impression in the history of IR and in disciplinary canons that women did not think seriously about international politics.[2] She counters this exclusion of women from the field of international politics by finding evidence against it in her study and analyses of texts of historical IR and disciplinary history. She chalks out a new research agenda for developing the history of women's international thought by employing the tools of feminist historiography and archival research work to prove that women thought deeply about international politics. However, their thoughts and contributions have been repeatedly left out from the disciplinary writings amounting to their erasure from the field of study. It is because of this constant erasure that when asked "where are the women?," the answer is more often than not an awkward silence.[3]

DOI: 10.4324/9781003036708-3

This chapter expands on the research agenda outlined by Owens to locate Indian women envoys in the early history of the UN. The women figures studied here are amongst the earliest envoys of an independent India. These women with astute political acumen were prominent nationalist leaders and were active participants in transnational women's and anti-colonial networks. The UN was not their first appearance internationally. However, until 1947, when they spoke internationally, it was against the colonizers and for the cause of Indian independence. Then they became diplomatic representatives of the first government of an independent India.

In the following sections of the chapter, we will revisit the international thought of Vijaya Lakshmi Pandit, Hansa Mehta, Begum Shareefah Hamid Ali, and Lakshmi Menon by employing a close study of their inaugural appearances at the UN. I hope to impress upon the readers that though these women were spokespersons of their governments, they were nonetheless speaking their own minds. They believed in the causes they were chosen to represent and were personally invested in these issues. This interest was not a mere instance of chance but was a product of years of political experience. Thus, when these women envoys represented India at the UN, they were not merely taking orders from New Delhi. Rather, they were actively informing and influencing the Indian government with their knowledge and conversations at the UN. These individuals were no ordinary envoys. They had a special role in history. While they were implementing and influencing the making of the early Indian foreign policy, they were also significantly transforming international diplomacy itself, as writes Swapna Kona Nayudu in her work on Indian diplomatic history.[4] The experiences of Pandit, Mehta, Ali, and Menon are discussed broadly around their work on issues of race, human rights, and women's rights. The archival study of primary sources include newspaper archives, autobiographies, and private papers of these women to briefly outline their world view and their hopes for the UN by bringing these figures of history to life.

The most remembered: Vijaya Lakshmi Pandit

We are the trustees of the future, architects of the new world. — Vijaya Lakshmi Pandit.[5]

Pandit was informed that she was to lead the first delegation of an independent India to the UN shortly after her return to India from her lecture tour in the US and the successful advocacy of Indian independence outside the gates of the UN conference in San Francisco, where she was leading the unofficial delegation representing India before it had won its independence.[6]

The key issue to be raised by India at the General Assembly was of the Asiatic Land Tenure and Indian Representation Act, also called the "Ghetto Act," passed by the Union of South Africa. The legislation divided Natal into two areas, the controlled and the uncontrolled, disallowing the Indian residents to own property in the controlled "white areas" of Natal. To soften the blow of these restrictions, the South African government offered the Indian population a superficial appeasement in the form of "political representation." This was a hollow promise as the representatives to the Assembly and the Senate had to be white. The Natal

Indian Congress took strong objection to this racially discriminatory policy and approached both the Indian Government and also the newly constituted United Nations.[7]

The Indian interim government wanted to send a strong delegation to the UN where India was to register on the UN agenda its protest against the treatment of Indians in South Africa. Pandit was a suitable choice to lead this mission. Before she departed for the US, she had a private meeting with Gandhi, the Indian nationalist leader. He told Pandit why it was important for India to take up the South African issue at the UN. He told her that the task entrusted upon her delegation was not merely to come back victorious, but they had upon them the responsibility to set an example.[8] Pandit too shared this vision of possibilities for a new world order that the UN could provide. In her own writings and various public addresses, she spoke of the hope of what the UN could be and how the great powers had to be careful with the conduct of their business because if the wrongs of the past are not corrected, the UN would be met with the same fate as its predecessor, the League of Nations.[9]

The Indian opposition to the South African legislation had put the question of racial discrimination right in front of the world assembly. It was a test for the great powers to prove their talks of a more equal world were not mere hollow promises. In Pandit's own words, "The disposal of this issue will be watched closely by the non-European peoples of the world who are an overwhelming majority of the human race."[10] Pandit's close association with the African American leadership in the past and with organizations like the National Association for the Advancement of Colored People (NAACP) added to the already high levels of excitement across "coloured" networks. When Pandit announced the Indian intention to appeal against the South African legislation, she prefaced it with India's belief that, "the independence of all colonial peoples in the world is the vital concern of freedom loving peoples everywhere."[11] She warned that peace and freedom are indivisible and denial of freedom anywhere in the world undermines peace. The most likely outcomes in such an unjust scenario would be war and conflict. She clearly stated that India fiercely disapproved of the "Nazi doctrine of racialism wheresoever and in whatsoever form it may be practiced."[12] She told the assembly that the South African legislation was not just racially discriminatory but was also an absolute and "continuing outrage against the principles enshrined in the UN Charter."[13] Thus, Pandit internationalized the issue by invoking the moral promises the Member States had made to the UN. James Reston of the New York Times reported that as these words were spoken:

> [S]ome American delegates turned pale or bright red at the thought that the UN might have the power to discuss the plight of an oppressed minority anywhere in the world, say the Negroes [*sic*] in the US for instance.[14]

The debate on the South African issue was an important one as it was essentially rooted in the contradictions within the UN Charter.[15] The conflict arose in the invocation of Article 1(3) by India, calling upon the members of the UN to preserve the spirit of the Charter. Article 1(3) states that the purpose of the UN is to:

> [A]chieve international co-operation in solving international problems of an economic, social, cultural, or humanitarian character, and in promoting and encouraging respect for human rights and for fundamental freedoms for all without distinction as to race, sex, language, or religion.[16]

It was this spirit of the UN that Pandit invoked as she held South Africa and the UN accountable to the promises made in the Charter. The escape from account-ability sought by South Africa lay in the Charter clause pertaining to state sover-eignty. Article 2 (7) states that:

> Nothing contained in the present Charter shall authorize the United Nations to intervene in matters which are essentially within the domestic jurisdiction of any state or shall require the Members to submit such matters to settle-ment under the present Charter; but this principle shall not prejudice the application of enforcement measures under Chapter VII.[17]

The South African delegation selectively took shelter under the first part of the above-mentioned clause, thus making the claim of domestic jurisdiction rather unsatisfactory. However, both South Africa and Britain realized the powerful impact that Pandit's advocacy had on the audience, inside and outside the UN. They proposed that the matter be taken to the International Court of Justice to decide whether the South African legislation violated Article 2(7). This was unac-ceptable to India as Pandit called on the UN to censure the South African Gov-ernment.[18] Both Nehru and Gandhi had asked Pandit to be true to the spirit of the world assembly and the vision of a better future it stood for. Nehru had outlined the guidelines for their conduct in the international forum and emphasized upon India's total acceptance of the UN Charter and its utmost determination to make it a reality. The Charter was almost India's pledge to the world. These were not mere words for Pandit.[19] Responding to South Africa, she insisted that India's concern on the issue raised was not on the question of legality. Rather, it was a matter of "dignity" and "self-respect." She fiercely articulated, "What the world needs is not more charters, not more committees to define and courts of justice to interpret, but a more willing implementation of the principles of the Charter by all governments."[20]

Pandit called upon the "collective conscience" of the world which she believed was represented in the UN Assembly. She did not treat the issue as a mere bilat-eral disagreement but reminded the Member States of the commitment to sol-idarity on grounds of humanity and a shared responsibility to work towards a better and more humane world; hers was "an appeal of conscience."[21] In her final response to the South African defense, Pandit spoke with passion emanating from the hope for a new and better future:

> I want to carry the Assembly with me in these matters which, I submit, are common ground. If I do, as I must, unless the 54 nations assembled here place on the Charter a meaning and a significance far below what its words convey, what its spirit demands, and indeed what we have asked the world to

accept (…) then the Issue (…) rests with us, the nations of the world assembled, who have taken upon themselves the defense of the law of ethics and morality (…) We are the trustees of the future, architects of the new world (…) and it is only on the foundation of justice that we can erect a new world order (…) Mine is an appeal to conscience, to the conscience of the world which this Assembly is. I will say no more.[22]

She was received with a thunderous applause and ovations from the audience.[23] It was no surprise that when the UN General Assembly went to vote at 2 a.m., the Indian Resolution was passed with two-third majority. This marked the first official victory of Pandit in the world of international diplomacy and more importantly, a victory of the spirit of the UN and of the coloured peoples across the world. Pandit called this an "Asian Victory." When asked by the press how she felt, Pandit responded by expressing India's gratefulness to its Asian and African friends through whose help this feat was made possible. She said that this was a success "shared by us all."[24] For India, Pandit's effective leadership had delivered the first victory of the Indian vision and idea of internationalism, rooted in anti-imperialism and in building a peaceful and more equal world. For the UN, it was a litmus test that was just passed. As an American newspaper reported, the Indian resolution would determine whether "the new organization will, in fact defend the rights of all racial groups and dependent peoples."[25] This victory created ground for the world community to put principles to action and expand and codify human rights, which was also the next major discussion in the UN, where a crucial role was played by another woman envoy of India, Hansa Mehta.[26]

The most remembered: Hansa Mehta

The Bill of Human Rights is the corner-stone of the United Nations, and we shall be poor builders indeed if we set it at naught. — Hansa Mehta.[27]

The Universal Declaration of Human Rights (UDHR) was adopted in the year 1948. The declaration was a product of prolonged discussions and debates spanning over multiple meetings of the UN Commission on Human Rights (UNCHR). Mehta was a key voice in the conception of the declaration. She was also the only other woman member, along with Eleanor Roosevelt, and it was she who had nominated the latter for the chair-ship of the commission which was unanimously approved. After Pandit, Mehta is probably the most well-known early Indian woman representative to the UN. In 1947, she was appointed as the Indian delegate to the UNCHR. In her capacity as one of the drafters of the human rights declaration, through the various sessions of the commission and discussions and debates, Mehta worked relentlessly to make the Bill of Rights inclusive and potent. An ardent believer of an equal access to justice, in February, 1947, Mehta submitted a draft resolution on human rights that incorporated:

[R]ight to access the United Nations without risk of reprisal whenever there is an actual or theoretical infringement of human rights (…) the right to equality without distinction of (…) nationality or political belief (…) right to education (…) right to property.[28]

She viewed the declaration of human rights not as mere lip service but as a promise that the UN would do everything at its end to live up-to. Throughout her work in the UNCHR, Mehta insisted that the commission should not promise what it cannot deliver and the bill of rights should not be a mere declaration with no accountability on part of its signatories.[29] She wanted enforcement and not mere supervision of maintenance of basic standards of human rights by the Member States of the UN.[30] Mehta was aware of the need to look beyond the paradigm of state sovereignty. Not to say that she undermined it, but she was wary of the restrictiveness of a state-centered approach when it came to addressing human rights violations and the lack of an "implementation machinery" to enforce the Bill of Rights.[31]

Reporting to the Indian Government on the 1947 meeting of the Human Rights Commission in New York, Mehta expresses her disillusionment with the workings of the commission. She writes, "the impression I received (…) was that members evaded main issues and they talked round and round the subject without coming to a definite point."[32] She was also concerned about equal representation amongst the members of the commission and was wary of the representation on the sub committees, a process that she found arbitrary, a concern she says that was shared by some other members as well. She observed that "while some members were on more than one subcommittee, there were others who were not on a single committee."[33] It was due to a concern that the same procedure might get duplicated in the subcommittee to draft the Bill of Rights, that Mehta and her advisors, Dr. Lankan Sundaram and Mr. Natarajan, submitted a resolution that proposed composition of a drafting subcommittee of 11 members to be formally moved by the Indian delegation in appropriate time. These members were to be, "US Chairman, ex-officio; China; Egypt; France; India; Iran; Lebanon; Panama; Philippines Republic; UK; USSR and Uruguay."[34] Soon after, pending the discussion on the Bill of Rights the following day, Mehta also proposed a draft resolution to the General Assembly which was aimed at discussing "definite issues as raised in the draft resolution." These were, "(1) The form the Bill of Rights should take; (2) its contents, i.e., categorising rights; (3) its application and most important of all (4) its implementation."[35] Though Mehta had moved the resolution as a basis for further discussion, she was disappointed that the main points were lost in discussion on general issues, enunciating high principles and discussing social theories.[36] While the value of the aforementioned is not to be undermined, such observations of Mehta reflect her more direct and "practical" approach towards international negotiation. Her frustration was not so much with the discussions on values but on the delay that prolonged discussions without tangible outcomes caused in the advancement of proposed resolutions. Thus, reflecting a frustration with bureaucratic procedures that even Pandit alludes to in the recollections of her first interactions at the UN in her memoir.[37]

Mehta's main contention was concerning the effectiveness of the Bill of Rights. When Mrs. Roosevelt suggested that the Bill should be a "resolution in the form of a general discussion," Mehta disagreed stating that mere declaration would be unsatisfactory and meaningless unless there was an obligation on the Member States to adhere to it.[38] The absence of sanctions backing the resolution would fail to pursue the states in keeping their end of the promise even if they agreed to the resolution.[39] The solution to this problem, writes Mehta, lay in two parts, i.e., supervision and enforcement. Mehta repeatedly stressed upon the need for a machinery that would supervise the adherence of human rights and monitor instances of violation to hold the offending parties accountable.[40] Mehta saw a moral reason for India to take a stand in this matter. She wrote back home, asking the government to consider what attitude it wished to take upon the issue of the bill. She coaxed the Indian government further and as she acknowledged the complications of the question of implementation and the issue of national sovereignty, she signed off by subtly reminding the Indian government that it had recently raised the South African issue in the matter and now it was time for India to lead on this issue too.[41]

Mehta's speech at the UN Commission on Human Rights further illustrates her vision of human rights. She impressed upon the members of the commission that the bill had to be a simple and forthright document that could be easily understood, accompanied by an adequate machinery ensuring its enforcement in the member countries.[42] Mehta continued emphasizing on the need for a practical approach towards the issue, as was also witnessed in her insistence upon simple language.[43] The bill had to be comprehensible with a "precise legal and practical language" defining 'minority' and what counted as discrimination.[44] She insisted the proposed bill required "a proper and unequivocal definition of the relationships (…) to subsist inter-se the individual, the community, the state and international organization, is not attempted" by the commission and eventually by the UN.[45] She suggested the commission and the sub-commission to build a "comprehensive list of every country in the world, of legal and administrative measures which subtract from the right of human beings as guaranteed within the purview of the charter."[46]

Mehta continued her insistence upon implementation when the Drafting committee reconvened in Geneva (1947) to discuss the form of the Bill of Rights, whether it was to become a declaration only or convention only or both.[47] She told the committee that the form of the bill could be decided once the mechanism of implementation was agreed upon.[48] The bill, she said, should be both a declaration as well as a convention. It should be "an expression of faith; and also a programme of action to be carried out. It becomes a declaration as an expression of faith; it becomes a convention as a programme of action. Therefore, there should be no confusion."[49] Agreeing with the Australian delegate, she further brought to the committee's attention that the declaration should make no promises it did not intend to implement.[50] It is for this purpose of clarity and to avoid giving false hopes, the declaration would outline the general principles, whereas the convention would precisely define the rights guaranteed. It had to speak to every member of the public and should be comprehensible to all. At the third meeting of the commission, she continued to press upon the above concerns and proposed amendments to make the declaration concise and lucid while not being merely reduced to its skeleton form. She said that it was imperative for the declaration to have a human appeal.[51] Mehta also spoke favorably for continuing the provision of the League of Nations that would allow the UN to receive representations from individuals or groups in certain cases.[52] She said that she understood the difficulties in dealing with representation from individuals as there is always the concern of reliability with such petitions. However, she said that it would not be difficult to weed out the unreliable pleas. The right to petition to the UN, Mehta asserted, should not be denied to the people in individual capacity as that would protect their basic human rights and fundamental freedoms.[53]

When it came to implementation, the question was not merely of giving the declaration teeth in the form of a covenant but to also bring member countries on board. Being true to her place as representative of a third world country, Mehta cautioned the commission about the unsuitability of a singular covenant for the implementation of the declaration. The rationale, she wrote, was the inability of a single covenant to understand the ground realities and limitations of all member countries. It was for this reason that she proposed that the first covenant should not include economic and social rights within its ambit as for countries in dirt of resources, it would be impossible to meet the expenditure of guaranteeing these rights and that would keep them from signing the covenant.[54] Thus, she advised for the first covenant to be restricted to "a few important rights, i.e. rights to equality and liberty, so that it may be possible to get the largest measure of agreement."[55]

What one finds visible in Mehta's iterations in the course of the discussion on the UDHR is her conception of the role of an international organization, such as the UN and of human rights and the need for those making decisions at the UN to look beyond the state and concerns of national sovereignty. The latter most importantly highlights her commitment to serving the people of the member countries and not the governments that were being representative. Mehta understood the pitfalls of blind faith in the State as she cautioned that sometimes it would be the State itself that would have to be fought to safeguard the rights of its people. It can be viewed as a result of her experience as a nationalist leader that she was not satisfied with anything short of precise definition and robust mechanisms to uphold human rights. This spirit is in cognizance with the idealism enshrined in the Indian vision of the UN in its formative years.

The forgotten envoys: Begum Shareefah Hamid Ali and Lakshmi Menon

Equal Rights for Women are Not Enough. — Begum Shareefah Hamid Ali.[56]

Ali and Menon are the lesser known women envoys of India. Both were prominent Indian nationalist leaders. At the UN, Ali was a founding member of the UN Commission on the Status of Women in 1947. While discussing the aim of the commission with other members, Ali brought along her beliefs on the issue of women's rights that were situated in her experiences as an active leader of the Indian suffragette movement. Ali highlighted the need to define the meaning of women's rights by insisting that women should not halt at merely asking for rights "equal" to those of men.[57] She asserted that the realization of women's rights as conceived within such a framework of equality would be inadequate as "there were still countries in the world where men had negligible rights."[58] Ali was supported in her injunctions by the American representative to the commission, Dorothy Kenyon. The many weaknesses of the term "equality" were discussed upon as all "enslaved men" would be perfectly equal under slavery. Thus, making it imperative that the language of women's rights is rooted in the idea of human rights and not merely "equal rights." Ali prodded women to strive for "real rights" instead.[59] This was an insightful observation by her as it was reflective of the varied realities of women across the world. What 'equality' would mean for one section of women would not be applicable to another. By bringing the question of the substance of these rights to the center of the debate, Ali built ground for conversation between women of various backgrounds.

Ali's advocacy of women's rights was positioned in her prolonged association with the Indian nationalist struggle and suffrage movement. In July 1933, along with Rajkumari Amrit Kaur and Dr. Muthulakshmi Reddy, also Indian nationalist leaders, Ali represented Indian women before the Joint Select Committee on Indian Constitutional Reforms of the British Parliament. The memoranda submitted demanded the recognition of equality of the sexes on the Declaration of Fundamental Rights and made alternative franchise proposals pending the introduction of universal franchise in India.[60] During her visit, she spoke at a meeting convened by the London Committee of the Women's India Association, openly criticizing the British approach towards women's franchise as "timid, halting and inadequate."[61] Further on, Ali said that women did not seek a competition for power with men. That conceptualization of power and rights, in her view, was limiting in nature. She continuously laid stress upon the idea that women instead want "a voice in social legislation" that allows them to perform their civic duties. She added, "Indian women would continue to agitate as long as the franchise was not enlarged."[62]

Thereafter, Ali participated in the Third International Conference for India, in Geneva in November, 1933. The only Indian Muslim woman representative, Ali spoke at length about the strength of the women's movement in India. She also emphasized upon the attention that the Indian women's movement laid upon social reforms and its efforts towards securing franchise for women, that would enable them to serve the country.[63] Her argument for women's rights was situated in the language of the ability to serve the country. However, it was at the International Women's Conference at Istanbul in 1935 that one sees the fiery internationalist approach of Ali where she warned the Western feminists of committing the mistake of making "arrogant assumption of superiority or patronage on the part of Europe or America" as this would do nothing but alienate the fellow women in Asia and Africa.[64] The main points of discussion at the conference revolved around questions of political rights, economic and legal rights, equal moral standards and establishment of world peace.[65] These are a few important insights into Ali's ideas of transnational solidarity that enable us to understand what she brought to the table when she took charge as the Indian delegate at the

UN Commission on Women. Unfortunately, despite her pioneering role in the discussions on women's rights and as the only Muslim woman delegate from India,
Ali remains one of the least written about women figures in Indian diplomacy;
thus amounting her erasure not just as a woman, but also as a Muslim woman. A
more detailed study of her role in the UN could make significant contributions
to understanding the place of minority representatives of India and, representatives from the global South, in the making of the UN. This is imperative as the
post-colonial states like India were not homogenous blocks and while the idea of
a coloured representative at the UN is easier to work around, the exploration of
the voice of minorities within the third world countries in the making of the new
world warrants deeper consideration.

Lakshmi Menon was a teacher, lawyer, activist, politician, and an Indian envoy
to the UN. In 1948, she was appointed as a member of the alternative Indian delegation to the UN. Thereafter, she headed the UN Section on the Status of Women
and Children (1949–1950) and in 1952 was appointed as a Deputy Minister in the
Ministry of External Affairs of India.

In 1948, while Pandit headed the Indian delegation to the UN General Assembly meeting, Menon was appointed as a member of the alternative delegation. The
initial engagements of independent India at the UN were always characterized
with strong women envoys. Menon was amongst these important female figures
and she left an imprint at her very first appearance at the UN. In 1948, Menon
was a noticeable figure in Indian politics and women's movement. She was also
the editor of Roshni, a quarterly journal of the All India Women's Conference,
and her writing and oratorical skills were already established and well known.[66]
As already illustrated in the experiences of Mehta, India played a crucial role
within the UN in the discussions and drafting of the Universal Declaration of
Human Rights. Menon too was on the Third committee on the Draft Declaration
of Human Rights.[67] Menon's most remembered contribution in the early years
though is her time as the Chief of the Committee on the Status of Women at
the UN.

At her inaugural appearance at the UN, Menon was looked at by the delegates
and the press with great interest.[68] While the appointment of a woman to the alternative Indian delegation to the UN came to many as "interesting," the effectiveness of Menon as a capable envoy won much praise as she spoke on the Indian
stance on the continued South African debate at the UN and in the discussions on
the human rights declaration.[69] She reminded the committee that, "different countries have different beliefs and political systems. What they share though are the
same ideals of social justice and freedom" and this had to be kept in mind while
drafting the declaration, thus emphasizing upon the need for mutual understanding in the landscape of international cooperation.[70]

As the Chief of the UN Commission on the Status of women (1949–50), Menon
was committed towards the upliftment of women and was very vocal about her
passion for the cause.[71] When asked how the status of women would be improved
in India and the world, she laid utmost attention upon the value of education in
the course of this pursuit. She said in an interview, "When women have a chance
to learn, their homes will improve. When their homes will improve, their nations

will improve."[72] This emphasis of Menon on education, though restrictive, can be seen in the context of the nationalist struggle and political work as social uplift-ment. While attending the UN conferences, she also participated in various public meetings discussing advocacy of education and peace and upliftment of the status of women.[73] Many of her contemporaries in these discussions were other women envoys to the UN like, Minerva Bernardino (Dominion Republic), Ana Figueroa (Chile), Amalia Castillo Ledón (Mexico), Dorothy Kenyon (US), and Ruth Tom-linson (UK), amongst others.

Menon believed that if "real democracy and freedom was to be attained," then inequalities had to be removed from the world.[74] She was also an ardent advo-cate of the correlation of peace and women's struggle for equality. Speaking at a public meeting in June, 1950, she said, "When women gain equal status with men in their nations, they will use power to promote peaceful settlements (…), women are eager promoters of peace."[75] In this, she presaged the UNSCR on women, peace, and security by half a century. She was not though, it appears, recognized as such by the lobbiests for that resolution. However, she warned that peace should not be the end goal envisaged for the UN. It would provide a fertile ground where the "greater ideals of freedom, justice and love would be realized and that is the final aim of the United Nations."[76]

Conclusion

Pandit, Mehta, Ali, and Menon are four of the many women representatives who were part of the making of the UN.[77] A quick glance at their experiences at the UN brings to the forefront lost international thought of these women and their vision for the most important international organization of the twenty-first century. This is a crucial entry point into a larger exploration of the place of women actors in international politics. It is too long overdue to bridge the gap between the transnational women's networks and third world internationalism in the interwar period and its post-world war successors, allowing for a closer look at how values of suffragette movements and anti-colonial struggle found expression through the women of the third world in the formation of the new world of international politics. This chapter thus, provides a teaser of what lies hidden in the archives and how once the focus is changed from institutions to the people who build that institution, a new history of the UN would come to surface. A history written from the margins but which echoes the aspirations of equality, justice, and peace that the world organization was supposed to stand for. This history will not only reintroduce us to the possibilities of a more united world, but would also outline a new disciplinary inquiry that does not leave the women behind while chronicling the workings of world politics.

Notes

1 Bhagavan, Manu, "A New Hope: India, the United Nations and the Making of the Universal Declaration of Human Rights" , *Modern Asian Studies*, No. 44 (2) (2010): 311–347; Bhagavan, Manu, *India and the Quest for One World: The Peacemakers*

(New Delhi: HarperCollins Publishers, 2012); Glenda Sluga, *Internationalism in the Age of Nationalism* (Philadelphia: University of Pennsylvania Press, 2013); Ownes, Patricia, "Women and the History of International Thought", *International Studies Quarterly* (2018): 1–15; Rebecca Adami, *Women and the Universal Declaration of Human Rights* (New York & London: Routledge, 2019); Khan, R. , "Between Ambitions and Caution: India, Human Rights, and Self-Determination at the United Nations", in Moses, A. D., Duranti, M., and Burke, R. (eds) *Decolonization, Self-Determination, and the Rise of Global Human Rights Politics* (Cambridge: Cambridge University Press (Human Rights in History), 2020): 207–235; Murthy, C.S.R. , *India in the United Nations: Interplay of Interests and Principles (*SAGE Publications, 2020).

2 Ownes, Patricia , "Women and the History of International Thought", *International Studies Quarterly (2018):* 1–15.
3 Enloe, C. H., *Bananas, beaches and bases: making feminist sense of international politics* (Berkeley, Calif, University of California Press, 2014) ; Ownes, Patricia , "Women and the History of International Thought", *International Studies Quarterly (2018):* 1–15.
4 Nayudu, Swapna Kona, "India Looks at the World: Nehru, the Indian Foreign Service & World Diplomacy", *Diplomatica,* Vol 2 ((2020): 100–117.
5 Bhagavan, *India and the Quest for One World: The Peacemakers*, 66.
6 Pandit, Vijaya Lakshmi, *The Scope of Happiness: A Personal Memoir* (New York: Crown Publishers,1979).
7 https://www.sahistory.org.za/dated-event/ghetto-act-or-asiatic-land-tenure-and-indian-representation-act-no-28-1946-passed.
8 Pandit, *The Scope of Happiness: A Personal Memoir,* 206.
9 Pandit, *The Scope of Happiness: A Personal Memoir.*
10 "Article I vs. Article II The Colonial Question at UN", *Socialist Call,* 4 November, 1946, 5.
11 Cork, Jim, "Article I vs. Article II The Colonial Question at UN", *Socialist Call* , 4 November, 1946, 5
12 Cork, Jim, "Article I vs. Article II The Colonial Question at UN", *Socialist Call* , 4 November, 1946, 5
13 Cork, Jim, "Article I vs. Article II The Colonial Question at UN", *Socialist Call* , 4 November, 1946, 5
14 Cork, Jim, "Article I vs. Article II The Colonial Question at UN", *Socialist Call* , 4 November, 1946, 5.
15 Bhagavan, *India and the Quest for One World: The Peacemakers.*
16 UN Charter, Article 1, https://www.un.org/en/sections/un-charter/chapter-i/index.html.
17 UN Charter, Article 2, https://www.un.org/en/sections/un-charter/chapter-i/index.html.
18 "Hits South Africa", *Newark Star Ledger,* 22 November, 1946, 25.
19 Bhagavan, *India and the Quest for One World: The Peacemakers.*
20 Pandit, *The Scope of Happiness: A Personal Memoir.*
21 Bhagavan, *India and the Quest for One World: The Peacemakers.*
22 Bhagavan, Manu, *India and the Quest for One World: The Peacemakers*, 64.
23 Bhagavan, Manu, *India and the Quest for One World: The Peacemakers*, 64.
24 Bhagavan, Manu, *India and the Quest for One World: The Peacemakers*, 64.
25 "200 attend N. Y. reception for african leaders", *Michigan Chronicle* ,16 November, 1946, 2.
26 Rebecca Adami, *Women and the Universal Declaration of Human Rights* (New York & London: Routledge, 2019).
27 File 15 (i), 'Report on the Commission of Human Rights, Third Session', Hansa Mehta Papers, NMML, 24 May, 1948- 18 June, 1948.
28 "Backward Areas Held UN Province", *New York Times,* 1 February, 1947, 3.

29 Adami, R. (2019). *Women and the Universal Declaration of Human Rights*. Routledge: New York, 72.

30 Ibid.

31 McLenan, Nancy, "UN Asked to Speed World Press Unit", *New York Times*, 15 March, 1947, 3; File 15 (i), 'Speech by Mrs. Hansa Mehta Before Commission on Human Rights', Hansa Mehta Papers, NMML, 27 January, 1947; File 15 (i), 'Report of Human Rights Commission-From 2 December 1947-17 December 1947', Hansa Mehta Papers, NMML.

32 File 15 (i), Human Rights Commission Report: 27 January to 10 February 1947, Hansa Mehta Papers, NMML, 25 Feb, 1947.

33 File 15 (i), Human Rights Commission Report: 27 January to 10 February 1947, Hansa Mehta Papers, NMML, 25 Feb, 1947.

34 File 15 (i), Human Rights Commission Report: 27 January to 10 February 1947, Hansa Mehta Papers, NMML, 25 Feb, 1947.

35 File 15 (i), Human Rights Commission Report: 27 January to 10 February 1947, Hansa Mehta Papers, NMML, 25 Feb, 1947.

36 Adami, R. (2019). *Women and the Universal Declaration of Human Rights*. Routledge: New York. P.70.

37 File 15 (i), Human Rights Commission Report: 27 January to 10 February 1947, Hansa Mehta Papers, NMML, 25 Feb, 1947 ; Pandit, *The Scope of Happiness: A Personal Memoir* ; Shulz, Simone, "*Diplomats of the Global South and the UDHR-Plurality and Universality*", in Miguelángel Verde Garrido, Philani Mthembu, Adam S. Wilkins (Eds.) The Global Politics of Human Rights, The Berlin Forum on Global Politics (2020).

38 Adami, R. (2019). *Women and the Universal Declaration of Human Rights*. Routledge: New York, p.71.

39 File 15 (i), Human Rights Commission Report: 27 January to 10 February 1947, Hansa Mehta Papers, NMML, 25 Feb, 1947.

40 File 15 (i), Human Rights Commission Report: 27 January to 10 February 1947, Hansa Mehta Papers, NMML, 25 Feb, 1947.

41 File 15 (i), Human Rights Commission Report: 27 January to 10 February 1947, Hansa Mehta Papers, NMML, 25 Feb, 1947.

42 Adami, R. (2019). *Women and the Universal Declaration of Human Rights*. Routledge: New York, p.66.

43 Ibid.

44 File 15 (i), "Speech by Mrs. Hansa Mehta Before Commission on Human Rights", Hansa Mehta Papers, NMML, 27 January, 1947.

45 File 15 (i), "Speech by Mrs. Hansa Mehta Before Commission on Human Rights", Hansa Mehta Papers, NMML, 27 January, 1947.

46 File 15 (i), "Speech by Mrs. Hansa Mehta Before Commission on Human Rights", Hansa Mehta Papers, NMML, 27 January, 1947.

47 File 15 (i) , "Report of Human Rights Commission-From 2 December 1947-17 December 1947", Hansa Mehta Papers, NMML.

48 File 15 (i) , "Report of Human Rights Commission-From 2 December 1947-17 December 1947", Hansa Mehta Papers, NMML; File 15 (i), "Speech at the Second Session of the Human Rights Commission", Hansa Mehta Papers, NMML, 2 December, 1947.

49 File 15 (i), "Speech by Mrs. Hansa Mehta, Indian Delegate for Human Rights", Hansa Mehta Papers, NMML, 3 December, 1947.

50 Adami, R. (2019). *Women and the Universal Declaration of Human Rights*. Routledge: New York, p.71.

51 File 15 (i), "Speech Made by Hansa Mehta, Delegate from India in the Commission on Human Rights, Third Session", Hansa Mehta Papers, NMML, May 27, 1948.

52 File 15 (i), "Indian Delegation, Proposal on Implementation", Hansa Mehta Papers, NMML, 18 June, 1948.

53 File 15 (i), "Indian Delegation, Proposal on Implementation", Hansa Mehta Papers, NMML, 18 June, 1948.

54 File 15 (i), "Human Rights Commission Fifth Session, Report by Mrs. Hansa Mehta, Representative of India", Hansa Mehta Papers, NMML, 9 May 1949-20 June 1949.

55 "Human Rights Commission Fifth Session, Report by Mrs. Hansa Mehta, Representative of India", 9 May 1949-20 June 1949, File 15 (i), Hansa Mehta Papers, NMML.

56 *Plainfield Courier News,* 22 February, 1947, 6.

57 Adami, R. (2019). *Women and the Universal Declaration of Human Rights.* Routledge: New York, 97.

58 "U.N. Women Balk at 'Equal' Rights With Men, Saying These Are Sometimes Not Enough", *New York Times,* 12 February, 1947, 10; "Would Guarantee Rights to Women", *The Gazette,* 13 February, 1947, 4.

59 "Ask for Real Rights", *Pittsburg Press,* 22 February, 1947, 9.

60 "Indian Women's Case in England", *Times of India,* 8 July, 1933, 9 ; "Women's Franchise", *Times of India ,* 25 July, 1933, 11; "Indian Women's Demand- Joint Electorates", *Times of India,* 2 August, 1933, 9.

61 "Women's Franchise", *Times of India,* 25 July, 1933, 11 ; "Indian Women Delegates", *The Manchester Guardian* (6 September, 1933): 12; "Faith in Non Violence- Geneva Discussion on Indian Situation", *Times of India ,* 21 September, 1933, 9.

62 "Women's Franchise", *Times of India,* 25 July, 1933, 11.

63 "Third International Conference for India Held in Geneva", *China Weekly Review* (11 November, 1933): 432.

64 Winslow, Barbara, "Feminist Movements- Gender and Sexual Equality". in Teresa A. Meade and Merry E. Wiesner (ed.). *A Companion to Gender History* (Blackwell Publishing, 2013): 202.

65 "Indian Affairs in England", *Times of India,* 19 June, 1935, 15.

66 "Habeas Corpus: India at the UN", *Times of India,* 19 August, 1948, 6.

67 Metz, Homer , "UN Debate on Human Rights Holds Vast Promise for World", *The Christian Science Monitor* (20 October, 1948): 7.

68 "South Africa Attacked For Racial Discrimination", *Times of India* (27 October, 1948): 7; Metz, Homer , "UN Debate on Human Rights Holds Vast Promise for World", *The Christian Science Monitor* (20 October, 1948).

69 "South Africa Attacked For Racial Discrimination", *Times of India* (27 October, 1948): 7.

70 Homer , 7; Roberts, Graham, "UN Reflects from Geneva", *A America,* 80 (8) (27 November, 1948): 203.

71 "Women Take to Skies in Seeking UN Jobs", *Los Angeles Times,* 25 September, 1949, 10; "UN Women Hold Meeting on Plane", *New York Herald Tribune.* 25 September, 1949, 21.

72 "World Brings Toughest Worries to L.I", *Newsday.* 6 December, 1949, 5.

73 "Day Education Symposium Opens at Wellesley Oct. 16", *The Boston Globe,* 9 October, 1949, C9; "Woman's Forum", *Newsday,* 25 March, 1950, 7.

74 "'Voice' is Reported Upsetting Kremlin", *New York Times,* 28 May, 1950, 3.

75 "Women's Struggle For Equality Linked With Peace Cause", *The Hartford Courant,* 2 June, 1950, 21.

76 "Women's Struggle For Equality Linked With Peace Cause", *The Hartford Courant,* 2 June, 1950, 21.

77 See Adami, 'International Welfare Feminism' this volume, ch. 4; Marino, 'From Women's Rights to Human Rights' this volume, ch. 1; Dietrich Luhr and Sator, 'The Latin American Women' this volume, ch. 2; and Burke, 'Universal Human Rights for Women' this volume, Ch. 5.

Bibliography

Adami, R., *Women and the Universal Declaration of Human Rights* (New York & London, Routledge, 2019).

Ahluwalia, S., *Reproductive Restraints: Birth Control in India, 1877–1947* (Urbana, University of Illinois Press, 2008).

Ankit, R., "In the Twilight of Empire: Two Impressions of Britain and India at the United Nations, 1945–47", *South Asia: Journal of South Asian Studies*, 38(4) (2015): 574–588.

Bhagavan, M., *India and the Quest for One World: The Peacemakers* (New Delhi, Harper Collins Publishers, 2012).

Bhagavan, M., 'India and the United Nations: Or Things Fall Apart', in David M. Malone, C. Raja Mohan and Srinath Raghavan (eds.) *The Oxford Handbook of Indian Foreign Policy*. (Oxford, Oxford University Press, 2015).

Bhagavan, M., "A New Hope: India, the United Nations and the Making of the Universal Declaration of Human Rights", *Modern Asian Studies*, 44(2) (2010): 311–347.

Enloe, C. H., *Bananas, Beaches and Bases: Making Feminist Sense of International Politics*. (Berkeley, University of California Press, 2014).

Glenda, S., *Internationalism in the Age of Nationalism* (Philadelphia, University of Pennsylvania Press, 2013).

Guthrie, A., *Madame Ambassador: The Life of Vijayalakshmi Pandit*. (London, Macmillan & Co Ltd, 1963).

Itty A., "From Bandung to NAM: Non-alignment and Indian Foreign Policy, 1947–65", *Commonwealth & Comparative Politics*, 46(2) (2008): 195–219.

Hoffmann, S.-L., *Human Rights in the Twentieth Century* (Cambridge, Cambridge University Press, 2011).

Jain, D., "Women of the South: Engaging with the UN As a Diplomatic Manoeuvre" in Jennifer A. Cassidy (eds.) *Gender and Diplomacy* (London and New York, Routledge, 2018).

Khan, R., "Between Ambitions and Caution: India, Human Rights, and Self-Determination at the United Nations', in Moses, A. D., Duranti, M., and Burke, R. (eds) *Decolonization, Self-Determination, and the Rise of Global Human Rights Politics* (Cambridge, Cambridge University Press (Human Rights in History), 2020): 207–235.

Khipple, R.L., *The Woman Who Swayed America: Vijayalakshmi Pandit*. (Lahore, Lion Press, 1946).

Mitoma, G. T., *Human Rights and the Negotiation of American Power* (Philadelphia, University of Pennsylvania Press, 2013).

Mukherjee, S., *Indian Suffragettes: Female Identities and Transnational Network* (New Delhi, Oxford University Press, 2018).

Murthy, C.S.R., *India in the United Nations: Interplay of Interests and Principles* (New Delhi, SAGE Publications, 2020).

Nair, J, "The Lateral Spread of Indian Feminist Historiography", *Journal of Women's History*, 20 (4) (2008): 177–184.

Nayudu, S. K., "India Looks at the World: Nehru, the Indian Foreign Service & World Diplomacy", *Diplomatica*, 2 (2020): 100–117.

Nehru, J., *Selected Works of Jawaharlal Nehru* (New Delhi, Jawaharlal Nehru Memorial Fund, 1993).

Nijhawan, Shobhna, "International Feminism from Asia Center: The All Asian Women's Conference (Lahore, 1931) as a Transnational Feminist Movement", *Journal of Women's History*, 29 (3) (2017): 12–36.

Ownes, P., "Women and the History of International Thought", *International Studies Quarterly*, 62 (3) (2018): 467–481.

Pandit, V. L., *The Scope of Happiness: A Personal Memoir* (New York, Crown Publishers, 1979).

Radha, K., *The History of Doing: An Illustrated Account of Movements for Women's Rights and Feminism in India 1800–1990* (New Delhi, Kali for Women, 1993).

Scott, J. W., *Gender and the Politics of History*, (New York, Columbia University Press, 1988).

Shulz, S., "Diplomats of the Global South and the UDHR-Plurality and Universality", in Miguelángel Verde Garrido, Philani Mthembu, Adam S. Wilkins (eds.) *The Global Politics of Human Rights, The Berlin Forum on Global Politics* (2020). https://bfogp.org/publications-and-projects/the-global-politics-of-human-rights/

Sponberg, M. et al. (eds.), *Companion to Women's Historical Writings* (New York, Palgrave Macmillan, 2005).

Thakur, V., "The "Hardy Annual": A History of India's First UN Resolution", *Indian Review*, 16(4) (2017): 401–429.

Winslow, B., "Feminist Movements-Gender and Sexual Equality", in Teresa A. Meade and Merry E. Wiesner (eds.). *A Companion to Gender History* (Oxford, Blackwell Publishing, 2013).

Zachariah, B., *Nehru* (London and New York, Routledges, 2004).

4 International welfare feminism

CSW navigating cold war tensions 1949

Rebecca Adami

Introduction

Early Cold War frictions after the end of the Second World War influenced the possibilities for advancement of an international human rights framework in the United Nations. The joint-effort in 1949 of the only two women delegates to the UN Commission on Human Rights (UNCHR), Eleanor Roosevelt (US) and Hansa Mehta (India), to draft an international convention on human rights that would connect political and civil rights with economic, social and cultural rights was hampered and its adoption prolonged due to Cold War rivalry. The reductionist narrative of an incompatibility of USSR communist and US capitalist ideological systems that shaped the first and second generation of human rights in the United Nations has, however, neglected to place in the foreground of such narratives the women diplomats who argued for women's economic and social rights based on other concerns than could be reduced into early East-West tensions. What is needed is a concept on international feminist efforts in the history of International Relations (IR) that sought to advance welfare rights in a patriarchal and colonial world order. Disagreements on the scope of human rights—of whether they would apply to women and people living under colonial rule—were also felt in the Commission on the Status of Women (CSW). How were efforts in the CSW to advance equal pay for women coloured by political and ideological strains in 1949—the sequent year when the UDHR had been adopted?

Based on United Nations meeting protocols from the third session of the CSW in 1949, the alliances and conflicts *within* the CSW sketched in this chapter contribute to unearthing the role of non-Western women in advancing welfare rights in the early Cold War years. Earlier studies on the feminist internationalization of economic and social rights have included women representatives in the International Labour Organisation (ILO), the World Federation of Trade Unions (WFTU), and the Women's International Democratic Federation (WIDF); [1] however, these international organizations sent representatives to the meetings of the CSW in 1949. The debates within this all-female UN commission at its outset are thus of great interest.

By introducing the concept of "international welfare feminism," the post-war frictions within the UN with regard to international law-making on human rights in 1949 are contextualized in this chapter as international women alliances on welfare rights that disrupted patriarchal and colonial interests relative to women's labour. Before turning to the debates within the CSW on the notion of equal pay

DOI: 10.4324/9781003036708-4

in 1949, I will consider the resistance that Latin American women delegates in the UN faced when trying to advance equal pay in the male-dominated ILO as well as the opposition by American women's organizations to the creation of an all-female commission in the ILO. I then expand upon the initial marginalization in the UN of the Commission on the Status of Women (CSW) and their appeal to become a division within the UN Secretariat before examining how equal pay was being debated within the CSW, pointing to the ways in which Western women delegates seemed to undermine the competence of the CSW from within by wanting to refer the debate on equal pay back to the ILO. Finally, I explore how matters like "equal pay" were discussed within the CSW by Western women delegates who had historically sought to advance women's rights but now seemingly retreated on the issue of gender equality in 1949. I conclude by arguing that "international welfare feminism" can be used to initiate further critical debates into hitherto overlooked women's history of the UN regarding struggles against colonialism, patriarchal structures, and capitalist exploitation of women's labour.

"International welfare feminism" – a hidden historical narrative in the UN?

The history of women in the UN has primarily centred on the role of Western female delegates and has largely assumed a shared feminist interest amongst women delegates.[2] This oversight has allowed for the contestations regarding different understandings of women's rights amongst female delegates—women who did not share ideological, political, and cultural interests and ideas—to be left unproblematized.[3]

Peter Waterman[4] has addressed the lack of focus on women's movements with internationalism in historical and contemporary feminist studies and has argued that studies either fail to problematize the relationship amongst women globally or assume a shared outlook and commonly agreed-upon approach to women's rights issues.[5] In earlier work,[6] I have focused on particular value conflicts within the CSW from 1945 during the drafting of the UN Charter to 1948 and the drafting of the UDHR. I have thus questioned the simplified view of North-South relations amongst the women representatives in the UN by describing the conflicts as well as the alliances across these divisions. Female delegates in the CSW took different positions on women's rights during the drafting of the UDHR in 1946–48 along class and ethnic lines, as well as along ideological lines of the various women and national independence movements they belonged to, which predicted their stances on the economic and political rights of women.

In this chapter, I explore what I conceptualize as "international welfare feminism" during the Cold War years as a critical counternarrative of feminist socialist struggles for women's rights within the CSW in 1949. The post-war period has been portrayed as the "doldrum years" in American feminism,[7] and the narrative of welfare internationalism has been dominated by the conformity, conservatism, and antifeminism of Stalinism and McCarthyism.[8] Pieper Mooney calls for a more nuanced 'understanding of the gendered politics of the Cold War'[9] and historian Franscica de Haan notes that assumption that women's organizations such as the WIDF and the WFTU's striving for international welfarism were Communist has invited scepticism from Western historians that these organizations were therefore not deemed feminist.[10] "International welfare feminism" is thus defined in contrast to "red feminism"[11] and "communist internationalism and feminism"[12] by not resting on the presumption that the women delegates to the UN who advanced women's economic and social rights by arguing for the need to create welfare institutions for day-care, preschool, and social security services necessarily adhered to a particular political perspective, nor had been acting representatives of Soviet countries. "International welfare feminism" in the early Cold War years has been mired in dichotomies that have obscured the links between welfarism and feminism on the one hand and internationalism and feminism on the other. Feminism was under Stalinism seen as a "bourgeois term that obscured the capitalist oppression of women."[13] Thus, initiatives for women's rights such as rights connected to the woman worker, including equal pay, when labelled communist in the Cold War years, were then not labelled as feminist initiatives. The perception that women could promote feminist internationalism and not merely reflect their own national interests has especially in research on UN diplomacy in the late 1940s been overlooked. "International welfare feminism" is developed to question the presumed incompatibility between advancing socialist feminist issues in the international arena during the postwar period. Southern women delegates in the UN advancing women's economic rights could represent other interests than East-West ideologies.

Feminist agency seems furthermore to have been characterized as Western in historical narratives. For example, US delegate to the CSW, Dorothy Kenyon (1888–1972)—a lawyer, socialist, and journalist labelled by Joseph McCarthy as communist affiliated—has been understood to have advanced women's economic rights through her long-term commitment to these issues in the League of Nations and the UN.[14] Her role in 1949 in the CSW was, however, complex in the debates on equal pay for women.

In the course of my earlier work on the UN Charter and the UDHR, I found that other prominent US and UK female figures (including the first female US delegates to the UN, Virginia Gildersleeve and Eleanor Roosevelt) have been given kudos for advancing women's rights within the UN when several proposals were suggested initially by women delegates from India, Brazil, Mexico, and the Dominican Republic.[15] Similar conclusions have been drawn by Skard, Marino, Dietrichson and Sator, Burke, and Rathore in this volume. It has been assumed that *Western* feminist welfarism was internationalized through the UN and the role of American women unionists' work in the ILO has been broadly acknowledged. However, the Southern feminists who also pushed for economic and social rights—in the Indian National Trade Union Congress and elsewhere—have been overshadowed in historical studies. A woman representative from the above-mentioned congress, Indira W. Bose, would declare in the 1950 ILO Conference that "Some of the representatives of so-called progressive governments, including my own, have thought it fit to oppose a Convention for men and women getting equal remuneration for work of equal value."[16] The wording opposed by the ILO members in that upcoming convention was itself a step back from what

Indian and Latin American women delegates to the CSW had proposed in 1949—namely an international convention covering equal pay for women.

Equal pay for women and the need for a separate female division within the ILO

The ILO meetings were comprised of internal debates containing different understandings of equality for women at the adoption of the Philadelphia Declaration on women's's rights 1944.[17] American women unionists had argued for a 'same but different' approach on women's labour which aimed at advancing protective legislation for women workers rather than the equal opportunities that Latin American Bertha Lutz was proposing 1944 in Philadelphia.[18]

Bertha Lutz (Brazil) felt that the stipulations for protection reduced the advancement of equal pay and equal opportunities. The ILO had formulated "equal remuneration" for (male) workers and "rate for the work" which had been the labour unions' definition of fair salaries. The use of cheap female labour was increasingly perceived as a threat to earlier labour standards. Instead of taking on equal pay for women, trade unions did not actively encourage employers to employ women workers. It was instead held that male workers' salaries should be decent and allow for the economic maintenance of a whole family.

> 'Equal remuneration for work of equal value' stood as a founding principle of the ILO. (...) 'remuneration without discrimination' reflected a dominant trade union position that sought to maintain men's wages and discourage employer use of cheaper female labour. In contrast, feminists cast equal pay as essential to women's rights.[19]

Bertha Lutz wanted to establish a sub-commission with only women in the ILO in order to ensure a language in its resolutions that reflected women's shared global struggle for gender equality.[20] Her suggestion was poorly received in the organization.

Resistance from US women's organisations of all-female UN body

Though they failed to create an all-female sub-commission within the ILO in 1944 to advance equal pay for women worldwide, Latin American women delegates including Bertha Lutz (Brazil); Minerva Bernardino (the Dominican Republic); and Amalia Castillo de Ledón (Mexico) sought at the United Nations Conference on International Organization (UNCIO) 1945 in overturning US and UK women's resistance to an all-women commission in the UN under ECOSOC, in addition to the CHR. The ILO had not been officially invited to participate at the conference in San Francisco but only "allowed to send an unofficial five-person delegation" for "informal consultation."[21] There was no woman on the delegation.

With a commission dedicated to women's rights within the UN, there was a renewed hope amongst Latin American women delegates of ensuring that gender equality became an inseparable part of an international framework of human rights. Historian Helen Laville has shown how US women's organizations opposed the idea of a separate commission for women.

> Members of the Women's Bureau coalition present at San Francisco immediately saw the proposal to establish a CSW as a threat to protective legislation, fearing the activism of such a commission in the hands of equalitarian feminists.[22]

The resistance reflected domestic battles in the US regarding the Equal Rights Amendment to the Constitution to which there were opponents stating that gender equality would lead to women losing the legislative protections related to work, bearing children, and economic privileges for women choosing domesticity.[23] The stance reflected a liberal political context in which government spending on welfare was seen as socialist and without the necessary welfare institutions fundamental for women to combine work and child care, furthering formal "equality" risked leading to discriminatory legislation in public arenas when 'equal' was interpreted as being treated on the same terms 'as men' without the necessary conditions in place for women to combine work with family.

American feminist groups failed to prevent the establishment of the CSW and instead focused their efforts on lobbying for representatives appointed who were against the Equal Rights Amendment (ERA) in the commission.[24]

> The coalition group Committee on Women in World Affairs (...) lobbied the State Department for the appointment of Kenyon to the commission. Kenyon was a long-time opponent of the ERA and had served as a representative on the League of Nation's Committee of Experts.[25]

The national political landscape in the US at the time seemed here to have haltered international feminist alliances through the CSW, as women representing other countries in the commission saw these debates on the risks with formal equality as US specific and were not as convinced of the supposed threat of socialism through the advancement of welfare institutions for women's economic and social rights.[26] Due to the conflict over the Equal Rights Amendment and early Cold War frictions between the opposing ideologies of capitalism and communism, women's equality turned out to be a sensitive topic for the US women representatives to the UN.

> [A]s the Cold War made women's rights an important battlefield in the early years of the CSW, Kenyon and her allies came to support international legislation on women's rights, less out of support for women in other nations, but out of a keen awareness of the need for the United States to sponsor women's rights as a national imperative.[27]

The establishment of a separate CSW was faced with opposition, not only from American and British women delegates but from within the Secretariat itself.

Underlying these reservations appears to have been other concerns: that a special woman's commission might empower women in unexpected ways, and perhaps even challenge the mainstream approach to violations of human rights.[28]

The CSW was devoted to the idea of convening in locations outside Europe and the US as a way to connect and assist national women's organisations and consequently held its third session in Beirut, Lebanon. The Commission had been invited there by Kenan Malik, chair of the Economic and Social Council (ECOSOC), who had played a vital role in the process of advancing the UDHR from the debates within the Council to the General Assembly vote in 1948.[29] Minerva Bernardino (the Dominican Republic) was chair of the CSW in 1949 who had lobbied for its establishment and been an unrelenting advocate for gender equality in the UN.[30] India was represented in the CSW by Lakshmi Menon[31] and the USSR by Elizavieta Alekseevna Popova. Lakshmi Menon had been one of the most outspoken critics of colonialism when debating human rights as she represented India in the Third Committee of the General Assembly. Elizavieta Alekseevna Popova had been a representative of the Soviet Union to the CSW and had participated in meetings of the CHR during the drafting of the UDHR. Mary Sutherland represented the UK and Dorothy Kenyon represented the US in the CSW.

The third session of the CSW was also open for the international women's organizations with consultative status, including the WFTU, represented by Marie Couette, and the WIDF, represented by Emelie Fares Ibrahim.

Specific conflicts concerned how different conceptions of equal pay for women were to be classified and whether the Commission could advance women's economic condition relative to other international bodies like the ILO and even the World Health Organization (WHO) but also whether the commission would gain more impact if turned into a division of the UN Secretariat. The low number of women appointed to higher positions in the Secretariat was of concern to the members of the CSW in 1949.[32] Bodil Begtrup (Denmark) and Minerva Bernardino (the Dominican Republic) had in 1948 discussed the possibility of transforming the CSW into a division in the Secretariat, and they shared the impression that the Secretary General was positively minded towards this. This suggestion was taken up for debate in the CSW at its third session in Beirut 1949. Minerva Bernardino believed that "such a measure would extend the Commission's possibilities of action."[33] Elizavieta Alekseevna Popova "recalled that ECOSOC had not approved the suggested change in the structure of the Secretariat."[34] Moreover, a division within the Secretariat would require a larger budget set aside for women's rights measures, which the Member States might not be willing to support. Mary Sutherland (UK) did not back the idea as she thought "the creation of a new division in the Secretariat would be badly received in certain quarters" since the "utility of the Commission itself was sometimes questioned."[35] Amalia Castillo de Ledón (Mexico) "warmly supported the Danish proposal" since the many resolutions of the Commission "had shown the necessity of having a large number of experts"[36] to facilitate the drafting of conventions proposed to strengthen the economic and legal status of women. The representatives of Greece and China also supported the proposal for transforming the Commission into a division in the Secretariat and to "insist on this request, in spite of the fact that it had not yet met with the approval of ECOSOC."[37] This suggestion did, however, not receive support within the UN, [38] which may have led to the marginalization of women's rights issues in the organization during the 1950s.

Reverting the notion of "equal pay" for women

The UK and US women delegates to the CSW during its third session in Beirut wanted to remove "equal pay" in a draft resolution on the rights for women workers by claiming it was a communist idea proposed by the WFTU. In doing so, they overlooked the fact that the CSW had advanced this idea on gender equality from its creation in 1946.[39] Mary Sutherland (UK) commented on WFTU's wording and expressed concern over "the term 'equal pay for equal work', for which 'rate-for-the-job' was a more easily understood clause."[40] Elizavieta Alekseevna Popova (USSR) responded that:

> In asking for the rejection of what she had termed 'an out-of-date' principle – equality with men who were raising a family – Mary Sutherland was going backward instead of forward and leading women to poverty. Many British women who had lost their husbands and fathers during the war were now heads of families, and should be considered as bread-winners.[41]

Marie Couette (WFTU) said that "the WFTU desired the Commission to re-affirm the principle of equal pay for equal work; and, secondly the procedure adopted by the ILO showed that it did not attach sufficient importance to this question."[42]

The Chinese representative Cecelia Sieu-Ling Zung tried to find a middle ground between these East-West conflicts over the issue of equal pay and agreed to withdraw her original text in favour of a UK amendment. Lakshmi Menon (India), however, was well aware of the consequences of this compromise:

> Lakshmi Menon (India) wondered whether the Representative of China had fully realized the implications of the United Kingdom amendment, since her original text had requested the Economic and Social Council to make recommendations to the Member States, which implied direct incentive to implement the principle of equal pay. The United Kingdom amendment, on the other hand, directed the whole of the question back to the International Labour Organization for an enquiry, which would take considerable time; in the meantime the Member States would not be obliged to take any action. That was a regressive step and she preferred the original Chinese text.[43]

The Chinese representative said she nonetheless accepted the UK amendment to the original proposal, which then lost its stronger support for equal pay. Elizavieta Alekseevna Popova (USSR) supported the statement by India. A compromise was met in which the UK amendment was placed as a second paragraph to the Chinese proposal, which was adopted.

These internal debates meant for US delegate Dorothy Kenyon that it was better to let the ILO study the issue of equal pay for women.

> Dorothy Kenyon (US) said the whole discussion (…) illustrated her view that it was premature to make recommendations concerning matters which obviously required lengthy study. The question of what was favourable or unfavourable to women was an extremely debatable point, and it was precisely on such points that the help of the International Labour Organization was required.[44]

Elizavieta Alekseevna Popova (USSR) "was opposed to any reference to study by the ILO."[45] The USSR had re-entered as members to the ILO in 1945. At the 1947 ILO Conference in which social policy in nonmetropolitan territories was discussed, it had been an Indian worker, Sharita Mukherjee, who had insisted "on the inclusion of the word 'sex' in the definition of discrimination" related to work.[46]

The CSW had, in the words of its former chair Bodil Begtrup (Denmark), been granted its status as full commission since the ECOSOC had realized that experts on human rights were not necessarily experts on the rights of women.[47] Nevertheless, the idea of "expert-status" was continuously placed outside the mandate or scope of the commission in the arguments laid out by American and British female delegates in the CSW in 1949 when the notion of equal pay was debated—they felt the discussion should be held in the ILO instead. But it would be thanks to the CSW that ILO finally included in its resolutions a mention of the equal rights of women after 30 years of advancing the rights of the male worker. The CSW had in 1948 "adopted a resolution calling for action by the ILO with respect to equal pay for equal work."[48]

Another division within the CSW was concerned with whether women's economic rights should be advanced through development agencies and whether other agencies should be advised to raise the standard of living through charity projects by Western NGOs. The representative of the WIDF, Emelie Fares Ibrahim, expressed surprise during the third session in 1949 that "relations with WHO had found a place on the agenda."[49] She argued that:

> In considering the protection of the health of populations, the first concern of the Commission should be measures for raising the standard of living and not questions such as the functions of specialized agencies, distribution of food through the Red Cross, the granting of scholarships, etc.[50]

This concern, raised already in 1949 by the WIDF, finds a contemporary critical analogue in colonial discourse analyses that question whether colonial development-projects, rationales, and structures can by any meaningful sense lead to change as they sustain inequality? As Emilie Fares Ibrahim formulated this concern:

[T]he Commission should give more careful study to the underlying conditions responsible for the state of health of the peoples before considering the function of WHO. The trouble must be attacked from the roots.[51]

This position questioned the patriarchal, colonial, and capitalist structures within which women, people living under colonial rule, and the working class suffered from economic exploitation. It was a controversial issue to bring up in the UN as the colonial powers were willing to debate the rights of women workers in Member States but not its overseas territories. Both France and the UK would later refrain from voting for the Convention on the Political Rights of Women because of the explicit mention of Non-Self Governing Territories.[52] When Emilie Fares Ibrahim drew attention at the third session to "the situation of women in Iran"[53]—members of the Iranian branch of the WIDF had been arrested and the branch dissolved—Lakshmi Menon (India) called it "a propaganda speech in which [Emilie Fares Ibrahim] had violently attacked a State Member of the United Nations."[54] The UK, Syria, Australia, and US made similar comments during the meeting.[55] At the following session of the CSW in New York, the WIDF was not granted visas to attend the session by the US government.

Equal pay for women—a question for the Commission on the Status of Women?

Dorothy Kenyon (US) and Mary Sutherland (UK) wanted the CSW to refer the 1949 draft on equal pay for equal work back to the ILO. This suggestion was met with criticism by Lakshmi Menon (India) and Elizavieta Alekseevna Popova (USSR) who indicated that the ILO had consistently prolonged the process by placing the issue of women's equal pay last on their conference agendas, and consequently running out of time before discussing the issue until a later meeting. This way the issue of equal pay travelled from meeting to meeting without receiving due consideration.

> In the early post-WWII years, the ILO focused on items that appeared genderless, like 'free association' and collective bargaining, which disproportionately benefited male workers, who were more likely to be in unionized occupations.[56]

International bodies and organizations that were all-male or predominantly male seemed to have been advancing (intentionally or unintentionally) the ideas and interests of its member base. An all-female commission in the UN would at least deal exclusively with women's rights. In 1949 Soviet and US women delegates seemed to increasingly use the CSW as a battleground for Cold War politics. When the Soviet delegate Elizavieta Alekseevna Popova relied on reports and information on the status of women around the world provided by the WFTU and the WIDF, these international feminist organizations were seen as part of a Soviet lobby. Both organizations held consultative status in the CSW while WIDF lost this status when listed as a communist enemy of the US. However, it was not only the US who felt threatened in their domestic affairs by the Soviet and supposedly communist-led international organizations.

What may initially have united the Soviet and Indian representatives in the CSW was the understanding that women's rights could not be secured without equal pay for working women, nor with a continued economic exploitation of women's labour. The divide between the Soviet and Indian female representatives grew in 1949 as the newly independent India felt that Soviet delegates used the UN as a forum to criticize other nations. The representative of India, Lakshmi Menon, also raised her concerns that WFTU was used as a lobby by the Soviets. [57] Elizavieta Alekseevna Popova (USSR) insisted in the CSW's third session that "The majority of international workers' organizations, of which WFTU was an outstanding example, had supported the principle [of equal pay]"[58] while the employer's organizations had opposed this principle. Her remark was followed by an observation by Lakshmi Menon (India) who maintained that:

> WFTU had many times distorted the facts in order to suggest that perfection only existed in the Soviet Union and that elsewhere all was confusion and misery. Lakshmi Menon had no doubt that the data brought forward by WFTU came from unofficial sources or from an organization working to overthrow the Indian government.[59]

When the US was criticized later in the meeting by Elizavieta Alekseevna Popova (USSR) for women's salaries only amounting to half of those of men workers Dorothy Kenyon (US) retorted by asking "whether the women in the Soviet slave labour camps received equal pay for equal work?"[60] Elizavieta Alekseevna Popova (USSR) had argued that gender equality was pivotal for human rights in the years following the Second World War, as British women had been laid off and thus discriminated against in their right to work. Mary Sutherland (UK) in rebutting this criticism from the Soviet Union countered that:

> In citing the fact that a million women had left factories in the UK since the end of the war, Elizavieta Alekseevna Popova had said that that had been caused by discrimination. The truth was quite otherwise. The UK, which did not maintain a large army on war footing, had enabled three million demobilized men to take up their places in industry by freeing a large number of women who devoted themselves to their households.[61]

This statement was a stance shared by both US and UK women representatives in the CSW in 1949, coloured of course by their commitment to national sentiments at the time; that women's freedom of choice included freely choosing domesticity. Dorothy Kenyon had, in a speech to Women's City Club of New York, argued that the right to work attained by women in the Soviet Union was nothing more than slavery.[62] Despite having made such anti-communist remarks, Dorothy Kenyon was later accused by McCarthy of being affiliated with communist organizations. Labelling women's international engagement in women's right to work as communist seems to have led to the silencing of international welfare feminism backed by Nordic, Latin American, and South Asian women delegates on women's economic and social rights in the late 1940s. A year later in 1950, Senator Margaret Chase Smith would hold the "Declaration of Conscience" speech expounding that people who exercised the freedom of speech—including the right to criticize, hold unpopular beliefs, protest, and think independently—risked being unfairly labelled as communists in America.

International welfare feminism and its relevance today

International welfare feminism—the advancement of women's rights with the understanding that women's equality and political freedom is linked with and dependent upon their economic liberation from unpaid or forced labour under capitalist, colonial, and patriarchal power structures—was advanced not only by Western women active in the international labour movement and Soviet women delegates in the UN in 1949 but also by Indian, Brazilian, Mexican, and Iranian women delegates through the CSW. The greatest divide regarding women's equal pay seemed to be between the US and UK women delegates on the one hand—whose governments re-employed millions of male workers after the Second World War—and Soviet and Indian women delegates on the other, the latter argued that women had become sole breadwinners in families and who also saw the economic upliftment of women living under colonial rule as vital for the advancement of gender equality. The French female delegates who had proposed non-discrimination based on sex in the UDHR abandoned their support for non-discrimination when it would mean the inclusion of people in the French territories.

Women's double role of unpaid domestic worker and also exploited underpaid and under-represented worker in international labour organizations became apparent in the post war years. Women were not yet organized in labour unions and their interests were not being advanced by male-dominated organizations. The employer organizations on the other hand seem to have avoided the issue of women's equal salaries as this would have meant higher costs, especially from providing social benefits for women workers with children. International welfare feminism would require recognition by private and state actors of the need for child welfare and social benefits for women workers to obtain and sustain paid work. It must also incorporate the understanding that women's unpaid labour in the home folded into full-time salaries of men with families.

Samuel Moyn[63] has claimed that human rights history starts in the 1970s when the utopian politics of communism and decolonization collapsed but he has, as Margarite Poulos[64] rightly argues, overlooked women's history. I agree here with Poulos that what is needed in order to understand the history of human rights through the UN are new looks at women's perspectives and histories.

> Seen within this framework the long traditions of internationalism, as well as the challenging shift to gender analysis in human-rights definitions and instruments at the UN, the claim of UN irrelevance to the 'true' story of human rights appears thin at best.[65]

Nevertheless, "women's perspectives and histories" are complex and the role of prominent feminists who advocated international welfare feminism from a third perspective of democratic socialism against colonialism in the Cold War years have been overlooked. Sondra Herman and Doris Linder have noted how Scandinavian women diplomats like Alva Myrdal—a Swedish socialist appointed the highest position as director of the social division within the UNESCO Secretariat—treated the UN as a platform to internationalize welfare feminism.[66] "She saw a worldwide, welfare-state feminism with women's efforts supported by community structures."[67]

As Wendy Pojman notes, the end of the Second World War did not mark an end or beginning of women's internationalism, but rather a turn in which national and international collaboration across divides was highly politicized and limited the international dimension of feminist alliances.[68] Colonial and patriarchal domination may have silenced historical narratives of southern women's resistance and struggles, which does not preclude their existence. Further research is needed into the international welfare feminism of the south advanced in the late 1940s through progressive feminist movements in African states that were still under colonial rule in order to challenge a dominant Western feminist perspective—as keeping with earlier findings sketched in this volume.

Notes

1 Francisca de Haan, "Continuing Cold War Paradigms in Western Historiography of Transnational Women's Organisations: The Case of the Women's International Democratic Federation (WIDF)," *Women's History Review* 19, no. 4 (2010): 547–73; Margarite Poulos, "Transnational Militancy in Cold-War Europe: Gender, Human Rights, and the WIDF during the Greek Civil War," *European Review of History* 24, no. 1 (2017): 17–35; Jadwiga E. Pieper Mooney, "Fighting Fascism and Forging New Political Activism: The Women's International Democratic Federation (WIDF) in the Cold War," in *De-Centering Cold War History: Local and Global Change*, ed. Jadwiga E. Pieper Mooney and Fabio Lanza (Routledge, 2012), 52–72; Melanie Ilic, "Soviet Women, Cultural Exchange and the Women's International Democratic Federation," in *Reassessing Cold War Europe*, ed. Sari Autio-Sarasmo and Katalin Miklóssy (Routledge, 2010), 157–74; Eileen Boris, Dorothea Hoehtker, and Susan Zimmermann, eds., *Women's ILO: Transnational Networks, Global Labour Standards and Gender Equity, 1919 to Present* (Leiden & Boston: BRILL, 2008); Eileen Boris, *Making the Woman Worker: Precarious Labour and the Fight for Global Standards, 1919–2019* (Oxford: Oxford University Press, 2019); Dorothy Sue Cobble, "International Women's Trade Unionism and Education," *International Labour and Working-Class History*, no. 90 (2016): 153–63.
2 See other chapters in this volume problematizing this idea.
3 See other chapters in this volume addressing this earlier gap.
4 Peter Waterman, "Hidden from Herstory: Women, Feminism and New Global Solidarity," *Economic and Political Weekly* 28, no. 44 (October 30, 1993): WS83–100.
5 Waterman, WS-83.
6 Rebecca Adami, "On Subalternity and Representation: Female and Post Colonial Subjects Claiming Universal Human Rights in 1948," *Journal of Research on Women and Gender* 6 (2015): 56–66; Rebecca Adami, "Counter Narratives as Political Contestation: Universality, Particularity and Uniqueness," *The Equal Rights Review*

15 (2015): 13–24; Rebecca Adami, *Women and the Universal Declaration of Human Rights* (New York & London: Routledge, 2019).

7 Leila J. Rupp and Verta Taylor, *Survival in the Doldrums: The American Women's Rights Movement, 1945 to the 1960s* (New York & Oxford: Oxford University Press, 1987).

8 Kate Weigand, *Red Feminism: American Communism and the Making of Women's Liberation* (Baltimore and London: The John Hopkins University Press, 2001), 10.

9 Pieper Mooney, "Fighting Fascism and Forging New Political Activism: The Women's International Democratic Federation (WIDF) in the Cold War," 66.

10 de Haan, "Continuing Cold War Paradigms in Western Historiography of Transnational Women's Organisations: The Case of the Women's International Democratic Federation (WIDF)."

11 Weigand, *Red Feminism: American Communism and the Making of Women's Liberation.*

12 Celia Donert, "From Communist Internationalism to Human Rights: Gender, Violence and International Law in the Women's International Democratic Federation Mission to North Korea, 1951," *Contemporary European History* 25, no. 2 (2016): 313–33.

13 Donert, 333.

14 Jaci Eisenberg, "The Status of Women: A Bridge from the League of Nations to the United Nations," *JIOS* 4, no. 2 (2013): 8–24.

15 See for example the inclusion of gender equality in the Charter and the UDHR, equal rights in marriage and to equal pay in the UDHR, Adami, *Women and the Universal Declaration of Human Rights.*

16 Carol Riegelman Lubin and Anne Winslow, *Social Justice for Women: The International Labour Organization and Women* (Durham and London: Duke University Press, 1990), 95.

17 Riegelman Lubin and Winslow, *Social Justice for Women: The International Labour Organization and Women.*

18 Eileen Boris, *Making the Woman Worker: Precarious Labour and the Fight for Global Standards, 1919–2019* (Oxford: Oxford University Press, 2019), 53.

19 Boris, 55.

20 Boris, 60.

21 Daniel Maul, *The International Labour Organization: 100 Years of Global Social Policy* (Berlin: de Gruyter, 2019), 137.

22 Helen Laville, "A New Era in International Women's Rights? American Women's Associations and the Establishment of the UN Commission on the Status of Women," *Journal of Women's History* 20, no. 4 (2008): 38.

23 Adami, *Women and the Universal Declaration of Human Rights*, 40–62.

24 Laville, "A New Era in International Women's Rights? American Women's Associations and the Establishment of the UN Commission on the Status of Women," 40.

25 Laville, 41.

26 Adami, *Women and the Universal Declaration of Human Rights*, 127–44.

27 Laville, "A New Era in International Women's Rights? American Women's Associations and the Establishment of the UN Commission on the Status of Women," 52–53.

28 Felice Gaer, "Women, International Law and International Institutions: The Case of the United Nations," *Women's Studies International Forum* 32 (2009): 61.

29 Adami, *Women and the Universal Declaration of Human Rights*, 66.

30 See introduction note, Chs. 1, 2, and 3 in this volume.

31 For more context on Menon, see Rathore 'Excavating Hidden Histories', this volume, Ch. 3.

32 E/CN.6/SR 41, Commission on the Status of Women, Third Session, Summary record of the 41st meeting, Beirut, Lebanon 22 March 1949, p. 2.

33 E/CN.6/SR 55, Commission on the Status of Women, Third Session, Summary record of the 55th meeting, Beirut, Lebanon 1 April 1949, p. 2.
34 E/CN.6/SR 55, Commission on the Status of Women, Third Session, Summary record of the 55th meeting, Beirut, Lebanon 1 April 1949, p. 3.
35 E/CN.6/SR 55, Commission on the Status of Women, Third Session, Summary record of the 55th meeting, Beirut, Lebanon 1 April 1949, p. 3.
36 E/CN.6/SR 55, Commission on the Status of Women, Third Session, Summary record of the 55th meeting, Beirut, Lebanon 1 April 1949, p. 3.
37 E/CN.6/SR 55, Commission on the Status of Women, Third Session, Summary record of the 55th meeting, Beirut, Lebanon 1 April 1949, p. 3.
38 As of today, 2020, there is no division within the Secretariat dealing specifically with the rights of women. UN Women is a body with limited budget and its work is remote from the UN Secretariat.
39 Adami, *Women and the Universal Declaration of Human Rights*, 74–85.
40 E/CN.6/SR.50, Commission on the Status of Women, Third Session, Summary record of the 50th meeting, Beirut, Lebanon, 28 March 1949, p.8.
41 E/CN.6/SR.50, Commission on the Status of Women, Third Session, Summary record of the 50th meeting, Beirut, Lebanon, 28 March 1949, p. 8.
42 E/CN.6/SR.50, Commission on the Status of Women, Third Session, Summary record of the 50th meeting, Beirut, Lebanon, 28 March 1949, p. 10.
43 E/CN.6/SR.52, Commission on the Status of Women, Third Session, Summary record of the 52nd meeting, Beirut, Lebanon, 29 March 1949, p. 4.
44 E/CN.6/SR.52, Commission on the Status of Women, Third Session, Summary record of the 52nd meeting, Beirut, Lebanon, 29 March 1949, p. 6.
45 E/CN.6/SR.52, Commission on the Status of Women, Third Session, Summary record of the 52nd meeting, Beirut, Lebanon, 29 March 1949, p. 7.
46 Riegelman Lubin and Winslow, *Social Justice for Women: The International Labour Organization and Women*, 76.
47 Adami, *Women and the Universal Declaration of Human Rights*, 51.
48 Riegelman Lubin and Winslow, *Social Justice for Women: The International Labor Organization and Women*, 94.
49 E/CN.6/SR.56, Commission on the Status of Women, Third Session, Summary record of the 56th meeting, Beirut, Lebanon, 31 March 1949, p. 7.
50 E/CN.6/SR.56, Commission on the Status of Women, Third Session, Summary record of the 56th meeting, Beirut, Lebanon, 31 March 1949, p. 7.
51 E/CN.6/SR.56, Commission on the Status of Women, Third Session, Summary record of the 56th meeting, Beirut, Lebanon, 31 March 1949, p. 7.
52 E/CN.6/SR.136, Commission on the Status of Women, Seventh Session, Summary record of the 136th meeting, New York, 25 March 1953.
53 E/CN.6/SR.59, Commission on the Status of Women, Third Session, Summary record of the 59th meeting, Beirut, Lebanon, 1 April 1949, p. 3.
54 E/CN.6/SR.59, Commission on the Status of Women, Third Session, Summary record of the 59th meeting, Beirut, Lebanon, 1 April 1949, p. 5.
55 E/CN.6/SR.59, Commission on the Status of Women, Third Session, Summary record of the 59th meeting, Beirut, Lebanon, 1 April 1949, p. 5.
56 Boris, *Making the Woman Worker: Precarious Labour and the Fight for Global Standards, 1919–2019*, 56.
57 E/CN.6/SR 49, Commission on the Status of Women, Third Session, Summary record of the 49th meeting, Beirut, Lebanon 28 March 1949, p. 2.
58 E/CN.6/SR.48, Commission on the Status of Women, Third Session, Summary record of the 48th meeting, Beirut, Lebanon 26 March 1949, p. 3.
59 E/CN.6/SR.49, Commission on the Status of Women, Third Session, Summary record of the 49th meeting, Beirut, Lebanon, 28 March 1949, p. 2.
60 E/CN.6/SR.49, Commission on the Status of Women, Third Session, Summary record of the 49th meeting, Beirut, Lebanon, 28 March 1949, p. 7.

61 E/CN.6/SR.49, Commission on the Status of Women, Third Session, Summary record of the 49th meeting, Beirut, Lebanon, 28 March 1949, p. 8.
62 Boris, Hoehtker, and Zimmermann, *Women's ILO: Transnational Networks, Global Labour Standards and Gender Equity, 1919 to Present*, 106.
63 Samuel Moyn, *The Last Utopia: Human Rights in History* (Cambridge: Harvard University Press, 2012).
64 Poulos, "Transnational Militancy in Cold-War Europe: Gender, Human Rights, and the WIDF during the Greek Civil War."
65 Poulos, 26.
66 Doris Linder, "Equality For Women: The Contribution of Scandinavian Women at the United Nations, 1946-66," *Scandinavian Studies* 73, no. 2 (2001): 165–208; Sondra Herman, "From International Feminism to Feminist Internationalism: The Emergence of Alva Myrdal, 1936–1955," *PEACE & CHANGE* 18, no. 4 (1993): 325–46.
67 Herman, "From International Feminism to Feminist Internationalism: The Emergence of Alva Myrdal, 1936–1955," 341.
68 Wendy Pojman, "For Mothers, Peace and Family: International (Non)-Cooperation among Italian Catholic and Communist Women's Organisation during the Early Cold War," *Gender & History* 23, no. 2 (2011): 415–29.

Bibliography

Adami, Rebecca. "Counter Narratives as Political Contestation: Universality, Particularity and Uniqueness." *The Equal Rights Review* 15 (2015a): 13–24.

Adami, Rebecca. "On Subalternity and Representation: Female and Post Colonial Subjects Claiming Universal Human Rights in 1948." *Journal of Research on Women and Gender* 6 (2015b): 56–66.

Adami, Rebecca. *Women and the Universal Declaration of Human Rights*. New York & London: Routledge, 2019.

Boris, Eileen. *Making the Woman Worker: Precarious Labor and the Fight for Global Standards, 1919–2019*. Oxford: Oxford University Press, 2019.

Boris, Eileen, Dorothea Hoehtker, and Susan Zimmermann, eds. *Women's ILO: Transnational Networks, Global Labour Standards and Gender Equity, 1919 to Present*. Leiden & Boston: BRILL, 2008.

Cobble, Dorothy Sue. "International Women's Trade Unionism and Education." *International Labor and Working-Class History* 90, no. 90 (2016): 153–163.

Donert, Celia. "From Communist Internationalism to Human Rights: Gender, Violence and International Law in the Women's International Democratic Federation Mission to North Korea, 1951." *Contemporary European History* 25, no. 2 (2016): 313–333.

Eisenberg, Jaci. "The Status of Women: A Bridge from the League of Nations to the United Nations." *JIOS* 4, no. 2 (2013): 8–24.

Gaer, Felice. "Women, International Law and International Institutions: The Case of the United Nations." *Women's Studies International Forum* 32 (2009): 60–66.

Haan, Francisca de. "Continuing Cold War Paradigms in Western Historiography of Transnational Women's Organisations: The Case of the Women's International Democratic Federation (WIDF)." *Women's History Review* 19, no. 4 (2010): 547–573.

Herman, Sondra. "From International Feminism to Feminist Internationalism: The Emergence of Alva Myrdal, 1936–1955." *Peace & Change* 18, no. 4 (1993): 325–346.

Ilic, Melanie. "Soviet Women, Cultural Exchange and the Women's International Democratic Federation." In *Reassessing Cold War Europe*, edited by Sari Autio-Sarasmo and Katalin Miklóssy, 157–174. London: Routledge, 2010.

Laville, Helen. "A New Era in International Women's Rights? American Women's Associations and the Establishment of the UN Commission on the Status of Women." *Journal of Women's History* 20, no. 4 (2008): 34–56.

Linder, Doris. "Equality For Women: The Contribution of Scandinavian Women at the United Nations, 1946–66." *Scandinavian Studies* 73, no. 2 (2001): 165–208.

Maul, Daniel. *The International Labour Organization: 100 Years of Global Social Policy.* Berlin: de Gruyter, 2019.

Moyn, Samuel. *The Last Utopia: Human Rights in History.* Cambridge: Harvard University Press, 2012.

Mooney, Jadwiga E. Pieper. "Fighting Fascism and Forging New Political Activism: The Women's International Democratic Federation (WIDF) in the Cold War." In *De-Centering Cold War History: Local and Global Change*, edited by Jadwiga E. Pieper Mooney and Fabio Lanza, 52–72. Routledge, 2012.

Pojman, Wendy. "For Mothers, Peace and Family: International (Non)-Cooperation among Italian Catholic and Communist Women's Organisation during the Early Cold War." *Gender & History* 23, no. 2 (2011): 415–429.

Poulos, Margarite. "Transnational Militancy in Cold-War Europe: Gender, Human Rights, and the WIDF during the Greek Civil War." *European Review of History* 24, no. 1 (2017): 17–35.

Riegelman Lubin, Carol, and Anne Winslow. *Social Justice for Women: The International Labor Organization and Women.* Durham and London: Duke University Press, 1990.

Rupp, Leila J., and Verta Taylor. *Survival in the Doldrums: The American Women's Rights Movement, 1945 to the 1960s.* New York & Oxford: Oxford University Press, 1987.

Waterman, Peter. "Hidden from Herstory: Women, Feminism and New Global Solidarity." *Economic and Political Weekly* 28, no. 44 (October 30, 1993): WS83–W100.

Weigand, Kate. *Red Feminism: American Communism and the Making of Women's Liberation.* Baltimore and London: The John Hopkins University Press, 2001.

5 Universal human rights for women

UN engagement with traditional abuses, 1948–1965

Roland Burke

Introduction

Across the 1950s and early 1960s, while the UN became progressively more riven by contests on the right to self-determination, racial discrimination, and the relationship between development and political rights, there was another battle on the proper character and bounds of universality—the personal status and bodily integrity rights of women within marriage. In December 1954, shortly after the sixth anniversary of the Universal Declaration of Human Rights (UDHR), the General Assembly proclaimed a sweeping programme against "ancient customs" which prevented the realization of the UDHR for women. Resolution 843 affirmed the supremacy of the UDHR over any custom, and demanded "elimination of such customs, ancient laws and practices," notably in marriage and family law, which were "inconsistent" with the precepts set down in 1948.[1] By 1961, the animating spirit of Resolution 843 was set into a draft treaty, adopted a year later as the Convention on Consent, Minimum Age, and Registration for Marriage.[2] The Marriage Convention was one of the first binding treaties on human rights protection passed by the UN, preceding its more celebrated siblings, the International Convention on the Elimination of All-Forms of Racial Discrimination (1965), and the two International Covenants (1966), by several years.

These campaigns have received little scholarly attention, despite the abundance of academic interest on the history of human rights and the impressive array of work on feminist internationalism.[3] Although the influence of women in the United Nations, and more widely across international institutions, has been widely recognized, the centre of gravity for most prior research has been on the 1940s, and the developments of the 1970s and beyond. By comparison, the intervening period has been less thoroughly surveyed.[4] In her superb examination of UN attention to corporeal abuses of African women, primarily in the 1950s, Giusi Russo has demonstrated the importance of the 1950s and 1960s in appreciating the configuration of rights, women, and colonialism.[5] Yet across the cumulative scholarship, the two flagship UN initiatives on traditional abuses in the 1950s and 1960s remain marginal. Resolution 843 is barely cited at all, beyond its gazetting in UN periodicals, and the Convention on Consent to Marriage is mostly consigned to passing reference.[6] Given the salience of this earlier effort on "traditional abuses" to many of the priorities which emerged as definitive

DOI: 10.4324/9781003036708-5

of the debates around the 1979 Convention on the Elimination of All-Forms of Discrimination Against Women (CEDAW), the 1989 Convention on the Rights of the Child (CRC), and the 1993 World Conference on Human Rights in Vienna, their absence is a striking ellipsis in the interlaced narrative of human and women's rights.[7]

This chapter examines the first two decades of UN human rights endeavours around traditional, social, and cultural practices, principally those which prevented the realization of the UDHR for women. It argues that the animating impulse was a profoundly hopeful vision of universality, advanced by a small but effective cohort of women, many from the newly independent states. The Marriage Convention, its precursors, and their associated sentiments represented an effort to translate the grand abstractions of 1948 into lived reality. Their campaign was not conceived of as any kind of special status renovation to universality—but a pragmatic endeavour to translate global norms to rural nuptials, and to extend the bold, abstract statement of human equality to some kind of daily symmetry in interpersonal and intimate relationships. While focussed on abuses which were experienced by women, the optic was not understood as any kind of sectional advocacy. It was instead a reflexive attempt to advance the enjoyment of human rights worldwide, to make universality a real, experientially meaningful, truth.

Unlike many other forums of the UN, the human rights and humanitarian arena was a place where women found sustained presence, and substantial influence. In part, this was a configuration that stemmed from highly gendered assumptions about the nature of rights, welfare, and humanitarian questions, all which had been established as the acceptable political space for women well before 1945. Across the Commonwealth, and the United States, arguments in the terms of strategic maternalism had been something of an over-success. Early suffragists had claimed authority in democratic politics that rested, in part, on an essentialized facility for caring.[8] Transnational organization between women had a still more established lineage.[9] Human rights and humanitarianism were, therefore, a sphere where there was some prospect for seizing opportunities, particularly given the limited interest most foreign services had in these forums.[10]

While still grossly unequal, the role and impact of women in the UN's human rights enterprise was much greater than in the notionally masculinist forums of the Security Council, and the economic components of the new international organization. The bespoke forum for women's rights, the Commission on the Status of Women (CSW), which shared personnel, and agenda items, with the larger human rights apparatus, was well-regarded for its commitment. John Humphrey, Director of the Human Rights Division, flatly declared in his memoir that "there was no more independent body in the United Nations."[11] The women of the General Assembly, often working across the CSW, the Commission on Human Rights, and the Committee on Social, Cultural, and Humanitarian Affairs, were amongst the first to migrate from grandiose ideals to the micro-scale practice and conditions of daily life outside Geneva and New York. Amongst the earliest of the UN's travelling advisory seminars on human rights, held across the late 1950s and early 1960s, were devoted to the pragmatic questions of women's freedoms and welfare. They convened well outside the conventional circuit of international organization, assembling, for example, in Bangkok, Bogotá Addis Ababa, and Lomé.[12]

Although on balance a mixture of liberal feminists, with the Western countries represented by a range of Christian and Social Democratic, Labor, and various reformist Conservative voices, there was also strong participation from Soviet aligned women. As Kirsten Ghodsee has shown in her excellent analyses, their perspective was distinct, drawn from state-managed women's organizations and the academy.[13] As with the majority of Soviet representation, they typically avoided concession on their own national deficiencies. Nevertheless, the alignment between Soviet international positioning as a champion of women's advancement, and their own experiences, did tend to place the Soviet bloc in a less obstructionist mode in women's human rights questions, especially when the rights involved demanded a strong, activist role for the state. Their own experiences were a demonstration of what had been possible for at least some women in the Soviet system. Zoya V. Mironova (USSR), a proponent of women's rights initiatives at the UN in the early 1960s, had been a champion ice skater—and went on to become a pioneering surgeon in some of the most intricate reconstructive procedures in elite Soviet athletes. Zofia Dembinksa (Poland) had worked for childhood education and welfare in the 1930s as a left-wing academic, and pursued the same priorities under Władysław Gomułka's Soviet-backed dictatorship. They were far from liberal reformers, but they provided another reliable constituency for some measures to improve women's status, unlike the general case obstructionism and diversion that characterized so much of Soviet activity on other human rights questions.

Beyond the opportunities seized by women from the political West and the Soviet bloc, the small but growing set of Asian, Arab, and African women played a prominent role in leading debate.[14] This was a cohort which generally had strong nationalist credentials, and had fought against colonialism, traditional social patterns of discrimination, and the repressive affinities between each system.[15] India's Hansa Mehta and Lakshmi Menon traversed the spectrum of activism, from organization at the village, as part of the All-Indian Women's Conference (AIWC), through to election to the Indian parliament, all the way to the General Assembly.[16] Ra'ana Liaquat Ali Khan founded the All-Women's Association of Pakistan (AWPA), the first major feminist assembly, and a major force in driving family law reform in the newly established state.[17] Badia Afnan represented the technocratic modernization of pre-Baathist Iraq, which had adopted sweeping family and personal status law liberalization, one of the few durable reform measures of its troubled 1950s polity.[18] Lebanon's Angela Jurdak, serving on the Commission on the Status of Women, had been an avowed advocate for women's education, and family law reform, measures which required more than the high political transformation of suffrage rights.[19] Their most conspicuous early triumph was in precipitating the most obvious shift in the 1948 Universal Declaration's language of rights compared to its Atlantic ancestors. Over the reservations of Eleanor Roosevelt, who initially viewed the measure as redundant, they ensured the new human rights of the post-war era spoke of "all," rather than "all men.["20] This early cohort of women also ensured there was an expressly stated affirmation of equal rights in marriage.[21]

In the 1960s, African women joined the other newly independent representatives. From the Francophone Togo, there was able representation from Marie Madoe Sivomey. Prior to independence, Sivomey had been engaged in Togolese social work for women and girls, and work in the civil service. As co-founder of Togo's first feminist organization, the Union of Togolese Women (UFEMTO), she would bring her experience to New York, before being elected Mayor of Lomé in 1972.[22] Alongside her counterpart Jeanne Martin Cissé, a senior party official from the radically anti-imperialist Guinea, serving the former trade union leader, and incipient dictator, Sekou Touré, Sivomey would be a leading advocate of equal marriage rights in the UN.[23] With an appreciation of the experience of women in rural settings, often desperately poor, and with highly constrained capacity for exercising rights, these delegates approached the soaring words of the UDHR with an insistence on pragmatism. Their perspective was less juridical and infused a practicality to often ethereal and evasive claims from Western powers on "levels of civilization" and the apparent infeasibility of advancing social and attitudinal change through international action. In their proximity to the community, the local, this Third World cohort were somewhat closer to the balance of interests that would become more characteristic of the 1970s and early 1980s, across the various International Women's Year Conferences, and their NGO Tribunes, in Mexico City,[24] Copenhagen, and Nairobi.[25]

Manufacturing monolithic cultures: Colonial cynicism on human rights for women

From 1949, as soon as work began to step beyond the exhortatory project of the UDHR, equal treatment for women and questions of family became a pivot for arguments about the extent and intensity of universality. Arguments which countries would not openly countenance on, for instance, signature abuses of state power, such as extrajudicial killing and torture, were strategically advanced by emphasizing those rights which entailed wider social and attitudinal reform, foremost marriage practices. The intricacy, for instance, of reconfiguring family law and personal status code to bring into compliance with a universal human rights standard were an endlessly useful diversionary question. Supposed deference to local customs was a superficially plausible, and somewhat respectable, defensive claim against universal application of various draft human rights measures. These claims were encapsulated in a proposed colonial application clause, which allowed metropolitan power to exempt their colonies from treaties. Insistence on the inclusion of a colonial application clause in the draft human rights covenant was amongst the highest priorities for the European powers, bolstered by Australia, Canada, and the US, who had their own federal state provisions which they sought to inscribe on the various texts.[26]

Across 1949 and into the 1950s, defences of the colonial exemption in the covenant produced some of the most spectacular contests on the bounds of universality.[27] France and Britain delivered studiously well-composed ventriloquism on the interests and cultural practices of colonial peoples, and a pretended respect for tradition. Cassin, combining roles of defensive advocate for imperial France, and a sincerely engaged jurist on human rights, was the most eloquent example. In commending the colonial clause on the draft covenant in June 1949, he warned that while there was a seductive logic to universal application to colonies, it risked "a general alignment at the level of the most backward people." [28] He identified equality as the signature example of why a colonial exception should be permitted. "It was certain," he argued, "that the principle of the equality of the sexes could not be applied immediately in all such territories in so far as family law was concerned."[29] Cassin claimed that "it was not possible to impose upon them progressive steps" for women, given these were "not understood by the people on account of their attachment to their own traditions."[30] France itself seemed attached to its traditions, given that women's suffrage had only been secured after the Liberation in 1944, against a considerable reactionary campaign opposing the reform.

Nevertheless, there were easy assertions that decades under imperial custodianship were the path to enlightenment. This colonial rationale against universality might have been credible—were it not for the presence of actual women from the regions that were being so comfortably and confidently essentialized. When raised again in 1950, Cassin met strong opposition from Lakshmi Menon, and, more forcefully, Badia Afnan. In a sharp riposte, Afnan stated her disappointment that Cassin "had used the backwardness of the peoples of equatorial Africa as an argument for the inclusion of the colonial clause in the covenant."[31] She explained, "differences of culture and tradition" should not foreclose "universal application."[32] Despite repeated efforts to revive it, there would be no colonial clause in the two human rights covenants that were eventually adopted in 1966. While the inclusion of a colonial clause in the covenant was defeated, the instrumental deployment of custom would continue across the 1950s, commencing with the December 1952 Convention on the Political Rights of Women (CPW).[33]

Striking for its clear, parsimonious statement of electoral equality, the CPW was amongst the most anodyne texts to emerge from the UN. It presented no normative novelty, and no extension of the precepts set down in the UDHR, instead serving as an international legal sequel to the suffrage won nationally in much of the world since the 1890s. With the second tranche of suffrage triumphs in the 1940s, the equal right for women to elect and to be elected had become amongst the less fraught human rights propositions. Amongst the few independent Asian and African states, universal suffrage was embraced as part of the national emancipation project. Nevertheless, women from outside the political West were again the terrain for testing what, precisely, was meant by universality. Against a coalition that included major Western powers, who cited apparently insuperable attitudes in their colonies, and the men representing Syria, Egypt, and Iran, it was the women from Pakistan and Iraq who insisted that suffrage was essential. Begum Rana Liaquat Ali Khan, who had faced such tests at home, spoke persuasively of the support for equality lent by the late Mohammed Ali Jinnah, father of Pakistani independence.[34] Iraq's Afnan spoke of the nationalist modernization effort underway across Asia, Africa, and her own Arab region, and the affirmation of equality it presented.[35] For all the verbiage about the need to hasten cautiously, the CPW was, like the UDHR, adopted without a single opposing vote. When kept within the austere frame of formal political institutions, translating philosophical vision to legal verité for women was contentious, but not catastrophically so.

However, when the UN began to engage in social and customary restrictions of women's human rights, the difficulties were markedly greater. In late 1954, as the first dedicated effort to contend with customs which impeded the realization of the UDHR was taken up, the clash over "tradition" became acute. Led by the imperial powers, and amplified by some of the Third World states, the initiative, which sought action on "customs, ancient laws and practices," was the arena for a wide-ranging contest on how real the UDHR should be for women.[36] Its origins were in an initiative which had emerged from the CSW, across March and April 1954.[37] Compelled by their observation "that certain practices, ancient laws and customs," notably marriage conditions, were "impediments to the attainment by women of their basic rights," the CSW urged "all necessary measures to ensure the abolition of such customs, ancient laws and practices."[38]

In the General Assembly debate of the CSW proposal, women from Asia, Latin America, and the Arab region served as the most effective advocates. Aziza Hussein, the first woman representative from Egypt, contested essentialized ideas on tradition and religious custom. In her debut intervention on 15 December 1954, Hussein related a catalogue of errors in Western presumptions about Islam, and the confusion between religion and an abuse that resided in social pathologies. She pointed to the first feminist success for Egyptian women at the turn of the century, and a national project to "recapture the original liberal spirit of Islam" as part of "the gradual intellectual and social regeneration of Egyptian society." Hussein described recent developments across education, welfare, and women's organizational work, of "forty years of struggle," and reforms in family law.[39] Her passionate advocacy of the resolution, and the nuanced manner in which she recounted Egypt's course, cast the problem in terms of the abuses of tradition.

Artati Marzuki, a future Indonesian minister for education under Sukarno, prepared a similarly complex account, with particular attention to the ways in which Dutch colonialism had sought to codify what had been a dynamic and evolving customary law. Her account was not triumphalist. There were obvious injustices in the practice of bride price. Child marriage persisted. Yet her diagnosis was not of immutable custom, but one that was being contested by Indonesian women, with substantial success. Marzuki gestured to the momentum that was emerging in the Indonesian Republic, citing a long dormant effort to reform marriage law had recently "been unanimously accepted by the women's organizations."[40] Carmela Aguilar, the legendary Peruvian feminist, and the first woman to accede to Ambassadorial rank in her country, was still less merciful in dispensing with claims of tradition. Fluent in Quechua, she embraced both her Incan heritage and a blunt human rights universalism.[41] With a career devoted to advancing equality through multiple domains—national, the regional system of the Inter-American Commission, and the international forums of the UN—Aguilar promptly dispensed with the excuses, and exalted the supremacy of the UDHR. "Women," she declared, "should not be deprived of fundamental rights merely because of prejudice and tradition."[42] Accordingly, while "sociologists often said that customary law was very difficult to change," and others had prophesized "that the fabric of society would disintegrate if women left their homes," these were hardly sufficient given the fundamental quality of the issue.[43] For Aguilar, "the Universal Declaration of Human Rights unequivocally proclaimed the principle of equal rights."[44] It was straightforward, or in her phrase, "unexceptionable," that "practices prejudicial to the human dignity of women should therefore be eradicated."[45] The proposal, which was limited to encouragement and promotion, was adopted—the first text which explicitly identified the need to align family law and marriage to the principles of the UDHR.

"Awaiting release from the yoke imposed on them by custom:" Navigating custom in the convention on marriage

Over the course of the 1950s, the CSW and various other arms of the UN wandered into marriage and family, and the perilous question of how rapidly, and by what mechanism, the architecture of human rights could be infused into customary practices. Exhortatory enterprises, such as the 1954 resolution, allowed a degree of evasion on how far and how fast social and attitudinal change could be achieved. A binding treaty would demand specificity, a difference which had already left the UDHR's sequel, the human rights covenant, foundering. Yet proposals for a Convention on Marriage emerged, and advanced, even as the covenant was first split into two instruments, and then trapped in endless, seemingly hopeless, debates across the later 1950s. Positioned in between the new post-war concept of universal human rights, and older traditions of protectionist humanitarianism, the marriage convention had antecedents in the 1950 Convention for the Suppression of the Traffic in Persons and of the Exploitation of the Prostitution of Others, and more directly, in the 1956 Supplemental Convention on Slavery.[46]

Deliberations on the 1956 text had explicitly drawn out the parallels between chattel slavery and slavery-like practices associated with marriage and indicated the need for a dedicated instrument.[47] The CSW promptly responded, preparing a proposed text across 1958 through 1960, which found a place on the General Assembly agenda for 1961. The essence of the task was encapsulated in the CSW's summative report, which observed the core problem—attitudinal and social systems which defeated the experience of equality. "Even in countries where the law recognized equality of rights for women," the CSW recorded, "traditions and customs based on the idea that the husband was the head of the family were still deep-rooted, with the result that in practice women did not exercise the rights accorded them by the law."[48] Equality and agency in marriage were perhaps the prime expression of the dynamic—and remedy, the CSW proposed, was in a formal treaty. Exhortatory Declarations were well, but insufficient. Supporters of an ambitious rights effort, "felt that only the adoption of an international instrument such as a convention was likely to set up a genuine current of public opinion."[49] Only international law might "stimulate Governments to take steps to bring their national legislation into harmony with the principles enunciated in the Universal Declaration of Human Rights."[50] The proposal was agreed without opposition.[51]

In determining the apportionment of time for the General Assembly's 1961 session, Togo's Marie Sivomey "stressed the very great importance attached by her delegation" to the draft Convention.[52] She found powerful supporters. Both Gladys Tillett, the US representative, and Poland's Zofia Dembinksa, a surrogate for the wider Soviet bloc, endorsed Sivomey's position. Nigeria's Jaiyeola Aduke Moore, who had worked for women's advancement at home, and practiced as a barrister, expressed her support for the Convention.[53] While aided by bipartisan Cold War agreement, the most emphatic proponents of the draft Convention were the two African women representatives, Togo's Sivomey, and Guinea's Jeanne Martin Cissé. Both spoke for states which were still in the optimistic early moments of independence. Both women urged the Convention's adoption in powerful, personalistic terms—an advocacy that stemmed from the immediacy and proximity of child marriage and bride price, which their new states were committed to eradicate.[54] Where Soviet and Western delegates pondered candidly ideological sub-amendments and juridical nicety, Sivomey gestured primarily to the UDHR, and what the text would mean for African women and girls. Her positioning in the discussion went well beyond Togolese delegate, and instead a kind of collective proxy for the young women across the African region.

As General Assembly deliberations opened on 4 October 1961, Sivomey "thanked the Committee for having agreed to give priority to the draft Convention on marriage, on behalf of the millions of African women who were awaiting release from the yoke imposed on them by custom."[55] Cissé spoke poignantly on what "custom" could mean for the rights of African women. She openly professed her faith that international resolve on marriage "would help to improve the lot of African women who still, only too often, were regarded as a chattel which the parents could dispose of without the girl concerned having to give her consent."[56] In a hopeful vision of what a formal treaty could deliver, Cissé argued the UN would be furnishing, however poorly and partially, some kind of defensive shield for women across her country. "African girls," she proclaimed, would be armed with a new confidence. Inspirited by the knowledge "they were protected by an international instrument," those far distant from New York and Geneva "would not hesitate to refuse their consent to anyone who attempted to exert pressure on them."[57]

Across the first afternoon devoted to the draft Convention, numerous delegates spoke in favour of the text from an ecumenical spread of Cold War alignments. The contest between anti-colonial Third World and the Western delegations was comparatively subdued, a tranquillity that had become rare by the early 1960s. Soviet bloc representatives took the opportunity to boast of their progressive ideological credentials on women's rights. Israel's Shulamit Nardi, building on the record established by her predecessor, Zena Harman, argued for the Convention as part of building the nation state. Nardi emphasized her experience within developing a protective family law across customs. Nardi, a Labor Zionist and academic, argued that the Convention "ought not to present insuperable difficulties."[58] With large inflows of co-religionists into her new country, many "from regions where the very customs and practices which the Convention was intended to abolish prevailed," Israel had found protections for women in marriage were an integral part of stitching together some shared vision, and facilitated a "new generation's adjustment to a different way of life."[59] Despite most recognizing the need for cautious drafting, the fundamental validity of setting a constellation of social attitudes and practices as the proper subject for human rights law appeared—at first—to mark a rare point of consensus.

The promise, however, was punctured in the final substantive intervention of the afternoon meeting—from Nigeria's most senior representative, Prince Jaja Wachuku, who rescinded the support originally extended by Jaiyeola Aduke Moore. Educated at Trinity College, Dublin, Wachuku was emerging as a major figure in the Nigerian government, and a rising star in the UN. After a decade of advancing the cause of independence, Wachuku had been appointed as Foreign Minister by Nigeria's anti-colonial icon, Nnamdi Azikiwe. Wachuku, whose own background comprised a distinguished Igbo royal descent line, the Student Christian movement in Britain, and a childhood playing the stereotypical Commonwealth sports of cricket and rugby, rehearsed objections to the draft Convention on the basis of an essentialized African tradition. He authored his own authoritative variant of African interests, one sharply at odds with the principles advanced by Sivomey and Cissé. Wachuku chided the proponents of consent to marriage, and stated "that the Western conception of marriage was not the only valid one," with the implied pejoration that Sivomey and Cissé were insufficiently authentic as African representatives.[60]

Despite spending his formative years abroad, and recent years ensconced in the Federal Parliament and Ministry of Foreign Affairs, Wachuku nevertheless assigned himself arbiter of what was definitively African. Paying no deference to the arguments of his Togolese and Guinean colleagues, he flatly stated that "whereas in the West the consent of the two intending spouses only was required, that was not the case in Africa."[61] He defended bride price, and extolled polygamy, stating what he perceived was a self-evident virtue, it "permitted a man whose wife was sterile to beget an heir."[62] An expert practitioner in international law, admitted to the King's Inn, Wachuku still seemed sceptical of its application to African women. Even as he professed his support for the two human rights covenants, he was almost contemptuous of the draft Convention on marriage, which he dismissed as "completely pointless."[63] A universalist when it came to fighting for Nigerian independence, when it came to local social and cultural institutions, he recited the sort of language more typically associated with Lord Frederick Lugard's vision of indirect imperial rule, and the determinative role of "the physical, economic, cultural and traditional factors in each country."[64] His speech closed with a demand the draft Convention be deferred, and the promise Nigeria would vote against it were it to proceed.

As the meeting drew it to its close, Sivomey and Cissé were deeply disappointed to encounter precisely the attitudes they were fighting at home were so readily transported to the General Assembly. Cissé responded that she was "very concerned" to encounter such claims. "To hear the statement of the Nigerian representative" was a real source of dismay, "since the women of Africa looked for encouragement in their efforts to improve the status of women."[65] She sidestepped the canard on polygamy, which was not expressly prohibited in the draft text, but added perfectly pitched barb which appeared to gesture to the Nigerian Prince's aristocratic heritage. Cissé opined "it was easy for a rich man who could afford ten wives to sing the praises of that system," and reiterated that their endeavours were designed "solely towards guaranteeing for women, and for African women in particular, a decent and happy existence."[66] Sivomey sought the intervention of another legation, "in view of the emotion which the Nigerian proposal caused her."[67] Rapid intercession from Iraq's Afnan, who promptly noted the hour, and the merits of adjourning, ensured the debate would continue across the remainder of the 1961 session. The Nigerian effort to terminate consideration of the Convention before it began failed, but the contest which followed did tend to reveal the extent of unease over the balance between the diversity of customs and circumstances, and draft text's effort to apply the plain meaning of the UDHR's articles to marriage.

What, precisely, constituted consent, who could provide it, and the official inscription of a specified age animated many of the speakers. Consent was the most profound question of the Convention process—in its most elemental sense, this entailed a serious reflection on what freedom and agency actually meant. Badia Afnan made the insightful observation that there were potentially serious structural defects which limited the meaning of consent in some countries. Though she had no immediate remedy at hand, Afnan's diagnosis of the problem of "consent without choice" was depressingly acute.[68] In the absence of wider social and economic opportunities, or any real protections from the state, the space for exercising a choice in a meaningful way was seriously constrained. Marriage consent was a crucial question—but it necessarily was stitched into the more sweeping poverty of rights enjoyed by women. The Marriage Convention could mandate consent with admirable clarity, but it inevitably left this massive wider context, which spoke to the structural lack of choice and freedoms, unresolved.

A definitive minimum age was perhaps the most severe test for the equilibrium between a maximalist universality, and one which held some nuance.[69] There was fairly sparing support for a binding specific age—which seemed too prescriptive, and not necessarily an absolute requirement for achieving the fundamental purpose of health, well-being, and the capacity to exercise some real agency. Most cited their own minima, often with evident pride; but conceded that there might be local conditions and circumstances in which other ages were reasonable. The eventual compromise was no mandated universal minimum—merely that a state determine and implement one. It was a concession to what seemed an impossible calibration, but kept the principle alive, in the hope of future augmentation.

Although not successful in the final Convention, there was almost immediately a supplemental campaign, which introduced the kind of hybrid human rights treaty that would become a mainstay for future UN projects. A proposed Recommendation, which was a kind of annexe to Convention, operated to enhance the original text, by stipulating 15 years old as the global minimum.[70] In so doing, it gestured to where the norm should be, while preserving the original wide consensus. The concept of a graded kind of state obligation, from modest to substantial, was a valuable mechanism for charting a line between pessimism and utopianism. As a strategy, the Recommendation furnished an approach which rapidly became a default solution to seemingly intractable differences in commitment and outlook; enacted in the Optional Article to the 1965 International Convention Against All-Forms of Racial Discrimination, and first Optional Protocol to the 1966 human rights covenants.

Although advanced most vigorously by African women, the addressed by the Marriage Convention was universal, even if manifestations differed. Daw Mya Sein, who led Burma's Women's Council, observed during the debate that discriminatory patterns were "a phenomenon unconnected with the level of civilization."[71] Privately, Australia, where suffragists had won the franchise early, and a substantial women's activism had emerged on peace, education, and welfare, there remained government resistance to adopting the Convention. The centre-right government of Robert Menzies and Attorney General Garfield Barwick were generally sympathetic, but blanched when they assessed its single colony, Papua New Guinea, which remained a decade from independence. Despite pressure from Australian women, and the opposition Labor party, the Convention was not recommended for adoption by the Commonwealth. Given that Australia had recently adopted structural reforms of its marriage and family law, and had once prided itself on progressive social legislation, it was a less than encouraging position. The abuses in the fabric of the "domestic" were still perceived as "overseas" problems—though as the 1974 Royal Commission on Human Relationships would reveal, violations in the "private" realm were also part of the "traditions" of Port Melbourne and Port Macquarie, and not a distant "custom" issue in Port Moresby.[72] What was recognized as proper human rights terrain by African women in the 1960s was the ground on which new struggles would be fought by Second Wave feminism in the 1970s.

Conclusions: Traditional abuses or abuses of tradition?

From the foundational years of the world organization, women working in the UN presented the challenge of universality of human rights in a different key, informed by experiential knowledge. Translation of the UDHR required national legislation, international cooperation, and education; the generic, often platitudinous, verbiage of UN debate. Yet it also necessitated attention to the least governmental, and most intimate; of the human-scale power relations, not merely the grand structures of constitutions, courts, and treasuries. The fledgling efforts on "custom" and "ancient law," specifically marriage, prefigured the sorts of arguments which became central, first to the 1967 Declaration on the Elimination of All-forms of Discrimination Against Women, and later to the drafting, and implementation, and monitoring of both CEDAW and the CRC.[73] To some extent, these early efforts were aided by the residual optimism of the post-war moment, and the hopeful, reformist spirit of the first post-independence governments, which embraced women as integral to national regeneration.

By contrast, the incorporation of a more "horizontal" view of human rights violations in CEDAW and the CRC did sit uncomfortably with the tenor of human rights in the 1980s and 1990s. Abuses that were diffusely perpetrated were increasingly the preserve of humanitarian dispensation, specialist technical assistance, and international development. In the austere reframing of human rights that emerged in the 1970s, this species of violations was positioned as worthy of effort, but not necessarily comparable to the central HR NGO priority of active state malignancy, foremost torture and extrajudicial killing. By the late 1990s, at least some post-colonial governments argued along grooves originally set down by imperial administrators, citing the apparent "backwardness" of their own citizens, and the inability of the government to do much with respect to custom or attitudes.[74] The necessary complexity of the task, and the shrunken vernacular of human rights, provided an ecosystem where such arguments could hope for a sympathetic hearing—a failure of ability, or, more credibly, ability and will, was a somewhat less provocative target for the large HR NGOs.

While a major and sustained social mobilization against socially and culturally mediated, and the attitudes which licensed them, would become a focal point of the UN programme on human and women's rights from the 1970s, historical study of the 1950s and 1960s suggests there were meaningful antecedents. The depth and sophistication with which "traditional" abuses were identified as priorities for remediation, in highly ambitious terms, from the earliest moments of the UN human rights programme is revealing. It demonstrated that the UDHR, particularly for women delegates from the Third World, was understood as integral to their own national projects to advance the rights of women in spaces which were not high political, or part of the formal institutional apparatus. For figures like Sivomey, Mehta, Aguilar, and Marzuki, it was axiomatic that human rights were women's rights—decades before the phrase was encapsulated by their contemporary heirs in the campaigns at Vienna and Beijing.

Notes

1 Status of Women in Private Law: Customs, Ancient Laws, and Practices Affecting the Human Dignity of Women, GA Resolution 843 (IX), 17 December 1954.
2 Convention on Consent to Marriage, Minimum Age for Marriage and Registration of Marriages, GA Resolution 1763 A (XVII), 7 November 1962; and its later elaborative comment, Recommendation on Consent to Marriage, Minimum Age for Marriage and Registration of Marriages, GA resolution 2018 (XX), 1 November 1965.
3 Leila Rupp, *Worlds of Women: The Making of an International Women's Movement* (Princeton: Princeton University Press, 1997); Nitza Berkovitch, *From Motherhood to Citizenship: Women's Rights and International Organizations* (Boston: JHU Press, 1999); Madeleine Herren, "Gender and international relations through the lens of the League of Nations (1919–1945)," in Glenda Sluga and Carolyn James (eds.), *Women, Diplomacy and International Politics since 1500* (London: Routledge, 2015), 182–201; Marie Sandell, "Regional versus International: Women's Activism and Organisational Spaces in the Inter-War Period," *The International History Review* 33: 4 (2011): 607–25; and Sluga, "'Add Women and Stir': Gender and the History of International Politics," *Humanities Australia* 5 (2014): 65–72. For excellent recent discussion on approaches to the field, see Karen Garner, *Women and Gender in International History: Theory and Practice* (London: Bloomsbury, 2018).
4 For wide survey coverage, see the comprehensive account from Anne Winslow (ed.), *Women, Politics, and the United Nations* (Westport: Greenwood Press, 1995); on the

general arc of the CSW, see *A Short History of the Commission on the Status of Women* (New York: United Nations Publication, 2019).

5 For compelling exception, see Giusi Russo, "Contested Practices, Human Rights, and Colonial Bodies in Pain: The UN's Gender Politics in Africa, 1940s–1960s," *Gender & History* 30: 1 (March 2018): 196–213. See also work on the earlier period, which specifically engages the colonial African dimension, Charlotte Walker-Said, "The Trafficking and Slavery of Women and Girls: The Criminalization of Marriage, Tradition, and Gender Norms in French Colonial Cameroon, 1914–1945," in Tiantian Zheng (ed.), *Sex Trafficking, Human Rights, and Social Justice* (New York: Routledge, 2010), 150–169.

6 For the most extensive study, see Egon Schwelb, "Marriage and Human Rights," *The American Journal of Comparative Law* 12: 3 (Summer 1963): 337–383; and more recently, Maja Kirilova Eriksson, *The right to marry and to found a family: a worldwide human right* (Uppsala: Iustus Förlag 1990); Ruth Gaffney-Rhys, "International law as an instrument to combat child marriage," *The International Journal of Human Rights* 15: 3 (2011): 359–373; and Annie Bunting, Benjamin Lawrance, and Richard Roberts (eds.), *Marriage by Force? Contestation over Consent and Coercion in Africa* (Columbus: Ohio University Press, 2016).

7 Charlotte Bunch, "Women's Rights as Human Rights: Toward a Re-Vision of Human Rights," *Human Rights Quarterly* 12: 4 (1990): 486–98; Arvonne S. Fraser, 'Becoming Human: The Origins and Development of Women's Human Rights', *Human Rights Quarterly* 21: 4 (1999): 853–906.

8 Seth Koven and Sonya Michel, eds. *Mothers of a New World: Maternalist Politics and the Origins of Welfare States* (New York: Routledge, 1993); Molly Ladd-Taylor, *Mother-work: Women, Child Welfare, and the State, 1890–1930* (Urbana: University of Illinois, 1995).

9 Marie-Hélène Lefaucheux and International Council of Women, *Women in a Changing World* (London: Routledge, 1966).

10 Roland Burke, "'Real Thinking': American Human Rights Diplomacy and the Perils of Anti-Emotionalism," *Diplomacy & Statecraft* 31: 2 (June 2020): 306–325.

11 John Humphrey, *Human Rights & the United Nations: A Great Adventure* (Dobbs Ferry: Transnational Publishers, 1986), 30–31.

12 See, for instance, Report of UN Human Right Seminar, Participation of Asian Women in Public Life; Bangkok, 5 – 16 August 1957, ST/TAA/HR1; Seminar on Participation of Women in Public Life, Bogotá, 16 – 29 May 1959; ST/TAO/HR/5; Seminar on Participation of Women in Public Life, Addis Ababa, 12–23 December 1960, ST/TAO/HR9; Seminar on the Status of Women in Family Law, 18 – 31 August 1964, Lomé, ST/TAO/HR22.

13 Kristen Ghodsee, *Second World, Second Sex: Socialist Women's Activism and Global Solidarity* (Durham: Duke University Press, 2019); and, earlier, Ghodsee, "Revisiting the United Nations Decade for Women: Brief Reflections on Feminism, Capitalism and Cold War Politics in the Early Years of the International Women's Movement." *Women's Studies International Forum* 33: 1 (January 2010): 3–12.

14 Rebecca Adami provides an impressively nuanced account of the role of this cohort in the drafting of the UDHR, see Adami, *Women and the Universal Declaration of Human Rights* (London: Routledge, 2018), 63–73.

15 Kumari Jayawardena, *Feminism and Nationalism in the Third World* (New Dehli: Zed Books, 1986).

16 Aparna Basu and Bharati Ray, *Women's Struggle: A History of the All India Women's Conference, 1927–1990* (New Delhi: Manohar, 1990); and Aparna Basu, "Feminism and Nationalism in India, 1917–1947," *Journal of Women's History* 7: 4 (Winter 1995), 95–107; for precis of Mehta's biography, see Mary Ann Glendon, *A World Made New: Eleanor Roosevelt and the Universal Declaration of Human Rights* (New York: Random House, 2001), 90.

17 Mehr Nigar Masroor, *Ra'ana Liaquat Ali Khan* (Karachi: All Pakistan Women's Association, 1980).

18 Amal al-Sharqi, "The Emancipation of Iraqi Women," in Tim Niblock (ed.) *Iraq, the Contemporary State* (New York: St. Martin's Press, 1982), 74–87; and Marion Farouk-Sluglett, "Liberation or Repression? Pan-Arab Nationalism and the Women's Liberation Movement in Iraq," in Derek Hopwood, Habib Ishow and Thomas Koszinowski (eds.), *Iraq: Power and Society* (Reading: St. Antony's College Oxford & Ithaca, 1993), 51–74.

19 Jurdak's Lebanon was an early expedition for the UN that took a major forum beyond the triumvirate of New York, Paris, and Geneva, with the CSW holding its third session in Beirut, see Report of the CSW, 21 March – 4 April 1949, 19 April 1949, E/CN.6/124.

20 Susan Eileen Waltz, "Human Rights: The Role of Small States in the Construction of the Universal Declaration of Human Rights," *Human Rights Quarterly* 23: 1 (2001), 63; see also, Summary Records of the CHR, 12 December 1947, E/CN.4/SR.34; see also Mehta's observations on any specific articulation of 'men' and 'women', which implied potential for some gender-derived exceptionalism, as opposed to the full generic phrase, 'everyone'. Summary Records of the CHR, 9 June 1948, E/CN.4/SR. 66.

21 Humphrey, *Edge of Greatness*, 50.

22 Ekoue Satchivi, "Farewell to Marie Madoé Sivomey," *UFC Togo*, 2 October 2008, available at http://www.ufctogo.com/L-adieu-a-Marie-Madoe-Sivomey-1961.html accessed 2 May 2019.

23 Jeanne Martin Cissé, *La fille du Milo* (Paris: Presence Africaine, 2009); and François Freland, "Guinea bereaved by the death of Jeanne Martin Cissé, figure of independence and women's rights," *Jeune Afrique*, 22 February 2017, available at at https://www.jeuneafrique.com/405868/politique/guinee-endeuillee-disparition-de-jeanne-martin-cisse-figure-de-lindependance-droits-femmes/ accessed 1 May 2019. accessed 1 May 2019. See, generally, Sylvia Serbin and Ravaomalala Rasoanaivo-Randriamamonjy (eds.), *African Women, Pan-Africanism and African Renaissance* (UNESCO: Paris, 2015).

24 For more context see Aoife and Rowe 'Feminism, Global Inequality and the 1975 Mexico City Conference', this volume, ch. 6.

25 See also Chesler 'Who Wrote the CEDAW?', this volume, ch. 7.

26 Roland Burke, *Decolonization and the Evolution of International Human Rights* (Philadelphia: University of Pennsylvania Press, 2010), 40–41; 116–121.

27 Ibid, 116–121.

28 Summary Records of the CHR, 15 June 1949, E/CN.4/SR. 129.

29 Summary Records of the CHR, 15 June 1949, E/CN.4/SR. 129.

30 Summary Records of the CHR, 15 June 1949, E/CN.4/SR. 129.

31 GAOR, 27 October 1950, A/C. 3/SR. 296.

32 GAOR, 27 October 1950, A/C. 3/SR. 296.

33 Convention on the Political Rights of Women, GA Resolution 640 (VII), 20 December 1952.

34 GAOR, 15 December 1952, A/C.3/SR. 478.

35 GAOR, 15 December 1952, A/C. 3/SR. 477.

36 Action Taken Upon Decisions Reached by the Eighth Session of the CSW, 22 March -9 April 1954, 24 January 1955, E/CN.6/261, para 27.

37 A strong interest in private law, custom, and wider social and attitudinal structures were, however, evident from the earliest sessions of the CSW, see Report of the CSW, 25 February 1947, E/281. for instance, Press Release, Roundup of the Fifth Session of the CSW, 14 May 1951, SOC/1201; CSW, Draft Report on the Fifth Session, 30 April – 12 May 1951, E/CN.6/L.57;

38 Action Taken Upon Decisions Reached by the Eighth Session of the CSW, 22 March -9 April 1954, 24 January 1955, E/CN.6/261, para 27.

39 GAOR, 15 December 1954, A/C. 3/SR. 621.

40 GAOR, 15 December 1954, A/C.3/SR.621.
41 On Aguilar's background, see Liliana Torres-Muga, Funeral Oration for Carmela Ayanz Aguilar, 5 June 2012, available at http://www.lilianatorresmuga.net/actividades/discursos-como-directora-de-la-academia-diplomatica accessed 1 May 2019.
42 GAOR, 15 December 1954, A/C.3/SR.621.
43 GAOR, 15 December 1954, A/C.3/SR.621.
44 GAOR, 15 December 1954, A/C.3/SR.621.
45 GAOR, 15 December 1954, A/C.3/SR.621.
46 It had some oblique relationship to features of the Convention on the Nationality of Married Women, GA Resolution 1040 (XI), 20 February 1957.
47 Supplementary Convention on the Abolition of Slavery, the Slave Trade, and Institutions and Practices Similar to Slavery, adopted by a Conference of Plenipotentiaries convened by Economic and Social Council Resolution 608 (XXI), 30 April 1956. On the Supplemental Convention, see especially the analysis from Joyce A. C. Gutteridge, 'Supplementary Slavery Convention, 1956,' *International & Comparative Law Quarterly* 6: 3 (July 1957), 449–471. Gutteridge, an eminent international lawyer for the British Foreign Office, would play a substantial role in shaping the eventual Marriage Convention.
48 CSW Report of the 28th Session, New York, 9 – 27 March -1959, 6.
49 Ibid, 7.
50 Ibid, 7.
51 CSW, Resolution 3 (XIII), Age of Marriage, Free Consent, and Registration of Marriages, E/CN.6/L.261/Rev. 1.
52 GAOR, Summary Records of Committee III, 2 October 1961, A/C.3/SR.1060.
53 GAOR, Summary Records of Committee III, 2 October 1961, A/C.3/SR.1060.
54 Burke, *Decolonization,* 128–130.
55 GAOR, Summary Records of Committee III, 4 October 1961, A/C.3/SR.1063, para 10.
56 Ibid, para 42.
57 Ibid, para 42.
58 Ibid, para 19.
59 Ibid, para 19.
60 Ibid, para 46.
61 Ibid.
62 Ibid.
63 Ibid.
64 Ibid.
65 Ibid, para 48.
66 Ibid, para 48.
67 Ibid, para 49.
68 GAOR, Summary Records of Committee III, A/C.3/SR.1068, 10 October 1961, para 5.
69 On the balance between universal principle and particular national circumstance, see the summation of Canadian representative, Jean Casselman, GAOR, Summary Records of Committee III, A/C.3/SR.1067, 9 October 1961, para 5.
70 *Recommendation on Consent to Marriage, Minimum Age for Marriage and Registration of Marriages* General Assembly Resolution 2018 (XX), 1 November 1965.
71 GAOR, Summary Records of Committee III, A/C.3/SR.1092, 2 November 1961, para 27.
72 Elizabeth Evatt et al., *Royal Commission on Human Relationships Final Report,* v. 1–5 (Canberra: Australian Government Printers, 1976).
73 On the 1967 Declaration, see discussion across GAOR, 5–13 October 1967, A/C. 3/SR. 1473–1483; and the final text as adopted, Declaration on the Elimination of Discrimination against Women, GA Resolution 2263 (XXII), 7 November 1967.

74 See the analysis presented in Sonia Harris-Short, "International Human Rights Law: Imperialist, Inept and Ineffective? Cultural Relativism and the UN Convention on the Rights of the Child," *Human Rights Quarterly* 25: 2 (2003): 130–81.

Bibliography

Adami, Rebecca. *Women and the Universal Declaration of Human Rights*. New York & London: Routledge, 2019.

Berkovitch, Nitza. *From Motherhood to Citizenship: Women's Rights and International Organizations*. Boston: Johns Hopkins University Press, 1999.

Bunch, Charlotte. "Women's Rights as Human Rights: Toward a Re-Vision of Human Rights." *Human Rights Quarterly* 12, no. 4 (1990): 486–498.

Bunting, Annie, Benjamin Lawrence, and Richard Roberts, eds. *Marriage by Force? Contestation over Consent and Coercion in Africa*. Columbus: Ohio State University Press, 2016.

Burke, Roland. *Decolonization and the Evolution of International Human Rights*. Philadelphia: University of Pennsylvania Press, 2010.

Burke, Roland. "'Real Thinking': American Human Rights Diplomacy and the Perils of Anti-Emotionalism." *Diplomacy & Statecraft* 31, no. 2 (2020): 306–325.

Cissé, Jeanne Martin. *La Fille Du Milo*. Paris: Presence Africaine, 2009.

Eriksson, Maja. *The Right to Marry and to Found a Family: A World-Wide Human Right*. Uppsala: Iustus Förlag, 1990.

Evatt, Elizabeth. *Royal Commission on Human Relationships Final Report*. Canberra: Cambridge University Press, 1976.

Fraser, Arvonne S. "Becoming Human: The Origins and Development of Women's Human Rights." In *Women, Gender and Human Rights: A Global Perspective*, edited by Majorie Agosin, 15–64. USA: Rutgers University Press, 2001.

Gaffney-Rhys, Ruth. "International Law as an Instrument to Combat Child Marriage." *The International Journal of Human Rights* 15, no. 3 (2011): 359–373.

Garner, Karen. *Women and Gender in International History: Theory and Practice*. London: Bloomsbury, 2018.

Ghodsee, Kristen. "Revisiting the United Nations Decade for Women: Brief Reflections on Feminism, Capitalism and Cold War Politics in the Early Years of the International Women's Movement." *Women's Studies International Forum* 33, no. 1 (2010): 3–12.

Ghodsee, Kristen. *Second World, Second Sex: Socialist Women's Activism and Global Solidarity*. Durham: Duke University Press, 2019.

Hannan, Carolyn, Aina Liyambo, and Christine Brautigam. *"A Short History of the Commission on the Status of Women."* New York: United Nations Publications, 2019.

Harris-Short, Sonia. "'International Human Rights Law: Imperilist, Inept and Ineffective' Cultural Relativism and the UN Convention on the Rights of the Child." *Human Rights Quarterly* 25, no. 2 (2003): 130–181.

Herren, Madeleine. "Gender and International Relations through the Lens of the League of Nations (1919–1945)." In *Women, Diplomacy and International Politics since 1500*, edited by Glenda Sluga and Carolyn James. London: Routledge, 2015.

Humphrey, John Peters. *Human Rights & the United Nations: A Great Adventure*. New York: Transnational Publishers, 1986a.

Humphrey, John Peters. *On the Edge of Greatness: The Diaries of John HUmphrey, First Director of the United Nations Division of Human Rights, Vol 1 1948–1949*. edited by A.J. Hobbins. Montreal: Carleton University Press, 1986b.

Jayawardena, Kumari. *Feminism and Nationalism in the Third World*. New Delhi: Zed Books, 1986.

Koven, Seth, and Sonya Michel, eds. *Mothers of a New World: Maternalist Politics and the Origins of Welfare States*. New York: Routledge, 1993.

Ladd-Taylor, Molly. *Mother-Work: Women, Child Welfare, and the State, 1890-1930*. Urbana, Illionois: University of Illinois Press, 1995.

Lefaucheux, Marie-Helene, and International Council of Women. *Women in a Changing World*. London: Routledge, 1966.

Rupp, Leila J. *Worlds of Women: The Making of an International Women's Movement*. Princeton: Princeton University Press, 1997.

Russo, Giusi. "Contested Practices, Human Rights, and Colonial Bodies in Pain: The UN's Gender Politics in Africa, 1940s–1960s." *Gender & History* 30, no. 1 (2018): 196–213.

Sandell, Marie. "Regional versus International Women's Activism and Organisational Spaces in the Inter-War Period." *The International History Review* 33, no. 4 (2011): 607–625.

Schwelb, Egon. "Marriage and Human Rights." *The American Journal of Comparative Law* 12, no. 3 (1963): 337–383.

Serbin, Sylvia, Rasoanaivo-Randriamamonjy, Ravaomalala. *"African Women, Pan-Africanism and African Renaissance."* Paris: UNESCO, 2015.

Sluga, Glenda. "'Add Women and Stir': Gender and the History of International Politics." *Humanities Australia* 5 (2014): 65–72.

Walker-Said, Charlotte. "The Trafficking and Slavery of Women and Girls: The Criminalization of Marriage, Tradition, and Gender Norms in French Colonial Cameroon, 1914–1945." In *Sex Trafficking, Human Rights, and Social Justice*, edited by Tiantian Zheng, 150–169. New York: Routledge, 2010.

Waltz, Susan Eileen. "Human Rights: The Role of Small States in the Construction of the Universal Declaration of Human Rights." *Human Rights Quarterly* 23, no. 1 (2001): 44–72.

Winslow, Anne, ed. *Women, Politics, and the United Nations*. Westport: Greenwood Press, 1995.

6 Feminism, global inequality, and the 1975 Mexico city conference

Aoife O'Donoghue and Adam Rowe

Introduction

The 1975 Women's Conference was significant, both as a single event but also in terms of its legacy across law, politics, and women's global campaigning within and outside of the UN structure.[1] While law was not created at the Conference what was established was momentum, contestation, and a demonstration that previous attempts to tackle women's issues, including via treaty writing, by a male dominated global diplomatic core, including the UN, were insufficient.

While women have always been present and active in the modern era of global campaigning and law-making, they were excluded, informally and formally from the official law and policy making table. But what is more, women's issues have been dominated by voices from the Global North. Global South women were, and are, excluded far more than their Western counterparts. The Mexico Conference brought this inequality and the tensions stemming from it, directly into the spotlight by virtue of the fact that it took place not only in the context of the Cold War but also at a moment when a surge of states from the Global South were seeking to reorient law, through the New International Economic Order, away from its imperial and colonial origins.

In the commentaries and histories regarding both the 1975 Conference, and those held since, the focus is often on the particular character of the disagreements and controversies. Debate and arguments are commonplace at all thematic global conferences, be that at the UN or other global bodies, such as the WTO. The Battle of Seattle, at the 1999 WTO Ministerial Conference, is a recent example of heated debate both inside and outside of a global conference on law and policy. In the narratives presented on the 1975 Conference, however, conflict amongst women is presented as fundamental and distinctive to women's events. That women should not agree on the best path towards equality, that their lived experiences are different, and that conflict may arise is seen as substantive rather than typical of international questions that deal with half the world's population. While it is accepted that theorists of positivism, of natural law or communism disagree, sometimes fundamentally, feminism's contestations are presented as a fundamental flaw born of emotionalism rather than reasoned disagreement. This is not to ignore the debates. The voice of Global South women demanding to be heard is critical as is the confrontation of Western feminist privilege, both issues are core to debates on legal reform. But a narrative that presents women's

DOI: 10.4324/9781003036708-6

conferences as essentially antagonistic because feminist campaigning is an exceptional argumentative space needs to be forestalled.[2]

In sum, then, this chapter examines the legal and political legacy of the 1975 Conference in several contexts. First, we can approach the Conference through the historical struggle of feminist activists to achieve official participation in the legal and policy forums addressing women's issues. But more than that, the Conference can be used to explore the internal relations and tensions within feminism itself. In this vein, the ongoing challenge to Global North feminists to cede space and end attempts at articulating and representing all women's lived experiences, the role of the New International Economic Order and international economic law within that context of the Global South to change global legal governance and the overarching impact of the Cold War, will be central themes of analysis.

History of international conferences on women

Since the advent of the modern international conference, women have played significant roles. Initially excluded from inter-state conferences, women organized their own parallel events. They were amongst the first non-state campaign groups to employ this tactic and, at times, succeeded in gaining legal change.[3] Moreover, women were also amongst the leaders of the anti-slavery, peace, and labour movements that arose in the 19th century and which continue to be essential debates within contemporary international legal discourse. Absent formal roles in inter-state conferences women as facilitators in salons and social events were so critical that the UK Foreign Office, into the post-World War II era, opposed diplomatic wives holding other careers so that they could focus on these social events.[4] Inevitably during an era of imperialism, these alliances and groups were dominated by white western women, a legacy that remains partly intact, particularly in formal institutions. Nonetheless women from beyond the Global North broke through formal barriers—a development that often led to significant changes which produced substantial shifts in international policy and law.

Global women's organizations of the late 19th and early 20th centuries were able to realize substantive legal change—change, moreover, that occurred contemporaneously with the evolution of modern international law. As was alluded to above, women were excluded from formal settings. To overcome such obstacles, they had to devise innovate strategies to effect legal change. In doing so, these first organizations were instrumental in setting the template for lobbying for change by NGOs outside the 20th century global institutions.

Outside of their demonstration of the potential effectiveness of NGOs in advancing legal reform, the early feminist organizations recognized the need for global coalitions. The Inter-Allied Suffrage Conference, The International Women's Congress for Peace and Freedom, and the Women's International League for Peace and Freedom emerged initially as national organizations but realized that issues, such as peace and trafficking of women, by necessity required an international response to effect legal change.[5] The Second International Congress of Women, held in parallel to the Versailles Peace Conference, is an important example of the potency of women's coalitions. They campaigned at Versailles to ensure women were eligible to work at the League of Nations and succeeded in inserting Article 7 into the Covenant of the League of Nations.[6]

Beyond NGO activity, several women, such as Rachel Crowdy, managed to gain roles within the League influencing work on the Advisory Committee on Traffic in Women and Children and the drafting of the Convention on the Traffic of Women and Children and the Convention on the Suppression of and Circulation of Obscene Publication.[7] But within the League, women were often limited to issues that were defined as concerning them—health, childbirth, nutrition, education.[8] What constituted women's concerns was judged by men. How women could influence these and other areas, as well as which women were able to gain influence, were all curtailed. When attempts were made within the League to examine the status of women, McKinnon Wood, an official in the Legal Department, wrote that he and the Secretary General agreed that "the question of the political and civil rights of women is unsuitable for international action" and that any movement towards raising issues were mere agitators such as Alice Paul' a US feminist.[9]

While some in the League made valiant efforts to advance women's issues, large populations of women, many of whom still lived under colonialism, were entirely excluded from the debate. Their specific issues were either not raised or defined by others. This was despite the fact that Latin American women often led campaigns to address issues of concern to women, demonstrating that critical Global South leadership is possible and necessary to address women's issues beyond a Euro-American gaze but also that women had to make these spaces for themselves. [10] Women achieved some success in the League's successor, the UN. Following the work of women such as Bertha Lutz, women were eligible for roles in the UN Secretariat and the leadership of women from Latin America was essential in ensuring that gender was on the UN's agenda.[11] This included the creation of the Commission on the Status of Women in 1946 led by Bodil Begtrup, the main avenue for feminist action within the UN structure.[12]

While Euro-American feminist organizations often dominated, after 1945, these NGO organizations were frequently divided between the West and Communist states. Additionally, the question of decolonization served to create tensions between Global North and South states. Rather than recognize that the Global South formed a distinct group with unique interests, their perspective has often been suppressed into the Cold War divide. The exclusion of women from the League of Nations and the UN, the defining of topics of interest to women, the exclusion of women from the Global South and decolonization all formed part of the legacies raised in Mexico.[13] But also, part of this legacy was the form and structure of these global conferences. Women had built networks of organizations and campaigns, had created and developed the processes of parallel conferences as a way to affect legal change when excluded from fora, but were also facing their own processes of exclusion and privilege, all of which would become apparent in Mexico City.

International women's year

The post-colonial context, including the legacy of the Bandung Conference and the debates on the New International Economic Order, the Non-Aligned Movement, and the Group of 77 meant that the Global South, was an increasingly significant voice within international conferences.[14] The Cold War, beyond women's rights, had made the Global South a site of confrontation. The tensions between the Western dominated International Council of Women and the socialist and anti-colonial basis of the Women's International Democratic Federation typified these tensions—albeit cooperation and progress on women's issues were still consistently made amongst these organizations.[15] By the time of the Mexico Conference, the domination of particular NGOs and their relationships with the UN structures was also a source of friction especially for those that did not have easy access to lobbying possibilities.

The Mexico Conference was the first inter-governmental global conference to focus on women, but the initial proposal was centred on a women's year. The first thematic year was in 1959/60 and focussed upon the human rights issues of refuges (such designations would become a feature of UN activity).[16] This initiative, as well as for the 1975 Conference, came to the UN Commission on the Status of Women (CSW) from NGOs. The CSW debates reflected both the vast array of issues that needed to be discussed, the differences amongst the NGOs, but also what types of events were likely to advance women's human rights and what topics should be included. The CSW ultimately declared its decision to "devote this year to intensified action to promote equality between men and women and to increase women's contribution to national and international development."[17]

The General Assembly Resolution, accepting the CSW proposal, focussed International Women's Year on three issues: (a) To promote equality between men and women; (b) To ensure the full integration of women in the total development effort, especially by emphasizing women's responsibility and important role in economic, social, and cultural development at the national, regional, and international levels, particularly during the Second United Nations Development Decade; (c) To recognize the importance of women's increasing contribution to the development of friendly relations and co-operation amongst States and to the strengthening of world peace.[18]

Outside of these three core points of focus, a partial aim was to highlight the lack of progress on legal reform, the continued domination of debate on liberal rights and of the Global North states in setting the terms of debate.[19]

A conference on women had been debated at the CSW since 1947. The specific proposal for the 1975 event came from Australian Julie Dahlitz and was coupled with eventual Australian government support though Elizabeth Reid, the first advisor to the Australian Prime Minister on women's issues.[20] The official proposal was put before the CSW by Patricia Hutar, a US delegate.[21] The proposal was not unanimously supported. Soviet bloc states argued it would be, like other themed conferences, a gimmick, due both to their expense—for the UN and for delegates, and their general lack of substantive outcome. They suggested that the General Assembly should include debate on IWY as a special agenda item, a process that had been used to discuss terrorism, as this would have a greater impact.[22]

Ultimately the resolution to hold a conference was supported by CSW and ECOSOC and adopted by the General Assembly.[23] Tensions on interpreting the themes, funding, location, and the content of what was to be debated immediately became sources of tension. This is perhaps unsurprising given the hitherto lack of focus on women at a major global event. Amongst these tensions, however, the question of which state would host became particularly serious.[24] Mexico City was the eventual location after Colombia withdrew their offer to host.

Mexico's hosting of the Conference was significant for a number of reasons. Most immediately, the decision to ratify its hosting came in the same session as Mexico's sponsorship of the *Charter on the Economic Rights and Duties of States*. The Charter was a key aim of the New International Economic Order. Given this context, Mexico's selection placed the Global South's international legal ambitions directly into the foreground of the Conference.[25] However, Mexican President Echeverría's poor human rights record resulted in Mexican feminists being unsupportive of the hosting as they argued the Conference would build his reputation by co-opting women's rights into his agenda.[26] It was from here that the idea of a parallel NGO event emerged (though as discussed above, such a feminist tactic was used as far back as the Paris Peace Conference in 1919).

Created by Mildred Persinger (US) and Marcia-Ximena Bravo (Ecuador), the NGO Tribune met five kilometres south of the main conference and contained many of the same delegates.[27] The NGO Tribune would be an open space for wider debate amongst feminists unconstrained by the structure of UN thematic conferences and critically would not seek to speak with one voice.

1975 conference on women

One commentator stressing the importance of the Mexico conference stated that "[n]ot since Adam and Eve ate the apple has this earth been faced with a social issue as complex as that which drew the delegates to the International Women's Year Conference in Mexico City." [28] Though this in its biblical referencing, and particularly mention of the human Fall, in many ways falls into the stereotypes of debates on women that would characterize much of the reportage on the event. Both the UN Conference and the parallel NGO Tribune commenced on the 23rd of June 1975. The task of the former was the promulgation of a World Plan of Action for addressing the inequalities facing women around the globe. The latter had no specific agenda and would constitute a forum for free debate. Attendance at the Conference, despite the costs, was encouraging. Notwithstanding a lack of funding and poor organization, 125 of the UN's member states sent delegations, numbering over 2000 individuals, with over 8000 people in total, almost 75% were women.[29] The NGO Tribune exceeded this total—being attended by 6,000.[30]

Of course, the number of women delegates deserves to be commended as an impressive achievement, but it is worth recollecting that the delegates in question were under the close control of their respective governments. Fraser (US), who attended the conference, recollected how US delegates were strictly instructed not to hold any communication with those delegates from the socialist bloc.[31] The USSR delegates and others from the socialist bloc, in turn, were likely under similar restrictions. What is more, the location of the Conference impacted upon the geographical spread of those who could attend. Being in Mexico City, attendance was dominated by US and South American members. Individuals from the continents of Africa and Asia struggled to find the resources to undertake the trip, were thus underrepresented, depriving the Conferences of an important intersectional element. The UN Conference got off to an unfortunate start, with the first two speakers being men. UN Secretary General Kurt Waldheim and President Luis Echeverría of Mexico were the first voices to be heard. Mexican Attorney General Pedro Ojeda Paullada was elected President of the Conference, a point that would become the centre of dispute between the US and Global South feminists. Even with a majority of women attending, the initial tone was male.

As the dual conferences got underway, the geopolitical tensions between the West and the USSR, and between the West and the recently decolonised states allied to the Non-Aligned Group, became manifest.[32] This was alongside the frictions already developing between Western feminists and those of the Global South, especially as US feminists began having their predominance challenged.[33] For these US and Western feminists, their core beliefs were in grass-root feminism, the creation of particular legal rights to achieve equality, and suspicion of what masculine dominated state-based structures could achieve in the emancipation of women. More specifically, they eschewed overtly political and economic considerations, seeking to centre debate around such issues as legal inequalities, sexual liberation, employment discrimination, education, and representation.[34] The lack of focus or even identification of what would subsequently be identified by Crenshaw as intersectionality would remain a problem for Western feminist leadership.[35]

To the US delegates' dismay, other delegates sought to refocus attention, with contemporary commentators remarking that the "women's revolution was immediately faced by what seemed like a counterrevolution."[36] Within the UN conference's plenary sessions, delegates from the Global South stressed the centrality of addressing economic concerns and the establishment of a fairer international economic system as a prerequisite to the realization of any gender equality. As Sirimave Bandaranaike, the Prime Minister of Sri Lanka, argued, the disputations of gender equality that characterize Western discourse were just not applicable to a polity that can scarcely guarantee subsistence for women.

This, predictably, was met by curt dismissals by Western delegates. France's Françoise Giroud, for one, condemned attempts to "divert the Conference from its true purpose into 'New Economic Order Problems'."[37] The reference to the New International Economic Order is significant. The Charter on Economic Rights was now adopted and significantly challenged the legal economic order dominated by the historical colonial powers and further change appeared possible (even if eventually it would not meet all its aims).[38] But the right to development as a distinct legal claim was already fomenting and it is unsurprising that feminists from the Global South would see the need to insert women into that right as being an essential aspect of their emancipation.[39] The New International Economic Order was regarded in the Global North as a threat and entirely negative prospect. The failure of the Global North feminists to see its possibilities became a key point of dispute.

The USSR, through their delegate Valentina Tereshkova, likewise rejected the ideas of equality espoused by the US feminists. To their perspective, the end of man's ability to exploit another man under the communist social model had realized equality for both men and women. While exaggerated, the achievements of the USSR and Eastern-bloc countries in achieving gender equality have been demonstrated in recent studies and within diplomacy. Indeed, communist states were amongst the first to appoint women as diplomats, including Alexandra Kollontai as one of the first senior woman diplomats in 1924.[40] Ghodsee, for one, points to the clear evidence of the USSR's "significant achievements in terms of women's literacy, education, legal equality, reproductive rights, and/or incorporation into the labor force."[41] For the USSR, the next step in securing equality was the integration of women's voices into those dialogues addressing questions of world peace (colonialism, neo-colonialism, nuclear proliferation). In response to this contribution, Whitaker (a contemporary commentator from the US) cursorily condemned the USSRs for abstaining "from the revolutions of both women and the poor."[42]

At the NGO Tribune, the tensions between competing claims emerged most clearly. Upon the Mexican Attorney General Pedro Ojeda Paullada being elected president of the UN Conference, US activist Betty Friedan denounced it. She argued that having a man preside over a conference concerning the condition of women was an absurdity. She established a Feminist Caucus within the Tribune to contest the presidency—though it should be noted that Friedan was not representative of the entirety of US feminists nor their diverse experiences at the Conferences.[43] Friedan, however, faced a significant backlash. Latin American women were in support of Paullada, a point that reflects their belief in the power of the state to effect change. Freidan's activities also raised concerns amongst delegates that the US representatives were attempting to dominate proceedings at the Tribune.[44] Mexican media lambasted Friedan as a caricature for privileged liberal Western feminism, in which the sole objective was the establishment of complete equality between men and women. In this vein, the press drew particular attention to her masculine features nicknaming her "The Terrible" and "The Threat," an often repeated trope used to undermine women's authority.[45]

Domitila Barrios de Chungara (Bolivia) represented an important rallying point for Third World frustration with US feminists. Coming from a Bolivian tin-mining community, Domitila expected the Conference and Tribune to be a space where women from economically depressed backgrounds could combine to campaign for substantial international economic reorganization. Upon arrival in Mexico, however, she felt immediately alienated by the various panels discussing what she characterized as First World concerns: sexual liberation and the fight to achieve equality.[46] The specific issues facing women from less industrialized economies and rural areas were being marginalized. Against this, Domitila, in a series of speeches, brought the question of economic advantage centre stage, highlighting the harsh conditions women like her faced.

The tensions within the NGO Tribune came to a head regarding the absence of a representative of the Tribune at the UN Conference. Growing frustrated at the inability of the Tribune to directly impact upon the proceedings of the UN Conference, the feminist caucus—lead by Friedan—restyled themselves the "United Women of the Tribune" and began holding private meetings and organizing to have petitions delivered to the UN conference.[47] While certainly a bold move, private side meetings have long been a feature of Global North proceedings at Conferences as epitomized by "Green Room" meetings at the GATT and WTO.[48] Notwithstanding that, Friedan was lionized in subsequent US accounts as bravely standing up to the UN delegates and as uniting the "women of the world," but her fellow tribunal members disagreed.

While certainly attempting to appear cosmopolitan, the United Women of the Tribune quickly became associated with US feminists. Rival groups established themselves to contest the usurpation of the Tribune's voice. These included the Coalition of Latin American Women (who rejected universalism, seeking to establish a distinctly Latin American Voice) and the Women Against Imperialism (a Marxist group that included Domitila amongst its members).[49] These disagreements were exploited by mainstream media commentators who emphasized the differences between the delegates following a traditional narrative of infighting feminists and emotional women which, as Olcott has pointed out, occludes much of the debate and misrepresents events.[50] This depiction of the Conference and Tribune, while fairly typical of reporting of women's' activism in this period, and while the disagreements remain fundamental to feminist debates today, such disagreements at world conference is not just the purview of those that address women.

Both Conferences concluded amicably. The juxtaposed viewpoints of the East and West, and the now vocal perspectives of the Global South, remained in conflict, but divisive episodes that took place were enlarged to obscure the genuine achievement that the Conference represented. Further, Western feminists were slow to take on board the issues of intersectionality that the Conference had brought to the foreground. In a highly dismissive survey of the proceedings, Whitaker described the Global South as being so singularly intent upon wealth redistribution, that feminists had to wonder whether "the Third World position did not reflect a disdain or hostility by their countries and their male-dominated governments for the goals of the conferences."[51] To be sure, she did admit of the unique economic difficulties that developing countries face and the privileged position Western feminists inhabit, (Whitaker 1975) but the tone is condescending. If anything, the recognition of the unique concerns of Third World Women merely reinforces the conviction that Western women "have led the way" in the fight for equality.[52]

The world plan of action

The adoption of the World Plan of Action was a tortuous process. While drafts of the World Plan had already been composed by a UN Consultative Committee based on principles of equality embodied in various Treaties, it remained a difficult task to gain agreement.[53] During the Conference the Drafting Committee heard over a hundred speeches detailing the global lived experiences of women. 894 amendments were proposed by the Committees, the Tribune, and feminist NGOs. The volume and variety are unsurprising given the hitherto inattention to women's issues and the inaudibility of women from the Global South that had been the norm up to this point.[54] In the final 24-hour sessions, the fatigued Conference demurred in debating these proposals and unanimously accepted the World Plan of Action.[55]

In addition to the World Plan of Action, and a testimony to the policy divides that characterized the proceedings in Mexico, the UN Conference adopted as a preamble to the Plan an additional Declaration of Mexico on the Equality of Women and Their Contribution to Development and Peace.[56] The proposal was brought by the Non-Aligned Movement and represents their particular concern of realizing a more equitable economic order. It passed by 89 votes to 2, with 19 abstentions. Revealingly, the US was included in the number of States voting directly against the proposal. Nonetheless, the influences of Western feminism within the document remain evident. The Declaration stresses "that women and men of all countries should have equal rights and duties and that it is the task of all States to create the necessary conditions for the attainment and the exercise thereof;"[57] and asserts the principle that "[e]quality between women and men means equality in their dignity and worth as human beings as well as equality in their rights, opportunities and responsibilities."[58]

However, the combined importance of the voices from the Eastern bloc and the Global South was critical. With respect to the latter, at principle 14, the Declaration asserts that:

> [t]he issue of inequality, as it affects the vast majority of women in the world, is closely linked with the problem of under-development, which exists as a result not only of unsuitable international structures but also of a profoundly unjust world economic system.[59]

From this postulate, article 18 declares that it is "essential to establish and implement with urgency the New International Economic Order."[60] This order is said to be founded upon the basic elements of "equity, sovereign equality, interdependence, common interest, co-operation among all States irrespective of their social and economic systems and on the principles of peaceful coexistence and on the promotion by the entire international community of economic and social progress of all countries, especially developing countries."[61] Finally, in article 19, the Declaration affirms "[t]he principle of the full and permanent sovereignty of every State over its natural resources, wealth and all economic activities, and its inalienable right of nationalisation as an expression of this sovereignty."[62] This language sits very much alongside the *Charter of Economic Rights and Duties* in focusing on economic sovereignty, natural resources, and nationalization but brings women's economic position to bear upon the New International Economic Order.[63]

The USSR's insistence on women's inclusion within international affairs, a space where women remained, and still remain, absent, is set out in principle 2, where states are required to ensure women's "participation in securing and in maintaining international peace" and in principle 25, that "[w]omen must participate equally with men in the decision-making processes which help to promote peace at all levels."[64] These quite general statements are supported by the comparatively bold principle 26, which declares that "[w]omen and men together should eliminate colonialism, neo-colonialism, imperialism, foreign domination and occupation, Zionism, apartheid, racial discrimination, the acquisition of land by force and the recognition of such acquisition."[65] The inclusion of such a programme is justified on the grounds that "such practices inflict incalculable suffering on women, men and children."[66]

Finally, in article 29, the ideas of sovereign equality and the right to non-intervention are reinforced:

> Peace requires that women as well as men should reject any type of intervention in the domestic affairs of States, whether it be openly or covertly carried on by other States or by transnational corporations... [and] that women as well as men should promote respect for the sovereign right of a State to establish its own economic, social, and political system without undergoing political and economic pressures or coercion of any type.[67]

This should be viewed alongside General Assembly Resolutions, led by the expanding number of Global South states which attempted to carve a place for the General Assembly in peace and security away from the dominance of the Permanent Five on the Security Council but also to re-assert that non-intervention was the norm.[68]

As to the World Action Plan itself, the document contains the concerns of the Global South and the Eastern bloc. The introduction to the plan includes references to the need for the elimination of "the last vestiges of alien and colonial domination, foreign occupation, racial discrimination, apartheid and neo-colonialism in all its forms"[69] and the inequalities within development. Its stresses the point that women subsisting in regimes—such as apartheid—struggle "tirelessly for the recovery of the most elementary rights of the human person."[70] Likewise, the need for the protection of state sovereignty is highlighted, and the "inadmissibility of acquisition or attempts to acquire territory by force, mutual advantage, the avoidance of the use or the threat of force, and the promotion and maintenance of a new just world economic order."[71] That being said, the USSR and Global South voices remain quite imprecise and general. Clear provision as to how these goals are to be realized was not given concrete expression. There are suggestions that States should ensure that women "are equitably represented among the principal delegates to all international bodies, conferences and committees"[72] and that the UN should focus upon the "preparation of international conventions, declarations, and formal recommendations, and the development of reporting systems."[73] Such statements, however, do not foist any clear mandate upon States to act. The *national* development goals that the Plan does set are, in contrast, much more precise and technical. For example, the plan envisages that in the next five-year period there should be achieved as a minimum:

i   "Marked increase in literacy and civic education of women, especially in rural areas."[74]

ii "Equal access at every level of education, compulsory primary school education and the measures necessary to prevent school drop-outs."[75]

iii "Provision for parity in the exercise of civil, social and political rights such as those pertaining to marriage, citizenship and commerce."[76]

iv "The establishment of interdisciplinary and multisectoral machinery within the government for accelerating the achievement of equal opportunities for women and their full integration into national life."[77]

None of these principles and propositions were binding. As one commentator described it, the Plan merely had "hortatory" force but after its adoption by the UN General Assembly the possibility of it morphing into soft law and becoming the basis of further legal and policy reform became extant. The Plan of Action also scheduled a further conference to be held at Copenhagen in five years' time in order to assess the progress made by States in the fulfilment of the agenda set out in Mexico City.

Outcome

Following the Conference, the General Assembly endorsed the World Plan of Action proclaiming 1976–1985 as the United Nations Decade for Women.[78] This was followed by additional conferences in Copenhagen in 1980 and Nairobi in 1985, though both conferences confirmed the lack of progress that had been made since Mexico City. That said, following the Mexico Conference, an existing UN body was renamed the Branch for the Advancement of Women. This institution would progress through several evolutions and now forms part of UN Women. The United Nations Development Fund for Women, though also evolving through several forms, would also emerge from the Decade for Women. There were also significant non-UN events and Conferences that eschewed UN structures, such as the International Tribunal on Crimes against Women.[79]

The Beijing Conference rivals Mexico in importance and significance and while it too had controversies and disagreements the established space to specifically discuss issues facing women and the impossibility of Western feminists dominating the narrative is evident.[80] It was also the last Conference of its specific type—though women activists have also utilized a series of 1990 UN sponsored Conferences to further their concerns.[81] Despite the fact that there remains an overarching concern as to whether these forms of conferences are the best avenue to affect legal and political change,[82] the Mexico Conference and the subsequent events in Copenhagen 1980, Nairobi 1985 and Beijing 1995 provided spaces for women to meet, to build alliances, and to learn from each other including about strategies and failures in campaigning.[83]

Conclusion

Differing perspectives on how to support women, what to forefront, what to fund, what to set into law, what to leave to policy, are fundamental to considering how to finally achieve full substantive equality for women. The 1975 Conference succeeded in forefronting that complexity and what was reported as an argumentative space was actually the first proper opportunity for women of the Global South to articulate their priorities within the formalised UN space. It would now be inconceivable that women of the Global North would dominate agendas and podiums, and while there is still a very long road ahead for Western feminism to finally cede space and end attempts to represent all women Mexico represented a first break in that (misguided) attempt to speak for all women.

The Mexico City Conference also demonstrated the complexity of women's lives and that the East-West divisions were not the only ones of consequence. The New International Economic Order in particular drew attention to the postcolonial realities of many women's lives, and while women in the Global South maintain their campaigns to be heard, to be participants, to set agenda, and to write policy and law, Mexico City ruptured a settled description of women's issues at the international level. Issues of sexuality, indigenous women's rights, and bodily autonomy or of simply being recognized as a valid voice at the table remain. Even within the UN secretariat, women's equality remains an outstanding goal. The UN and NGO level are also not the sole avenues of activism and change. Mexico City in 1975 was a critical moment where women infiltrated and created their own agendas and set-in motion a (slow) process of change. The UN did not create, nor has it supported, feminism to any great extent, and UN activities "are not substitutes for women's movements nor should they be expected to be so" or indeed advocated as such.[84] Such events are also, without funding and support, inaccessible to those women who face the hardest challenges. Nonetheless they have shone light on women's issues and built alliances and assisted in changes in policy, law, and most importantly lives and these should not be discounted.

Notes

1 Jean H. Quataert, Benita Roth 'Human Rights, Global Conferences, and the Making of Postwar Transnational Feminisms' (2012) *Journal of Women's History* 11, 15.
2 For an overview of media strategies and depictions of women in the media in this context see Jocelyn Olcott 'Empires of Information: Media Strategies for the 1975 International Women's Year' (2012) 24 *Journal of Women's History* 24.
3 See Marino 'From Women's Rights to Human Rights', this volume, ch.1.
4 Helen McCarthy, *Women of the World: The Rise of the Female Diplomat* (Bloomsbury, 2014).
5 Jill Liddington, The Road to Greenham Common: Feminism and Anti-militarism in Britain Since 1820 (Syracuse University Press, 1989).
6 Constitution of the International Labour Organisation Constitution under Article 9.3 on staff that '[a] certain number of these persons shall be women' and under Article 3.2 on Meetings and Delegates that, '2. Each delegate may be accompanied by advisers, who shall not exceed two in number for each item on the agenda of the meeting. When questions specially affecting women are to be considered by the Conference, one at least of the advisers should be a woman.'

7 Margaret E Galey, 'Forerunners in Womens Quest for Partnership' in Anne Winslow (ed), *Women, Politics, and the United Nations* (Greenwood Publishing Group, 1995) 5.

8 Margaret E Galey, 'Forerunners in Womens Quest for Partnership' in Anne Winslow (ed), *Women, Politics, and the United Nations* (Greenwood Publishing Group, 1995) 5.

9 Sandi E Cooper, 'Peace as a Human Right, The Invasion of Women into the World of High International Politics' (2002) 14 *Journal of Women's History* 9, 12.

10 Hilkka Pietilä, The Unfinished Story of Women and the United Nations (NGLS development dossier, 2009) 7–8.

11 ibid 9–10.

12 Jean H. Quataert, Benita Roth 'Human Rights, Global Conferences, and the Making of Postwar Transnational Feminisms' (2012) *Journal of Women's History* 11, 16.

13 Gayatri Spivak 'Can the Subaltern Speak?' in Rosalind C Morris (Ed) *Can the Subaltern Speak?: Reflections on the History of an Idea* (Columbia University Press, 2010) 33.

14 Introduction' in L Eslava, M. Fakhri, V. Nesiah (eds.) *Bandung, Global History, and International Law* Critical Pasts and Pending Futures (CUP, 2017) 17.

15 Jocelyn Olcot, *International Women's Year: The Greatest Consciousness-Raising Event in History* (OUP, 2017) 19.

16 United Nations International Years https://www.un.org/en/sections/observances/international-years/index.html

17 Commission on the Status of Women: Report on the Twenty-Fourth Session UN doc. E/CN.6/L.644, 29 February 1972, 157, 185.

18 The inclusion of development and peace followed sustained wrangling regarding extending the purview of what was a women's' issue beyond the traditional boundary of liberal rights. See: United Nations General Assembly Resolution 3010 (XXVII) A/RES/27/3010 (XXVII) 18 December 1972.

19 Olcott (n 14) 23.

20 ibid 27 – 33.

21 CSW, 25th session, 15 January 1974, UN doc. E/CN.6/L.658.

22 CSW, 25th session, 21 January 1974, UN doc. E/CN.6/L.659. Olcott (n 2) 44.

23 General Assembly Resolution A/RES/3277(XXIX) Consultative Committee for the Conference of the International Women's Year 10th December 1974.

24 Olcott (n 14) 42.

25 General Assembly Resolution A/RES/3281(XXIX) Charter of Economic Rights and Duties of States UN doc. E/L.1615, 18 November 1974.

26 Olcott (n 14) 58.

27 There was also an East Berlin Conference.

28 Jenifer Whitaker, 'Women of the World: Report from Mexico City' (1975) 54(1) *Foreign Affairs* 173.

29 Kristen Ghodsee, 'Revisiting the United Nations Decade for Women: Brief Reflections on Feminism, Capitalism and Cold War Politics in the Early Years of the International Women's Movement' (2010) 33 *Women's Studies International Forum* 244, Charlotte Bunch 'Opening Doors for Feminism: UN World Conferences on Women' (2012) *Journal of Women's History* 213, 214.

30 ibid.

31 Whitaker (n 28).

32 Quataert, Roth (n 11) 11–12.

33 Western feminists had already been anticipating such an eventuality. See https://www.nytimes.com/1975/06/19/archives/international-womens-year-world-conference-opening-in-mexico.html

34 Judith P Zinsser, 'From Mexico to Copenhagen to Nairobi: The United Nations Decade for Women, 1975-1985' (2002)) Journal of World History 139, 140.

35 Kimberlé Crenshaw, 'Mapping the Margins: Intersectionality, Identity Politics and Violence Against Women,' in Kimberlé Crenshaw, Neil Gotanda, Gary Peller, and

Kendall Thomas (eds), *Critical Race Theory: The Key Writings that Formed the Movement*, ed. (The New Press, 1995) 357.

36 Whitaker (n 28) 173.
37 Marguerite Rawalt, 'UN World Conference in International Women's Year and Tribune – Mexico City' (1975) 61 Women's Law Journal 184, 186.
38 S Chatterjee, 'The Charter of Economic Rights and Duties of States and the New International Economic Order' (1991) 40 ICLQ 669.
39 S Chowdhury, E M.G. Denters, P.J.I.M. de Waart, 'The Right to Development in International Law' (Martinus Nijhoff Publishers, 1992).
40 Diana Apcar of Armenia is recognised as the first in 1920.
41 Ghodsee (n 29) 247.
42 Whitaker (n 28) 173.
   For an account of the marginilisation of non-western voices to the development of feminism, see Kristen Ghodsee 'Research Note: The Historiographical Challenges of Exploring Second World–Third World Alliances in International Women's Movement' (2014) 14(2) Global Social Policy 244.
43 Olcott (n 14) 115, Charlotte Bunch 'Opening Doors for Feminism: UN World Conferences on Women' (2012) *Journal of Women's History* 213, 213.
44 ibid 120-121.
45 ibid 126.
46 ibid 140-142.
47 ibid 169.
48 Kent Jones, 'Green room politics and the WTO's crisis of representation' (2009) 9 *Progress in Development Studies* 349.
49 Olcott (n 14) 171.
50 Olcott (n 2) 2.
51 Olcott (n 14) 187.
52 ibid 180.
53 Though not all had sufficient ratifications to be legally binding Hermina Strauss, 'The Legal Issues Facing International Women's Year Conference in Mexico City on June 19, 1975' (1975) 61(2) *Women Lawyers Journal* 66.
54 Gayatri Spivak 'Can the Subaltern Speak?' in Rosalind C Morris (ed), *Can the Subaltern Speak?: Reflections on the History of an Idea* (Columbia University Press, 2010) 33.
55 UN General Assembly, Implementation of the World Plan of Action adopted by the world Conference of the International Women's Year, 12 December 1975, A/RES/3490.
56 UN General Assembly, Implementation of the World Plan of Action adopted by the world Conference of the International Women's Year, 12 December 1975, A/RES/3490.
57 Declaration   3.   https://www.un.org/womenwatch/daw/beijing/otherconferences/Mexico/Mexico%20conference%20report%20optimized.pdf
58 ibid 4.
59 ibid 5.
60 ibid.
61 ibid.
62 ibid 6.
63 General Assembly Resolution A/RES/3281(XXIX) Charter of Economic Rights and Duties of States UN doc. E/L.1615, 18 November 1974.
64 UN General Assembly, Implementation of the World Plan of Action adopted by the world Conference of the International Women's Year, 12 December 1975, A/RES/3490, 6.
65 Ibid.
66 ibid 7.
67 ibid.

68 UN General Assembly, Uniting for peace, 3 November 1950, A/RES/377.
69 UN General Assembly, Implementation of the World Plan of Action adopted by the world Conference of the International Women's Year, 12 December 1975, A/RES/3490.
    https://www.un.org/womenwatch/daw/beijing/otherconferences/Mexico/Mexico%20 conference%20report%20optimized.pdf 9.
70 ibid 11.
71 ibid 12.
72 ibid 36.
73 ibid.
74 ibid 16.
75 ibid.
76 ibid.
77 ibid 17.
78 UN General Assembly Resolution 3520 World Conference of the International Women's Year, Hanna Papanek, 'The Work of Women: Postscript from Mexico City' 1975 1 *Signs* 215.
79 Diana E. H. Russell, Nicole Van de Ven *Crimes against Women: Proceedings of the International Tribunal* (Les Femmes Pub., 1976).
80 https://www.unwomen.org/-/media/headquarters/attachments/sections/csw/pfa_e_ final_web.pdf?la=en&vs=1203
81 Marilyn Porter, 'Transnational Feminisms in a Globalized World: Challenges, Analysis, and Resistance' (2007) 33 *Feminist Studies* 43.
82 Hilary Charlesworth, 'Women as Sherpas: Are Global Summits Useful for Women?' (1996) 22 *Feminist Studies* 537.
83 Charlotte Bunch 'Opening Doors for Feminism: UN World Conferences on Women' (2012) *Journal of Women's History* 213, 213.
84 ibid 213.

Bibliography

Bunch, Charlotte. "Opening doors for feminism: UN world conferences on women." *Journal of Women's History* 24, no. 4 (2012): 213–221.
Chatterjee, S. K. "The charter of economic rights and duties of states: An evaluation after 15 years." *The International and Comparative Law Quarterly* 40, no. 3 (1991): 669–684.
Charlesworth, Hilary. "Women as Sherpas: Are global summits useful for women?" *Feminist Studies* 22, no. 3 (1996): 537–547.
Chowdhury, Subrata Roy, Erik MG Denters, and Paul JIM de Waart, eds. *The Right to Development in International Law*. Leiden: Martinus Nijhoff Publishers, 1992.
Cooper, Sandi E. "Peace as a human right: The invasion of women into the world of high international politics." *Journal of Women's History* 14, no. 2 (2002): 9–25.
Crenshaw, Kimberle. "Mapping the margins: Intersectionality, identity politics, and violence against women of color." *Stan. L. Rev.* 43 (1990): 1241.
Eslava, Luis, Michael Fakhri, and Vasuki Nesiah, eds. *Bandung, Global History, and International Law: Critical Pasts and Pending Futures*. Cambridge, New York: Cambridge University Press, 2017.
Galey, Margaret E. "Forerunners in women's quest for partnership Contributions." *Women's Studies* 151 (1995): 1–10.
Ghodsee, Kristen. "Revisiting the United Nations decade for women: Brief reflections on feminism, capitalism and Cold War politics in the early years of the international women's movement." *Women's Studies International Forum*, 33, no. 1 (2010): 3–12.

Jones, Kent. "Green room politics and the WTO's crisis of representation." *Progress in Development Studies* 9, no. 4 (2009): 349–357.

Liddington, Jill. *The Road to Greenham Common: Feminism and Anti-Militarism in Britain Since 1820*. Syracuse, N.Y: Syracuse University Press, 1991.

McCarthy, Helen. *Women of the World: The Rise of the Female Diplomat*. London: A & C Black, Bloomsbury Publishing, 2014.

Olcott, Jocelyn. "Empires of information: Media strategies for the 1975 international women's year." *Journal of Women's History* 24, no. 4 (2012): 24–48.

Olcott, Jocelyn. *International Women's Year: The Greatest Consciousness-Raising Event in History*. United States: Oxford University Press, 2017.

O'Donoghue, A. 'Article 7 of the Covenant of the League of Nations, 1919' in E Rackley and R Auchmuty *Women's Legal Landmarks*. Bloomsbury, 2018.

Papanek, Hanna. "The work of women: Postscript from Mexico City." Signs: *Journal of Women in Culture and Society* 1, no. 1 (1975): 215–226.

Pietilä, Hilkka, and Beth Peoch. *The Unfinished Story of Women and the United Nations*. United Nations Non-Governmental Liaison Service, 2007.

Porter, Marilyn. "Transnational feminisms in a globalized world: Challenges, analysis, and resistance." *Feminist Studies*, (2007): 43–63.

Quataert, Jean H., and Benita Roth. "Guest editorial note: Human rights, global conferences, and the making of postwar transnational feminisms." *Journal of Women's History* 24, no. 4 (2012): 11–23.

Rawalt, Marguerite. "UN world conference in international women's year and tribune-Mexico City, June 19-July 2, 1975." *Women Law Journal* 61 (1975): 184.

Russell, Diana EH, and Nicole Van de Ven, eds. *Crimes Against Women: Proceedings of the International Tribunal*. Frog in the Well, 1976.

Spivak, Gayatri 'Can the subaltern speak?' in Rosalind Morris, ed. *Can the Subaltern Speak?: Reflections on the History of an Idea*. Columbia University Press, 2010.

Strauss, Hermina. "The Legal Issues Facing International Women's Year Conference in Mexico City on June 19, 1975." *Women Law Journal* 61 (1975): 66.

Whitaker, Jennifer Seymour. "Women of the world: Report from Mexico City." *Foreign Affairs* 54 (1975): 173.

Zinsser, Judith P. "From Mexico to copenhagen to nairobi: The United Nations decade for women, 1975–1985." *Journal of World History* (2002): 139–168.

7 Who wrote CEDAW?

Ellen Chesler

Introduction

Educated in London in economics and law, Annie Jiagge became the second woman lawyer in the newly independent state of Ghana, and the second woman in Africa to serve as a justice of the courts. In 1962, she came to New York to represent her country at the United Nations Commission on the Status of Women, or in UN parlance, the CSW. Five years later, as rapporteur for the group, she stayed up one night and crafted together a draft of the Declaration on the Elimination of Discrimination against Women, known as DEDAW, a document that would help transform global understanding of the issue of sex discrimination and provide a framework for a binding women's rights treaty a decade later.[1]

DEDAW represents the UN's first attempt to define the meaning of women's rights as fundamental human rights and do so expansively. The agreement claimed that discrimination against women is "unjust and constitutes an offence against human dignity." It established the legal principle of equal protection for women, when only a few countries had done so. And it demanded that "all appropriate measures" be taken to abolish prejudice, not just in law, but also in customs and practices based on the "idea of women's inferiority."[2]

The UN General Assembly had bold aspirations for this undertaking. It endorsed the document expressing a confidence, radical for its time, that women's advancement is not just a moral obligation but also a necessary condition to secure global progress: "The full and complete development of a country, the welfare of the world, and the cause of peace require the maximum participation of women as well as men in all fields," the 1967 preamble to DEDAW proclaims in language credited to Annie Jiagge.[3]

Leticia Ramos Shahani joined the UN in 1964 as a young editor for the Secretariat in New York, where she worked on general human rights matters and then transferred to the division overseeing the advancement of women. A graduate of Wellesley College, Shahani, had also earned a doctorate in comparative literature at the Sorbonne, but she then changed course and decided to follow in the tradition of her father, a prominent diplomat from the Philippines. Just a few years later, in 1968, after the tragedy of her husband's sudden death, Shahani left her staff job at the UN and returned home to seek family assistance with the care of her three young children. In short order, however, she was back, representing her country as a diplomat at the CSW, the organization she had once staffed. She soon landed as chair of the body and became a rising star in the UN system.

The CSW had been asked to create a binding human rights instrument elaborating on the declaration. Shahani came up with a draft. This effort, after protracted

DOI: 10.4324/9781003036708-7

negotiation, produced the Convention on the Elimination of all Forms of Discrimination against Women (CEDAW), an international bill of rights for women, which was adopted by the General Assembly in 1978 and formally signed by member states in 1980.[4]

The convention enjoys a robust and diverse commentary, but it lacks a thoughtful history that identifies its principal authors, analyzes their personal and political motivations, explains the complex circumstances in which they worked, and engages with the many arguments arrayed for and against it.[5]

Finding the sources to construct that narrative, however, is a challenge. The archives are tragically sparse. An early proposal to fund a formal historical records office at the UN foundered on opposition from Americans concerned about costs and from Soviets worried about objectivity. Formal standards were never created for preserving the background correspondence and documentation that would have illumined the typically opaque transcripts that survive from official public proceedings. In the case of CEDAW, moreover, this institutional failure was compounded when the UN Division for the Advancement of Women, having moved to UN headquarters in Vienna during the late 1970s at the time CEDAW was negotiated, later returned to New York, and boxes of its records were unaccountably lost in transit.[6]

Only two prior analyses I could identify draw on primary sources or on interviews with participants in the drafting of these documents. The late American human rights activist and scholar, Arvonne Fraser, first wrote briefly on the subject.[7] The Dutch legal scholar Lars Rehof later mined incomplete records of the final CEDAW negotiating sessions available in the UN Library in Geneva for a *Travaux Preparatoire.* To the extent possible, Rehof identifies various state party contributions to the long and intense debate over the document's evolving structure and language and concludes that the animating principles and substantive approaches of the 1967 declaration and of the earliest CEDAW draft fundamentally shaped the outcome. Neither work, however, explores the women behind these drafts or investigates what informed their thinking and inspired their activism.[8]

This chapter begins an overdue effort to that end. It establishes necessary historical context and then zeroes in on the biographies of the two women identified as principal architects of the declaration and the convention respectively, Annie Jiagge and Leticia Shahani. Passing reference is made to others, such as Princess Ashraf Pahlavi, who energized and financed the UN's women's rights projects at the UN in these years, before the 1979 revolution in Iran sent her family into exile. The contributions of other important diplomats and civil society advocates from Western Europe, the Americas, and the Soviet bloc are mentioned only briefly. Within the confines of a single chapter, I offer only a snapshot of events that deserve an even richer portrait.

Getting to a declaration on women's rights

As the UN grew in membership, newly independent states lacked the capacity and resources, or the will, to enforce early agreements on gender equality. The need for a more robust approach became clear, as did the recognition that formal principles of political and civil equality would not be sufficient to address the economic obstacles facing women or to liberate them from patterns of discrimination with deep social and cultural roots. In 1963, at the urging of 22 developing world countries and the Soviet bloc, the General Assembly called on the CSW to prepare a declaration modelled on the UDHR that would address these many challenges. Drafting began at the commission's next scheduled meeting in Tehran in 1965, and a final document reached the General Assembly two years later.[9]

Twenty-three countries comprised the CSW membership at this time. The budget constrained body convened bi-annually in these years, and occasionally met abroad where a local host would cover costs. Princess Ashraf Pahlavi, twin sister of the Shah, presided as chair that year, representing the Iranian government, which had launched its "White Revolution" two years before, a program of social and economic reforms that promised to increase literacy, reform land ownership, grant long demanded worker's rights, and extend the franchise and the right to run for office to women. Contempt for this effort from the Ayatollah Khomeini, who likened women's voting to prostitution, was a principal factor in his expulsion from the country and fuelled the opposition movement he led from exile for the next 15 years. Rising tensions in Iran cast their shadow on the CSW proceedings, but in an ominous forewarning of the conservative religious alliance that would burden the UN women's agenda far into the future, opposition to the CSW agenda also came from Catholic countries like Mexico, even as its representative, Marina Lavelle Urbino, rotated into a term as CSW chair.[10]

According to Arvonne Fraser, working papers were prepared for the declaration's drafting committee by Marina Urbino, Annie Jiagge, and Zofia Dembinska of Poland. But differences arose quickly within the group over basic questions of legal philosophy and reach, including what should have been straightforward—the question of equal protection under the law. Inscribed in the UN charter and in the UDHR, that basic equality principle was again front and center in the two overall UN human rights conventions that had been hammered out over many years—the International Covenant on Civil and Political Rights (ICCPR), and the International Convention on Economic, Social and Cultural Rights (ICESCR)—both of which would finally reach the General Assembly for approval in 1966.[11]

But what would equal protection mean in circumstances where men continued to serve as legal guardians and heads of household? How would the formal claim of legal equality address the special burdens of women struggling to balance obligations of work and family? What would its impact be on developed countries where protective labor laws had already established minimum wages, maximum hours, and other ostensible safeguards for women workers?

Debate among the delegates was serious and intense. There were fractures across geographic and ideological divides, east-west, and north-south. Further work was put off until the next scheduled CSW meeting in 1967. Members of an expanded drafting committee were then invited to present alternative texts in writing, with the intent of avoiding further protracted discussion. Official proceedings were limited to up or down votes on proposed amendments.

In this manner, for example, a proposal was made to water down the document by suggesting that it "modify," rather than "abolish" discriminatory laws, but the stronger language prevailed. Where differences could not be resolved—as in how exactly to define what constitutes "discrimination" against women—the meaning of the term remained ambiguous. In one of history's great ironies, Afghanistan's delegate introduced the idea that "temporary special measures" could compensate for historic patterns of discrimination without violating the larger equality principle, therein introducing the concept that has since inspired national affirmative action policies that address race and gender. Absent agreement, the matter was tabled, as was another disputed question—whether to condemn the practice of female genital cutting as a rights violation.[12]

Credit for sorting through differences over content and language, and for putting forward a coherent and straightforward final text, went to CSW rapporteur, Annie Jiagge of Ghana. The final draft of the declaration she crafted follows the structure of the UDHR and includes the lofty preamble quoted above and eleven short articles. There is no equivocation over the basic tenets of the agreement: to "abolish" discrimination; to establish a strict legal standard of equal protection; to educate public opinion; and to "direct national aspirations" to eliminate prejudice.

The document reprises earlier CSW actions from the 1950s on suffrage, the right to hold public office, nationality rights, civil law governing marriage and divorce, and education, and adds clarifying detail. Claiming no prejudice to the "unity and harmony of the family, which remains the basic unit of society," for example, Article 6 spells out women's rights in the home to include equality in legal capacity, property and inheritance, child custody, and freedom of movement. Article 8 addresses prostitution and trafficking in women, presaging a later and more forceful engagement by the UN with the problem of sexual violence. Article 10 addresses the principle of non-discrimination in employment and enumerates specific recommendations, such as equal pay for equal work, paid maternity leave, and childcare, creating an ambitious public policy framework.[13]

Who was Annie Jiagge?

Annie Ruth Baeta Jiagge was born in 1918, in Lome, Togoland, now the Republic of Togo, one of four surviving children of Henrietta and Robert Domingo Baeta, a couple of mixed African and Brazilian/Portuguese lineage. Her mother was a schoolteacher, her father, a minister of the Presbyterian Church, educated in Germany, which had ceded the colony to France. As a girl demonstrating considerable educational promise, she was sent to live with her maternal grandmother in Accra, the capital of neighboring British Togoland, now Ghana, where better English-speaking schools were available. Widowed as a young woman, the grandmother, Barbara Sedode, had become a wealthy and influential merchant, trading local agricultural products for European imports.

The young Jiagge at age 15 entered Achimota College, an elite secondary institution, from which she graduated four years later with a teaching certificate, permitting her to work at the primary school she had attended, the Evangelical

Presbyterian School for Girls in the coastal town of Keta. She soon became head of the school, but with longstanding aspirations to continue her education, and with loans secured by her mother, she left for London in 1946, after the war in Europe ended, having been admitted to the London School of Economics and Political Science. The doors of the institution were opened for the first time to male students from the colonies and to refugees from continental Europe, but there were only three other women in her class, two British and one from India. Jiagge later recalled that she had struggled to succeed as a woman of colour in that setting. Whenever she complained, however, her male friends would strengthen her resolve by encouraging her to quit and study fashion in Paris instead. She persevered, earned a bachelor's degree in 1949, and was called to the Bar at Lincoln's Inn a year later.

A lone in London, Jiagge found a welcoming community at the Young Women's Christian Association (YWCA), an institution to which she remained devoted for the remainder of her life and long credited with having shaped her thinking about the injustices suffered by women and girls. She travelled through continental Europe, the Middle East, and India during college and in the years thereafter, as a member of the executive board of the international YWCA, which also became an important civil society partner on women's issues in the early years of the UN.

Back in Ghana as a young barrister, Jiagge established a local YWCA outpost after she was engaged to represent a young woman from the countryside who had been raped and robbed while seeking shelter. Through her campaign to raise awareness of this widespread problem, and to secure government support for a hostel, she met Kwame Nkrumah, who would soon become president of Ghana, the first British colony in Africa to gain independence in 1957. Like her, he had attended Achimota College but then went to the United States to complete his university degree.

In 1953, at age 35, still eager for a family of her own, Annie Baeta married Fred Jiagge, a local businessman, whom she had known years earlier at Achimota. Unable to conceive a child of their own, they adopted a son and, as had been her grandmother's custom, also raised several girls from rural villages in their household and provided them education. Seeking more manageable hours than her demanding legal practice allowed, Jiagge joined Ghana's courts as a magistrate that year; became a circuit court judge in 1959, a High Court judge in 1961, and a member of the Court of Appeal, then the highest court in the land, in 1969, where she presided as president from 1980 until her retirement three years later. Family and faith remained a central part of her life.[14]

In recent years, a body of scholarship has emerged examining the role of women in the shaping of African nationalism. The biographical elements of Jiagge's life follow the principal contours of this work, which generally holds that Europeans tried but did not fully succeed in introducing gender hierarchies into many African societies long distinguished by a tradition of complementarity between men and women in many facets of life that extended from the household into economic activities like farming and trade, and into civic and political affairs. This was especially true among elites, where authority in the family was commonly shared by husband and wife. Jiagge's family replicated this model.

Kwame Nkrumah rose to power in the 1950s with broad-based support across socio-economic classes and trades—those educated and those not—but also with special attention paid to women and young people, whom he organized through such traditional networks as markets, voluntary associations, and places of worship. One historian describes women as "the backbone" of Nkrumah's revolution. Having gained the right to vote under British rule, women became active in political parties in the run up to independence and were invited to stand for local office. In the first years after independence, ten women were also elected to the new national parliament, which debated social issues such as banning nudity, outlawing bigamy, and bringing marriage under civil rather than customary law.[15]

Nkrumah sought to make Ghana the model for a modern Pan-Africanism that also attracted prominent black Americans then in the throes of the U.S. civil rights movement, including W.E.B DuBois and Bayard Rustin, both of whom attended Ghana's historic Conference of Independent African States in 1958, which was meant to build unity and consolidate ties among countries newly freed from imperialism. The utopian vision set forth there incorporated egalitarian economic and social principles across class, cultural, and gender lines and put Ghana on a path that Nkrumah defined as non-aligned socialism.[16]

Ghanaian historian, Adwoa Opong, says this gathering inspired the Ghana Organization of Women, then the country's leading voluntary association, to convene a "Conference of Women of Africa and African Descent" that would examine "the struggles of Negro [*sic*] women across the continent and in the diaspora" and establish conditions for women's "emancipation, unity and advancement."[17] The meeting of 150 women convened in July of 1960. Representing the United States, among other notable black women, was Pauli Murray, a Howard University trained lawyer, whose innovative legal scholarship on race discrimination had contributed to Thurgood Marshall's arguments in his direct challenge to school segregation in the landmark case of *Brown v. Board of Education* in 1954.

Jiagge's speech to the conference offers a rare window into her thinking at the time. Ghana's women enjoyed few legal protections despite the prominent roles they played in agriculture, commerce, and civic life. "Only lip service is paid to the saying that a woman's place is in the home... there is hardly anywhere outside the home where she hasn't another special place," she observed, while acknowledging that competing systems of civil and customary law ceded full control to men over marriage, child custody, property, and inheritance.[18] Once women married, therefore, they suffered what she later referred to as "civic death." Other speakers addressed additional barriers, especially in rural villages, where whatever authority women may have enjoyed, they were denied education, expected to bear many children, and valued primarily as mothers.[19]

Pauli Murray used this platform to educate conference participants on the establishment of the UN CSW and its mandate to create universal standards for women's rights. She encouraged greater participation in the body and closed with a rousing peroration:

> ...the problems of women everywhere, without respect to color, or to nationality, or to religion, are common problems, and they must be solved many

times through common agencies, and when we have finished unifying the continent of Africa, we will then have to unify the world, and this will be done through the United Nations.[20]

Murray had been lured to Ghana by pan-African idealists including DuBois and his wife, who would soon lose confidence in U.S. institutions and become expatriates. Her experience, however, was disappointing. She taught at the newly created Ghana School of Law for a year, but immediately grew skeptical of Nkrumah's drift away from democracy—his surveillance and silencing of critics, censorship of the press, and declaration of one-party rule. And while she understood the allure of socialism for countries whose wealth had long been extracted by Europeans, she correctly predicted that Africans who rejected democratic practice and free enterprise would become pawns of the Cold War. Murray also questioned Nkrumah's support of women's rights, which she saw as a political calculation rather than a genuine commitment. He would soon consolidate all civil society organizations, including independent women's groups, under strict government authority.[21]

I could find no evidence whether the two women again crossed paths, even as their interests continued to converge. Jiagge joined the CSW in 1962, just as Murray returned to the U.S. and became a member of John F. Kennedy's U.S. Commission on the Status of Women at the invitation of its chair and her long-time friend, Eleanor Roosevelt. In that forum, she introduced the legal concept of "Jane Crow" for which she became famous, to illustrate the parallels she saw in how to confront sex and race discrimination. Her arguments helped persuade second wave U.S. feminist Betty Friedan to establish the National Organization of Women as an NAACP-like advocacy organization seeking legal reforms for women, and years later provided Ruth Bader Ginsburg, then a young civil liberties lawyer, with the case she made to claim equal rights for women using the equal protection clause of the 14th Amendment to the U.S. Constitution. How Pauli Murray may have also influenced Jiagge's thinking in these years is worth considering, as is the opposite proposition—that Murray's experiences in Africa may have shaped her new resolve about the intersections of rights of race and gender. Further research seems essential.[22]

What we do know is that by education, professional training, and lived experience, Jiagge was well prepared in her own right to understand the multiple constraints that burden women and to seek their resolution in law and public policy. In 1976, she assembled her thoughts on the "Exploitation of Women in Third World Perspective" for the *Ecumenical Review*, a World Conference of Churches publication, summarizing "the staggering evidence on the deprivation and degradation of all kinds suffered by women all over the world on account of their sex."[23] She condemned enduring traditions of male privilege but also offered confidence that education, legal reform, and birth control would liberate women.[24]

The article reinforces the view of family members and former colleagues interviewed for a recent biographical project in Ghana, who spoke of Jiagge's exceptionally good nature and of her deep religious conviction. Both attributes could only have served her well in contentious UN forums and as she navigated tortuous political currents at home. Temperament may have been her saving grace.

Jiagge survived the military coup that sent the Nkrumah into exile in 1966, an action in which the U.S. Central Intelligence Agency has since been implicated. She then became the choice of Ghana's generals to lead a high-profile investigation of corruption in his regime, an exercise that produced multiple charges and prevented many of the defendants from participating in politics, until it was reversed a decade later. Throughout this turmoil, she continued to represent Ghana at the CSW, and in 1968 was elected as its chair.[25]

At home, she went on to establish Ghana's Council on Women in Development—an early example of the "national machinery" the UN was then encouraging. The work of this organization later inspired Esther Ocloo, an Achimota school friend who had prospered as an entrepreneur, to travel with her to the UN women's forum in Mexico City in 1975, where they helped launch the network that became Women's World Banking, a pioneer in the micro-credit space that continues to work today with financial institutions in 32 countries, providing loans to some 24 million small entrepreneurs around the world, 80 percent of whom are women. These institutions, however, proved no immediate protections against Ghana's notorious generals, who ruled the country for nearly two decades with a heavy hand, inflicting successive reigns of terror and licensing sexual assault, especially on market women, whom they tried to hold responsible for their own failed economic policies.[26]

Jiagge last returned to the UN in 1980, at a moment when democracy in Ghana was briefly restored, and she took part in the formal passage of CEDAW. During the decades of revolving military rule, she remained on the appeals court, handling commercial and domestic disputes, some involving women's inheritance, with no evidence of any involvement in politics. When democracy was permanently restored, however, she was chosen to serve on the commission that wrote the country's new constitution. The 1992 document guarantees the:

> enjoyment by every person of fundamental human rights and freedoms, including freedom of speech, freedom from arbitrary arrest and detention, freedom of assembly and association, including the freedom to form political parties, women's rights, worker's rights and the rights of the handicapped.[27]

The following year, Jiagge accepted the invitation of UN Secretary General Boutros Boutros-Ghali to join an advisory planning group for the Fourth World Conference on Women planned for Beijing in 1995, which she was then too ill to attend. At her death, BBG paid tribute to Jiagge as "a driving force" in the advancement of women's rights, known for her "determination and ingenuity."[28]

Leticia Ramos Shahani and the drafting of the CEDAW

In 1968, the UN marked the 20th anniversary of the UDHR with a high-profile inter-agency conference in Tehran hosted by the Human Rights Commission. Annie Jiagge attended in her capacity as CSW chair. Leticia (Letty) Shahani, having left the UN after her husband's death, was not present, but a report she had written as her final staff assignment was among the official documents prepared for the event. It made the case for linking women's rights to community development.[29]

The Tehran meeting is now understood as a pivotal moment in the revision of human rights discourse to place greater weight on economics. Shah Reza Pahlavi set the tone in plenary remarks that boldly endorsed a revision in rights categories, privileging economic and social rights while leaving the matter of civil and political protections opaque, in what some saw as a thinly veiled rationalization for cracking down on opponents of his modernization efforts, but also on left-of-center antagonists of his aristocratic tendencies.[30]

In this context, women's rights provided a rare subject of agreement. The conference endorsed CSW recommendations to expand the UN's women's legal rights project and called for a unified effort across all agencies to advance women. Plans were outlined for greater investment in rural agriculture, where women's work remained informal, and for the development of the mechanism to support family planning that later became the UN Fund for Population Assistance (UNFPA). Countries were encouraged to set up national commissions on the status of women, and pledges were made to open more senior positions to women in the UN system, The General Assembly endorsed these objectives two years later. Subsequent provisions were also made for periodic, voluntary reporting on implementation of DEDAW by member states. Work on a proposed binding convention, however, languished, as Western Europeans and Americans came under the sway of conservative governments concerned about rising costs at the UN and averse to burgeoning human rights obligations.[31]

Back in Manila, Shahani became Assistant Secretary for the UN in the Philippine Department of Foreign Affairs and set up a national women's rights commission. She was also appointed to serve as a delegate to the CSW. With demonstrated facility in producing UN documents, she quickly became the group's choice to take over as rapporteur and within a few years to become chair.[32]

Born into an elite family in 1929, Shahani was the second of three children of Narcisco Ramos, a crusading lawyer and journalist, who became a diplomat in the early days of independence and ultimately the country's Secretary of Foreign Affairs. Her mother Angela Valdez-Ramos, a teacher and early advocate for women's suffrage, was aunt to President Ferdinand Marcos. Shahani's older brother, Fidel (Eddie) Ramos, to whom she was very close, was head of the country's constabulary police under Marcos, a position that put him in charge of arresting political dissidents when martial law was declared, a fact that did go unnoticed by skeptics of his sister's women's rights advocacy. He resigned in 1986, when he then led the popular movement to restore democracy under Corazon Aquino, before becoming president in his own right in 1992.[33]

Narcisco Ramos was a deputy in the Philippine embassy in Washington where his daughter attended her final years of high school and then went onto Wellesley. He then became ambassador to India, where, at age 22, she met and fell in love with Ranjee Shahani, a Karachi born intellectual, 25 years her senior, who had studied in France and lived for three decades in England. His many published works, ranging from a reflection on Shakespeare, to a popular portrait of Gandhi, to a volume on Indian sexual practices, earned him stature in elite British literary circles and appreciations from such prominent writers as H.G. Wells and Havelock Ellis.[34]

They married in 1962, following a decade-long courtship, once she had completed her doctorate, and he had divorced an estranged first wife. According to their daughter, Lila, the unconventional marriage was never fully accepted by her mother's family, which accounted for their decision to start a new life together in the United States, where they both initially found university teaching positions. He then died suddenly six years, and three children, later. Lila, the youngest, was still a toddler. Her mother never lacked for suitors thereafter, in Lila's memory, but buried her grief and her passions in her family and, perhaps, more completely in her work.[35]

In her first job at the UN, Shahani was fortunate to find a mentor in Julia Henderson, a former Wellesley professor of economics, who came to the institution in its early years and served as inaugural Director of the Bureau of Social Affairs. Shahani remembered Henderson as an eloquent advocate for "the social aspects of development and the need to look after the welfare of the human being and marginalized groups," and, in this regard, as an "intellectual" whose vision was not realized until the 1990s, when Cold War antagonisms diminished, and opportunities emerged to integrate social and economic concerns into a comprehensive human security framework.[36]

When Shahani transferred to the section of the Secretariat staffing the CSW in 1966, she gained a second valuable superior in Margaret Bruce, a British born veteran of the UN's early days, from whom she gained practical experience in how to prepare "thorough and precise" documents in clear language meant to inspire consensus. She credited this training for her later successes in drafting agreements, navigating the UN bureaucracy, and overcoming the resistance she encountered from the many men who still considered women's issues "a joke," as she put it.[37] Shahani may well have taken away a third lesson from her time at the UN—that she would be far more influential as a delegate in her own right than as a staffer. In 1966, she passed the Philippine foreign service exams that qualified her for the position she later assumed when she returned home.[38]

Unbowed by intellectual challenges or by strong political headwinds, Shahani first took it upon herself to prepare a working draft of a women's rights convention in 1972. She leaned on her own UN experience but also called on Minerva (Mina) Falcon, then a young lawyer on her staff in Manila, who would subsequently become a prominent ambassador in her own right, with postings in Turkey, Germany, Switzerland, and Canada. In a recent interview, Falcon observed that sheer will to advance her own career made up for a lack of formal training in human rights at the time.[39] With the benefit of youthful innocence and pluck, she simply assembled and referenced every relevant document she could find, a daunting research task in an era before the Internet, indeed, before computers.

Using DEDAW as a framework, she filled in essential details from printed material in Mrs. Shahani's possession and consulted other human rights instruments and national constitutions. She then produced a draft on a manual typewriter and made copies on carbon paper, in what she remembers as a tedious and cumbersome process. Especially important was the 1968 International Convention on the Elimination of Race Discrimination (ICERD), from which she derived an expansive definition of sex discrimination, like race, as a problem deeply embedded in cultural circumstances that formal changes in the law would not alone eliminate. This insight helped resolve the conundrum that had kept DEDAW's framers from clearly defining the term. Human rights scholars, Marsha Freeman and Christine Chinkin, observe the significance of CEDAW's distinction between formal equality in the law and substantive equality in everyday life, where male privilege has for so long been taken for granted, and women's inferiority assumed—a persistent pattern that public policies then often unconsciously replicate. The treaty extends state action to private behaviors in the community, business, and the family. Sex discrimination, distinct from race, is especially intractable in this respect because it occurs within families bonded by ties of genuine affection.[40]

Falcon also identified dimensions of her own upbringing that shaped her thinking. As was true in the circumstances that produced Annie Jiagge. Filipino women across class lines traditionally enjoyed influence within their families and communities and routinely balanced formal work and family obligations. Her own mother, like Shahani's, was a teacher. Universal English language education through the secondary level became available to boys and girls after the United States wrested the colony from Spain at the turn of the twentieth century. This produced a skilled female workforce and opened doors to university training and professional opportunities for women as well. Yet virtually no laws existed to address bias and secure women's rights, and a politically powerful Catholic Church, the legacy of Spanish rule, regulated family law, dictating the terms of marriage and divorce, and prohibiting birth control and abortion. Falcon deeply admired Shahani, whose family came from the country's Protestant minority, for her courage in taking on these challenges, and for her intellect, values, and diplomatic skill.[41]

As Shahani herself would tell the story on many occasions thereafter, she returned to New York, with a preliminary CEDAW draft in hand, having never mentioned the matter to her superiors. This was a serious breach of protocol. At CSW meetings that year, she found only one willing co-sponsor in Tatiana Nikolaeva, a respected senior member of the Russian Foreign Ministry, who was also willing to sign on without formal consultation and approval from her government. Consorting with Russians, however, constituted a second grave infraction for a U.S. aligned Filipino at the time.

The maneuvers resulted in what Shahani later characterized as a "kilometric" response from then Secretary of Foreign Affairs, Carlos P. Romulo, another veteran diplomat who had represented the Philippines at the UN's charter meetings and was a long-time colleague of her father. This personal relationship may explain why Romulo accepted her characterization of the document she had put together as an "unofficial working paper" and withdrew his objections. It may, however, also explain her subsequent posting in Bucharest in 1975, as her country's first ambassador to Soviet satellites, Romania, Hungary, and East Germany—a challenging job but hardly a plum assignment, in those dark and lean years under the dictatorship of Nicolae Ceausescu, with only one apparent advantage. It put her close to Vienna, where the UN Secretariat's Division on the Advancement of Women had relocated at the invitation of Austrian Secretary General Kurt Waldheim. In 1978, however, she became Ambassador to Australia, a happier place and an important Philippine trading partner that was also absorbing huge numbers of Filipino workers. But if was very far away from the UN.[42]

Meanwhile, the UN had designated 1975 as International Women's Year and organized a landmark conference in Mexico City that would begin to flesh out policy and programmatic agendas in the hope of realizing concrete gains for women—the first of four such gatherings that would culminate in Beijing 20 years later. For many years, the reputation of this event suffered from selective representations of what happened there. Journalists who covered the official sessions and the parallel civil society forum constructed a tumultuous narrative of conflict between first world feminists, whose concerns they treated contemptuously, and grassroots women from the developing world, whose victimization, however worthy of redress, they viewed as hopelessly intractable. A first generation of scholars then accepted these characterizations at face value.

A recent re-interpretation by the historian Jocelyn Olcott, however, takes a different view, emphasizing the ingenuity of the seasoned diplomats in charge of the conference, who were able to craft an agenda sensitive to the geographic, cultural, and class diversity of the assemblage.[43] Helvi Sipila of Finland, the first woman to be appointed as a UN Assistant Secretary General, served as presiding official at Mexico City, and Leticia Shahani worked closely with her as CSW chair. Ashraf Pahlavi provided critical funds for the event but kept a low profile.

As a Filipino, Shahani also belonged to the new and powerful alliance within the UN system—the Group of 77 non-aligned Nations (G77)—which had recently negotiated a document known as the New International Economic Order (NIEO) committing international institutions and donor countries to expand resources for development and secure conditions for human rights to flourish. The Mexico City conference incorporated these priorities in its outcome document and left institutional structures in place to help achieve them: INSTRAW, the UN training and research institute to advance women that has since provided valuable research and data to bolster advocacy; UNIFEM, a dedicated financing arm within the UN's development apparatus; and CEDAW, which the CSW was instructed to finalize.[44]

Working groups on CEDAW that included interested governments, specialized agencies, and NGOS, had been meeting since 1974. The negotiation process replicated procedures put in place years earlier in Tehran. Comments were accepted in writing and then consolidated into drafts displaying bracketed alternatives in language that was voted up or down. Sensitivities were high, and reservations extensive, give the ambitious reach of the document into matters governing family life, long controlled by religious or customary law.

The draft went from the CSW to the Economic and Social Council of the General Assembly, and then onto the main body itself in 1977, which circulated a largely favourable analysis signed by the Secretary General.[45] With many specific matters still unresolved, however, multiple subsequent meetings were necessary during the next two years to discuss and revise the substance and make final stylistic and technical changes before formal adoption by consensus in December of 1979, with only two countries at the time—Iraq and Morocco—expressing formal reservations. Plans were made for a signing ceremony at the second World Conference on Women scheduled for July of 1980 in Copenhagen.[46]

The treaty as adopted consists of a short preamble that largely follows the language of DEDAW in defining discrimination and in locating women's rights within larger aspirations for self-governance and for development inspired by the anti-colonial, independence movements of the day. The Philippine draft had not provided a preamble. A version first suggested by the Soviets was largely replaced after extensive negotiations, especially among Westerners who preferred Annie Jiagge's simpler, logical approach, and more elegant language.[47]

The substance that follows also tracks but expands considerably upon the declaration. Five articles seek to define discrimination and provide for concrete measures to address it through a positive, action-oriented government response— yet one with the flexibility to accommodate countries of vastly different economic and social circumstances. Much is made of the need for innovation beyond conventional legal remedies to confront the reality of attitudes and prejudices deeply embedded in families and cultures. Surviving from the Philippine draft, after extensive discussion and changes in wording, is the concept of granting temporary special privileges to women as amends for the past, which never made it into DEDAW. This includes an explanation of how to distinguish such interventions from permanent protective measures that segregate women and limit their opportunities.[48]

Ten more articles spell out "all forms of discrimination" in detail and catalogue necessary responses across sectors, including politics and civic life, education, employment, finance, agriculture, health care, sports, culture, the media, and criminal codes governing prostitution and sex trafficking. Article 11 on employment calls for legislation to guarantee equal pay and paid maternity leave. Article 12 obligates national governments to provide equal access to health care, including family planning, with the specification added by India that these programs include information and counselling, as well as technical services. These were ideas still far ahead of their time.

The most controversial section of the document, incorporated into Article 16, spells out the meaning of discrimination in marriage and family relations and calls for shared responsibility in decisions about age and consent in marriage and in the planning, spacing, rearing, and betrothal of children. Special emphasis is given to the "paramount" interests of children and extends protections to those born in and out of wedlock. Originating in the joint Philippine/USSR draft, these concerns are joined together with formal legal provisions for guardianship, for ownership and distribution of property, and for other aspects of personal legal capacity long denied women, such as choice of family name and of profession or occupation. Reservations on this article during the treaty's ratification would be even more extensive than during the negotiation, especially from Muslim majority countries with objections all around, but most emphatically to the protection of single mothers.[49]

Article 17 sets the terms for ratification of the treaty and addresses its implementation, matters the Philippine draft had left unattended. It calls for the election of a geographically balanced committee of 23 experts "of high moral standing and competence in the field," who would serve four-year terms and hold annual meetings to review enforcement by state parties on a revolving schedule. These procedures followed those established for ICERD and largely reflected the concerns of European, American, and Iranian delegates, who while cool to the idea of a treaty at the start, then fought to insure its rigorous execution. The change reflected the new emphasis on human rights and global development in Jimmy Carter's foreign policy. The Carter administration had established a women's initiative at the U.S. Agency for International Development run by Arvonne Fraser, then a prominent Democratic party activist and wife of a Minnesota congressman. She, in turn, recommended Koryne Horbal, who negotiated CEDAW as U.S. representative to the CSW.[50]

CEDAW has since won considerable praise as a tool of innovative feminist jurisprudence. The American legal scholar, Kathleen Sullivan, gives it credit for an expansive vision that sharply contrasts with the minimalist approach of traditional efforts to constitutionalize women's equality. "American constitutional law operates under strong conventions of constraint to general norms of formal equality, symmetrically interpreted, against state rather than private action, to promote negative not positive rights, that are capable of judicial enforcement," Sullivan writes.[51] CEDAW, adopts an explicitly female perspective and defines inequality on women's terms, without a male default. It acknowledges genuine biological difference but also prohibits socially constructed gender stereotypes; it permits consideration of matters like maternity, childrearing, and other family obligations, but dismisses cultural tropes of physical and intellectual inferiority that have long enforced male privilege and constrained women's opportunities, such as denying women physically demanding jobs or keeping them out of the military. In this respect, she notes, as have others, that CEDAW resolves historic conflicts in how best to adjudicate between sexual difference and equality and elaborates conditions to create an equal playing field for women. Sullivan concludes admiringly that CEDAW is "asymmetric, extended to private action and positive rights, and culturally aspirational."[52]

CEDAW is also celebrated for its contribution to global development theory and practice. The feminist economist, Devaki Jain, gives the women's movement credit for undertaking the critical research and making the necessary arguments to demonstrate that multiple constraints of sex, race, and class constrain economic growth, that progress does not just "trickle down." In doing so women reframed global understanding of social and economic inequalities as essential issues of human rights, or as she puts it, they "inscribed development into rights."[53]

In 1980, Kurt Waldheim rewarded Leticia Shahani for her intellectual contributions to CEDAW, and her instrumental role in its negotiation, by appointing her as the UN's second female Assistant Secretary General for Social Development and Humanitarian Affairs, filling the vacancy left by Helvi Sipila's retirement. Five years later Shahani would oversee the Third World Conference on Women in Nairobi, Kenya, ending the so-called UN Decade on Women and earning plaudits for producing an outcome document that continued to refine policy objectives and adopt "forward looking" strategies to shape programs on the ground. She also elided vocal tensions between the G77 alliance and the US government under Ronald Reagan, when the agreement nearly foundered over characterizations of "Zionism as racism," [*sic*] until Shahani managed to sit down with warring parties and negotiate less incendiary language to express concerns about the rights of Palestinians.[54]

Intending to spend a quiet Christmas holiday with her ailing father, Shahani instead returned home that year and made national headlines when she confided to a reporter that change was necessary and she would vote in the coming election for the Marcos challenger, Corazon Aquino. Marcos subsequently claimed victory despite allegations of largescale voter fraud, which led to the defections of Eddie Ramos and other senior military officials and forced him into exile.

Shahani left the UN and joined the Aquino administration as an undersecretary in the Department of Foreign Affairs, where she drafted a development plan that introduced gender analysis and programming across government agencies. She then held two, six-year terms in the Philippine Senate, passed legislation providing protection against sex discrimination and unfair workplace practices, built a vocational training and life skills program for women, and helped her brother improve family planning services in the country when he became president. In retirement, she returned to her family's home province of Pangasinan and organized a cooperative to train farmers, many of them women, in sustainable agriculture. "I'm in the grassroots now," she told an interviewer. She died in March of 2017.[55]

Conclusion

This history reminds us, if we need reminding, that the common characterization of women's rights as a western invention, imposed on innocents elsewhere in the world, is not only wrong but also insulting. It ignores years of commitment by the two distinctly talented individuals profiled in this chapter and by thousands of others from across the world who have assumed positions of leadership in global forums over the past half century.

They shaped laws and policies rooted in and relevant to their own experiences. They uncovered the common disadvantages women face across geographic and ideological divides—no matter what their circumstances. They framed the issue of women's rights as a moral imperative but also as a necessary condition for success in advancing prosperity and securing peace—along the way convincing a wary male establishment to take these arguments seriously. Too often, however, they became scapegoats for modernization's false promises and its discontents— condemned as disloyal to local cultures, as in Iran—their bodies made battlegrounds, as in Ghana.

Understanding that sex discrimination is deeply embedded in families and cultures, they insisted that measures be taken to abolish bias not just in the law, but also in customs and practices assuming women's inferiority that had long been taken for granted. They helped establish standards for legal scrutiny and protection of women's rights but also took on the challenge of changing attitudes and behaviors through education, media, and culture. Recognizing that rights cannot be realized in the absence of resources, they demanded social and economic investments to secure political freedoms and civil liberties, and they advanced the principle of indivisibility among rights categories.

Jiagge and Shahani may rightly be identified as cosmopolitan elites—well-bred and well-schooled—fluent in several languages and comfortable in often daunting situations—all necessary attributes for success as diplomats. But they also helped launch and left in place vast networks of grassroots activists, who in turn seeded local social justice work on the ground. They persisted as political and economic turmoil enveloped their home countries, confident that rights and opportunities for women are a necessary foundation for stable societies.

"What we have put in place is a revolution from which there is no turning back," Annie Jiagge proclaimed at Mexico City in 1975. "If we succeed, all humanity has a chance."[56]

Notes

1 Deborah Atobrah and Albert K. Awedoba, "A Trail-Blazer, An Outstanding International Jurist, A Humanitarian, An Ecumenical Christian and More: The Life of Justice Annie Jiagge (Nee Baeta)" in ed. Mercy Akrofie Ansah and Esi Sutherland-Addy, *Building the New Nation: Seven Notable Ghanaians* Accra: Institute of African Studies, University of Ghana, 2018, 3. Also see, "Jiagge, Annie (1918–1996) in *Encyclopedia.com* http://www.encyclopedia.com/women/ecncyclopedias-almanacs-transcr Also see Josephine Dawuni. "Jiagge, Annie Ruth(1918–1996) in *The Dictionary of African Biography*, accessed from the Oxford African American Studies Center Https://oxfordaasc.com/view/10.1093/acref/9780195390130173l.001.0001/

2 United Nations, *The United Nations and the Advancement of Women, 1945–1996*, United Nations Blue Book Series, Volume VI, UN Sales Publication, E.96.I.9, New York, 1996, 175.

3 UN and the Advancement of Women, 175.

4 Ramos-Shahani, Leticia V., interview by Richard Jolly, United Nations Intellectual History Project, New York, Columbia Center for Oral History Columbia University Rare Book Library, November 27 & December 11, 1999, 12.

5 See, for example: Marsha A. Freeman, Christine Chinkin, and Beate Rudolf, eds., *The UN Convention on the Elimination of All Forms of Discrimination Against Women: A Commentary*, Oxford, UK, Oxford University Press, 2012, and Schöpp-Schilling, Hanna Beate, ed., *The Circle of Empowerment: Twenty-Five Years of the UN Committee on the Elimination of Discrimination Against Women*, New York, The Feminist Press, 2007.

6 Weiss, Thomas G., Tatiana Carayannis, Louis Emmerij, and Richard Jolly, *UN Voices: The Struggle for Development and Social Justice*, Bloomington and Indianapolis: Indiana University Press, 2005, 162. Lars Adam Rehof, *Guide to The Travaux Preparatoires of The United Nations Convention on the Elimination of All Forms of Discrimination Against Women*, Dordrecht/Boston/London, Martius Nijohoff Publishers, 1993, references the loss of documents in his introduction.

7 Arvonne S. Fraser, "The Convention to Eliminate All Forms of Discrimination Against Women (The Women's Convention"), in ed. Anne Winslow, *Women, Politics and the United Nations,* Westport, Connecticut, Greenwood Press, 1995, 77–94.

8 Lars Adam Rehof, *Guide to The Travaux Preparatoires,* 3. The guide contains the original Philippine draft, the joint Philippine/USSR draft and as much documentation as exists in Geneva on the debate over specific articles.

9 UN and the Advancement of Women, 29,173.

10 Fraser, ""The Convention to Eliminate All Forms of Discrimination Against Women (The Women's Convention"), 80–81. Others among those present in Tehran were Helvi Sipila of Finland, Aziza Hussein of Egypt, Jeanne Chaton of France, Helena Benitez of the Philippines, Zofia Dembinska of Poland, Hannah Bokor of Hungary, Rachel Nason of the U.S., and Ashraf Pahlavi, along with representatives of UN technical agencies and from 22 NGOs. For background on Iran, also see a timeline prepared by the Foundation for Iranian Studies, https://fis-Iran.org/en/women/milestones/pre-revolution. Pahlavi pops up occasionally in UN archives. See for example, a cable dated October 25, 1971 with birthday wishes from Secretary General, U Thant in UN Archives in New York.

11 Fraser, "The Convention to Eliminate.", 80–81. For Articles 3 of the ICCPR and ICESR, see UN and the Advancement of Women, 174.

12 Arvonne Fraser, "The Convention to Eliminate," 82–83. Fraser's notes are sparse but reference UN, ECOSOC, 39th Session, Official Records, Supplement 7; CSW, Report on the 18th Session (1–10-March 1965, 23 and UN ECOSOC, and a CSW report on the 18th session (March 1–10, 1965) for her account.

13 UN and the Advancement of Women, 30, 175–176.

14 Biographical detail on Jiagge is from Atobrah and. Awedoba, Life of Justice Annie Jiagge, 8–15. Also see Abe and Edith Halperin, "It's Wonderful to Be a Woman: An Interview with Annie Jiagge," *The Rotarian,*" February, 1968, 36–38, and Seth Bokpe, https://www.theghanareport.com/she-called-the-bluff-of-chauvinists-to-become-ghanas-first-female-lawyer-judge/ Kate Skinner, "Women's rights as international human rights: Justice Annie Jiagge of Ghana," Birmingham Blogs, https://blog.gham.ac.uk/archiveofactivism/2019/07/23/womens-rights-as-international-hum-aights-justice-annie-jiagge-of-ghana/. Fred Jiagge had also been a teacher but then went to work for the Tema Development Corporation, an urban real estate development firm originally chartered in 1952 before independence. Atobrah and. Awedoba, Life of Justice Annie Jiagge, 15.

15 Adwoa Kwakyewaa Opong, "Rewriting Women into Ghanaian History, 1950–63" (Master's Thesis: University of Ghana, 2012), 30–53. Ms. Opong went on to pursue her Ph.D. at Washington University in St. Louis. Also see, Dennis Austin, *Politics in Ghana, 1948–1960* (New York: Oxford University Press, 1965). Also see, Naaborko Sackeyfio-Lenoch, "Women's International Alliances in an Emergent Ghana,"*Journal of West African History* 4, no 1 (Spring, 2018).

16 Opong, 67–68.

17 Opong, 72.

18 Opong, 72–74, with the quote on p. 75.

19 Opong, 72–74, with the quote on p 75. Opong found the remarks in private archives of Dr. Evelyn Amarteifio of the the Ghanaian Organization of Women, held at the Department of History, University of Ghana, Legon. Jiagge's quoteon "civic death" is from Annie R. Jiagge, "Exploitation of Women in Third World Perspective," *The Ecumenical Review,* Fall, 1976, 42.

20 Opong, 75. The most contentious debate of the gathering, however erupted over race, not gender, when a delegate proposed a resolution condemning both the United States and South Africa for their oppression of people of color. Murray and others beat back the measure by distinguishing America's constitutional system from apartheid on the grounds that the U.S. government had intervened in the federal courts to overturn state sanctioned segregation policies. See Rosalind Rosenberg, *Jane Crow: The Life of Pauli Murray* (New York: Oxford University Press), 2017, 227–228.

21 Rosenberg, 229-239.

22 Rosenberg, 244–252, 287–289308–309, 385–388. In an email exchange with the author, Rosenberg said she was able to find only one piece of correspondence about the conference in Murray's papers which reflects her concern about the anti-Americanism expressed there and says nothing about women's rights.

23 Annie R. Jiagge, "Exploitation of Women in Third World Perspective," *The Ecumenical Review,* Fall, 1976, 42.

24 Annie R. Jiagge, "Exploitation of Women in Third World Perspective," *The Ecumenical Review,* Fall, 1976, 42–48.

25 Atobrah and. Awedoba, Life of Justice Annie Jiagge, 28–30.

26 Atobrah and. Awedoba, Life of Justice Annie Jiagge, 16, 35. For more on Women's World Banking and Jiagge, see Margaret Snyder and Mary Tadesse, *African Women and Development,* Zed Books, London, 1995, and Michaela Walsh, *Founding A Movement, Women's World Banking, 1975–1990,* (New York: Cosimo Books, 2012), 11, 94–96. Also see Annie Jiagge, "Letter to Mildred Persinger, December 13, 1977," Mildred E. Persinger papers, 106, Hollins University, https://digitalcomons.hollins. edu/persinger-papers/106.

27 Atobrah and. Awedoba, Life of Justice Annie Jiagge, 26–28, 30. On the 1992 constitution, https://dailyguidenetwork.com/work-committee-experts-1992-constitution/

28 "Tribute by the United Nations Secretary-General, Dr Boutros Boutros-Ghali, memorial for Mrs. Justice Annie Ruth Jiagge, 3 August 1996, http://www.un.org/ women'swatch/daw/news/jiagge.htm

29 Leticia Shahani, "The UN, Women, and Development: The World Conferences on Women", in *Developing Power: How Women Transformed International Development,* (New York: The Feminist Press, 2004) 29. Shahani, Oral History, 12-14. When asked to identify outstanding women from this period, Shahani named Annie Jiagge among others, noting that the Soviet women were also exceptional but that their governments never stood behind them—their legal rights were never realized, nor would the USSR ever spend money to support the women's agenda at the UN.

30 Roland Burke, "Confronting 'Indivisibility' in the History of Economic and Social Rights: From Parity to Priority and Back Again," review of *Indivisible Human Rights* by Daniel Whelan, *Human Rights & Human Welfare,* 12, 2012, 61.

31 UN and the Advancement of Women, "Resolution IX adopted by the International Conference on the Human Rights in Tehran on measures to promote women's rights in the world and endorsing the Secretary-General's proposal for a unified long-term United Nations programme for the advancement of women," May 12, 1968, 117, and "General Assembly resolution outlining a programme of concerted international action for the advancement of women", December 15, 1970, 179.

32 A formal letter dated January 27, 1969 from Philippine Ambassador Privado Jimenez announcing Shahani's appointment is one of the few references I was able to find to her in the UN CSW archives in New York.

33 Biographical details are from Shahani, Oral History, 1–2; Elena Masilungan, "Leticia Ramos-Shahani, Diplomacy and initiative in and of the UN," *Shaping the Women's Global Agenda: Filipino Women in the United Nations,* ed. Olivia H. Tripon (Manila: National Commission on the Role of Filipino Women, 2007), 17–35; "Leticia Ramos-Shahani, "Be Strong Because You Are A Woman!" interview by Melvin C, Almonguera, in *Frontlines of Diplomacy: Conversations with Phillipine Ambassadors,* ed. J. Eduardo Malaya, (Manila, Anvil Publishing, 2011),197–199. My thanks to Patricia Licuanan, Filipino representative to the CSW and its chair during the 1995 World Conference on Women in Beijing, for copies of these publications. Also see Michael Bueza, "Leticia Ramos Shahani, 1929–2017, The woman who competed with the best," https://www.rappler.com/nation/164671-letitia-ramos-shahani-obituary. A short biography of Fidel (Eddie) Ramos is at www.Britannica.com/print/article/490745.

34 A bibliography and some biographical detail for Ranjee Gurdassing Shahani is at www.open.ac.uk/researchprojects/makingbritain/content/ranjee/g/shahani.

35 Author's interview with Lila Shahani in New York City, February 16, 2020. Also see Lila's eulogy of her mother at https://www.rappler.com/thought-leaders/165203-life-shahani-eulogy-leticia-ramos-shahani.

36 Author's interview with Lila Shahani in New York City, February 16, 2020.

37 Shahani Oral History, 12.

38 Shahani Oral History, 5–7.

39 Author's interview by phone with Mina Falcon in Calgary, Canada, October 12, 2020. Also see Minerva Jean Abuyuan Falcon, interview with Nomer Blevins, in *Frontlines of Diplomacy*. Freeman and Chinken, "Introduction," in *The UN Convention on the Elimination of All Forms of Discrimination Against Women: A Commentary*, 2–3, 8–9.

40 Author's interview by phone with Mina Falcon in Calgary, Canada, October 12, 2020. Also see Minerva Jean Abuyuan Falcon, interview with Nomer Blevins, in *Frontlines of Diplomacy*. Freeman and Chinken, "Introduction," in *The UN Convention on the Elimination of All Forms of Discrimination Against Women: A Commentary*, 2–3, 8–9.

41 Author's interview with Falcon.

42 Shahani in *Shaping the Global Women's Agenda,* 25–26; Shahani in *Developing Power*, 31–32.

43 Jocelyn Olcott, *International Women's Year: The Greatest Consciousness-Raising Event in History*, (2017), New York: Oxford University Press.

44 Jocelyn Olcott, *International Women's Year: The Greatest Consciousness-Raising Event in History,* (New York: Oxford University Press, 2017). Also see Ellen Chesler, "The Year of the Woman Again," review of Olcott, *The Women's Review of Books* 35, no 5, September-October, 2018. And for a competing view, see Roland Burke, "Competing for the Last Utopia? The NIEO, Human Rights, and the World Conference for the International Women's Year, Mexico City, June 1975", *Humanity,* 26, Spring, 2015, 47–61. INSTRAW got underway with a grant from Iran and was meant to be housed in Tehran, but was relocated to the Caribbean.

45 UN and the Advancement of Women, "General Assembly resolution calling on State Parties to ratify international conventions and other instruments concerning the protection of women's rights…and requesting the CSW to complete the draft convention on the elimination of discrimination against women." 217.

46 Rehof, 'Introduction to the Genesis of the Convention," *Guide to The Travaux Preparatoires,* 6–12.

47 Rehof, *Guide to The Travaux Preparatoires,* 15.

48 The UN and the Advancement of Women, "Convention on the Elimination of all Forms of Discriminatiion against Women, adopted by the General Assembly on 18 December 1979", 244. Rehof, *Guide to The Travaux Preparatoires,* 66–69. Freeman and Chinken, "Introduction," in *The UN Convention on the Elimination of All Forms of Discrimination Against Women: A Commentary*, 8–9.

49 Rehof, *Guide to The Travaux Preparatoires*, found the most records and provides its most extensive documentation of treaty deliberations on Article 16, owing no doubt to it's the controversial ground it covers, 168–186. Freeman and Chinken, "Introduction," in *The UN Convention on the Elimination of All Forms of Discrimination Against Women: A Commentary*, 10–11.

50 Rehof, *Guide to The Travaux Preparatoires*, as throughout, only identifies comments by country, not by individual. His discussion of Articles 17–21 on implementation is extensive, 187–223. Perhaps not surprisingly, USSR delegates wanted no committee. Also see, Arvonne S. Fraser, "Making History Word for Word," *Journal of Women's History,* 24, no 4, 193–200. Koryn Horbel's interest in strong monitoring was first expressed in a statement she made on April 2, 1978 published by the U.S. Mission to the UN, a copy of which was given to the author. Horbel's papers are collected at the Minnesota Historical Society in Minneapolis but not available online. Iran's concerns are notable, as this was, of course, a final intervention for representatives of the Pahlavis.

51 Kathleen M, Sullivan, "Constitutionalizing Women's Equality" *California Law Review*, 90 (3), 762.
52 Kathleen M. Sullivan, "Constitutionalizing Women's Equality," *California Law Review*, 90, no. 3, May, 2002, 735–764, with the quote on 762. At: http://www.jstor.org/stable/3481236.
53 Devaki Jain, *Women, Development, and the UN: A Sixty-Year Quest for Equality and Justice*, Indiana University Press, Bloomington and Indianapolis, 2005, 33.
54 Shahani in *Shaping the Global Women's Agenda*, 27–29. Shahani's appointment was treated as a big deal at the UN. See "LETICIA R. SHAHANI APPOINTED ASSISTANT SECRETARY GENERAL FOR SOCIAL DEVELOPMENT AND HUMANITARIAN AFFAIRS," UN Press Release, Department of Public Information, UN, New York; Kurt Waldheim to Shahani, January 16, 1981; Ambassador Alejandro D. Yango to Kurt Waldheim, transmitting the appreciation of Carlos P. Romulo, then Philippine Minister for Foreign Affairs, September 10, 1980, all in the Waldheim papers, UN Archives, New York.
55 Shahani in *Shaping the Global Women's Agenda*, 2–34. Shahani's name was raised as a qualified woman to become Secretary General when Kofi Annan got the job in 1996. See Roberto Ordonez, "Etcetera, Etcetera: 'Miss UN' Shahani a good bet for Sec-Gen at https: //search-proquest-com/docview/367855301? Also see Steven Erlanger, "Manila Journal: From a Life of Privilege, a Woman of Substance," *The New York Times,* November 9, 1989. Jennifer Jett, "Overlooked No More: Leticia Ramos Shahani: a Philippine Women's Rights Pioneer, *The New York Times,* June 4, 2018.
56 Annie Jiagge quoted in Jain, *Women, Development, and the UN,* 68.

Bibliography

Almonguera, Melvin. "Be Strong Because You are a Woman." In *Frontlines of Diplomacy: Conversations with Philipine Ambassadors*, edited by J. Eduardo Malaya. Manila: Anvil Publishing, 2011.
Atobrah, Deborah, and Albert K. Awedoba. "A Trail-Blazer, An Outstanding International Jurist, A Humanitarian, An Ecumenical Christain and More: The Life of Justice Annie Jiagge (Nee Baeta)." In *Building the New Nation: Seven Notable Ghanians*, edited by Mercy Akrofie Ansah and Esi Sutherland-Addy. Accra: Institute of African Studies: University of Ghana, 2018.
Austin, Dennis. *Politics in Ghana, 1948–1960.* New York: Oxford University Press, 1965.
Burke, Roland. "Competing for the Last Utopia? The NIEO, Human Rights, and the World Conference for the International Women's Year, Mexico City, June 1975." *Humanity* 26 (2015): 47–61.
Burke, Roland. "'Confronting "Indivisibility" in the History of Economic and Social Rights: From Parity to Priority and Back Again', Review of Indivisible Human Rights by Daniel Whelan." *Human Rights & Human Welfare* 12 (2012).
Chesler, Ellen. "'The Year of the Woman Again', Review of Olcott." *The Women's Review of Books* 35, no. 5 (2018): 25–27.
Fraser, Arvonne S. "Making History Word for Word." *Journal of Women's History* 24, no. 4 (2012): 193–200.
Fraser, Arvonne S. "The Convention to Eliminate All Forms of Discrimination Against Women (The Women's Convention)." In *Women, Politics and the United Nations*, edited by Anne Winslow. Westport; Conneticut: Greenwood Press, 1995.
Freeman, Marsha A., Christine Chinkin, and Beate Rudolf, eds. *The UN Convention on the Elimination of All Forms of Discrimination Against Women: A Commentary*. Oxford, UK: Oxford University Press, 2012.

Halperin, Edith, and Abe Halperin. "It's Wonderful to Be a Woman: An Interview with Annie Jiagge." *The Rotarian* February (1968).

Jain, Devaki. *Women, Development, and the UN: A Sixty-Year Quest for Equality and Justice*. Bloomington: Indiana University Press, 2005.

Jiagge, Annie R. "Exploitation of Women in Third World Perspective." *The Ecumenical Review Fall* (1976).

Kwakyewaa Opong, Adwoa. "Rewriting Women into Ghanaian History, 1950-63." Master's Thesis, University of Ghana, 2012.

Masilungan, Elena. "Leticia Ramos-Shahani, Diplomacy and Initiative in and of the UN." In *Shaping the Women's Global Agenda: Filipino Women in the United Nations*, edited by Olivia H. Tripon. Manila: Anvil Publishing, 2007.

Olcott, Jocelyn. *International Women's Year: The Greatest Consciousness-Raising Event in History*. New York: Oxford University Press, 2017.

Rehof, Lars Adam. *Guide to The Travaux Preparatoires of The United Nations Convention on the Elimination of All Forms of Discrimination Against Women*. Dordrecht; Boston; London: Martinus Nijhoff Publishers, 1993.

Rosenberg, Rosalind. *Jane Crow: The Life of Pauli Murray*. New York: Oxford University Press, 2017.

Sackeyfio-Lenoch, Naaborko. "Women's International Alliances in an Emergent Ghana." *Journal of West African History* 4, no. 1 (2018): 27–56.

Schöpp-Schilling, Hanna Beate, ed. *The Circle of Empowerment: Twenty-Five Years of the UN Committee on the Elimination of Discrimination Against Women*. New York: The Feminist Press, 2007.

Shahani, Leticia. "The UN, Women, and Development: The World Conferences on Women." In *Developing Power: How Women Transformed International Development*. New York: The Feminist Press, 2004.

Snyder, Margaret, and Mary Tadesse. *African Women and Development*. London: Zed Books, 1995.

Sullivan, Kathleen M. "Constitutuonalizing Women's Equality." *California Law Review* 90, no. 3 (2002): 735–764.

United Nations. "*The United Nations and the Advancement of Women, 1945–1996*." United Nations Blue Book Series. New York: UN Sales Publication, 1996.

Walsh, Michaela. *Founding A Movement, Women's World Banking, 1975–1990*. New York: Cosimo Books, 2012.

Weiss, Tom, and Pallavi, Roy. "The UN and the Global South, 1945 and 2015: Past as Prelude?" *Third World Quarterly* 37, no. 7 (2016): 1147–1155.

Weiss, Thomas G., Tatiana Carayannis, Louis Emmerji, and Richard Jolly, UN Voices: The Struggle for Development and Social Justice, Bloomington and Indianapolis: Indiana University Press, 2005.

8　Were children's rights ever a feminist project?

Linde Lindkvist

Introduction

International norm-making on women's rights and children's rights is often historicized as parts of a broader process of challenging the abstract vision of humanity that undergirds mainstream human rights discourse after the Universal Declaration of Human Rights. But women's rights and children's rights have distinct historical trajectories in international human rights politics, and their relationship has not always been free of friction. In 1992, the feminist legal scholar Frances Olsen attempted to make sense of this relationship in commentary on what was then the recently adopted United Nations Convention on the Rights of the Child (1989). Olsen noted how children's rights and women's rights were frequently discussed together in international human rights settings. More specifically, she addressed how women and children often appeared on the same lists of particularly vulnerable groups, and how they were frequently pulled together in provisions on the rights of maternity leave and maternity protection.[1] Olsen further argued that women's and children's rights are often mutually reinforcing in practice. In other words, where children's rights enjoy a high degree of protection, women tend to fare better too. At the same time, she suggested that international norms on children's rights often perpetuate age-old notions and stereotypes of motherhood, and how the abstract category of "the child" obscures the ways in which the structures of gender work unequally on boys and girls.[2] Children's rights thus seemed to reinforce the very same essentialist and conservative tendencies in human rights discourse that women's rights activists were trying to counteract.

Considering Olsen's work today raises the difficult question of how the history of children's rights relates to the history of women's rights for the UN. If these concepts are so closely intertwined but at the same time in a state of friction, then how are we to understand their historical relationship? This chapter approaches this question from within the UN's history of children's rights. In examining how children's rights evolved as a subfield of international human rights law and politics, it seeks to capture the contours of this history with an eye on the concept's relation to the ideas of women's rights and gender equality.[3]

Most international histories of children's rights have been set in the aftermath of World War I and have centered on the contributions of humanitarian entrepreneurs like Eglantyne Jebb of the Save the Children Fund. Their charity-based activism was sometimes mocked by radicals who claimed that it "reinforced the

DOI: 10.4324/9781003036708-8

age-old notion that women had no concern in public life except to wipe up the mess made by men."[4] However, it is now evident that interwar humanitarianism also functioned as a forcefield in which women could advance bold ideas for the enhancement of peace, justice, and civilization. Such ideas frequently revolved around the concept of childhood and, more specifically, the conviction that improved child protection in the present would help to bring about better versions of humankind in generations to come. This line of thought influenced the Geneva Declaration of the Rights of the Child, which originated in the Save the Children Fund and the International Women's Council in the early 1920s and was endorsed by the League of Nations Council in the fall of 1924. This short, five-paragraph manifesto on the essential goods that humankind owes to all children, regardless of race or national boundaries, received widespread circulation in its time and still serves as a source of inspiration for child rights activists.[5]

In 1959, the United Nations adopted its own updated version of the Declaration of the Rights of the Child. Three decades later, this was followed by the UN Convention on the Rights of the Child, which has since become the most ratified international treaty on human rights. The few histories charting the emergence of these later documents have so far paid little attention to the connection between children's rights and women's rights that is so prominent in the historiography of the 1920s.[6] This may partly reflect how the later UN processes were controlled mainly by states, allowing limited space for individual agency. There is, in short, no heroine to which the Convention can be accredited. Still, it is puzzling why the literature on international children's rights has thus far shown little concern for the contributions of women diplomats and activists and has offered almost no analysis of the relationship between children's rights and women's rights. This is all the more surprising given that the talks on the UN Convention on the Rights of the Child coincided with the UN Decade for Women (1975–1985) and the finalization of the Convention on the Elimination of All Forms of Discrimination against Women (1979). Is this just another instance of wiping out the traces of women and non-Western agency in UN treaty-making processes? Or is it indicative of a deeper skepticism among feminists towards the very concept of children's rights?

This chapter offers some observations on how and to what extent women diplomats and activists, and, more broadly, ideas of gender equality, helped to shape the norms on children's rights advanced by the UN between 1945 and the mid-1990s. More broadly, it seeks to determine whether it is justifiable to speak of international children's rights as a feminist project, or whether it is more accurate to see children's rights as clashing with projects of gender equality and women's liberation. The conclusion suggests that both of these assessments are true. On the one hand, women representatives repeatedly found ways to use the frameworks on children's rights to advance gender-sensitive conceptions of human rights and to challenge the private-public distinction in international human rights law. At the same time, the main UN instruments on children's rights upheld traditional understandings of the nuclear family as the fundamental social unit and the most conducive realm for promoting children's physical and mental development.

In doing so, the ways in which gender inequalities play into the lives of young human beings were disregarded. When approaching a document like the UN Convention on the Rights of the Child, we have to bear in mind that it did not resolve such tensions. Rather, the treaty itself contained fundamentally different views on the content and function of children's human rights, lending itself to multiple social and political uses.

From human rights to children's rights

If historians generally look to the late 1940s as a founding moment of the discourse on universal human rights, child rights scholars view it as an opportunity lost. In 1950, after much lobbying by the Save the Children movement, the UN's Social Commission issued resolution endorsing the fundamental principles of Geneva Declaration, while at the same time suggesting that if there ever would be a UN version of the declaration, it would first have to go through a state-led process of redrafting.[7] Nevertheless, in spite of some initial discussion, this process soon sputtered to a halt.

One reason for the lack of interest in a child rights instrument was the discourse of human rights. The decision of the newly established UN Commission of Human Rights to devote its energy to the creation of an international bill on the rights of individuals meant that the rights of particular groups—whether distinguished by age, race, gender, or nationality—acquired only limited attention. Still, the text of the Universal Declaration of Human Rights (UDHR) contained some clauses of direct relevance to children, including the right to education and an adequate standard of living. More directly, Article 25(2) announced that "motherhood and childhood are entitled to special care and assistance," further stating that "all children, whether born in or out of wedlock, shall enjoy the same social protection."[8]

Like all the individual passages that comprise the UDHR, Article 25(2) was the product of intense negotiation. The Danish delegate Bodil Begtrup insisted that the term "motherhood" was preferable to a previous proposal that spoke of the rights of "mothers," arguing that this would cover the rights of women both during and after pregnancy.[9] The word "childhood" was principally chosen for linguistic consistency, even though the Soviet delegate Alexei Pavlov grumbled that motherhood and childhood were, strictly speaking, "abstract ideas" rather than "legal entities" capable of holding rights.[10] The second part of Article 25(2) betrayed a more substantial disagreement on the status of children born out of wedlock. During the meetings of the General Assembly in the fall of 1948, Ratko Pleic of Yugoslavia—supported by, among others, Minerva Bernardino of the Dominican Republic—insisted that addressing discrimination on the basis of illegitimacy was paramount in an instrument that purported to advance universal rights.[11] The proposal was attacked by other delegates, such as Marga Klompé of the Netherlands, who feared that it might undermine "the importance of the marriage bond and (...) the principle that the family was the fundamental group unit of society."[12] The reference to the equal rights of social security that ended up in the final version of Article 25(2) was a compromise, acknowledging that "illegitimate children" were entitled to social welfare while stopping short of recognizing them as subjects of civil rights, most notably that of inheritance.[13]

The most striking feature of this part of the Universal Declaration, however, is the way it constituted children and women (in the capacity of mothers) as similarly vulnerable objects of benevolence and protection, but at the same time as ideas rather than persons.[14] As Jessica Whyte has recently shown, the UDHR's language on social and economic rights restated a Fordist idea of the family wage, i.e., the idea that the male head of household should be able to earn enough to provide for the needs of other members of his family. From this perspective, the language on motherhood and childhood mainly functioned as a stop-gap clause in covering the purportedly exceptional situation where a man is either absent or otherwise unable to fulfil his responsibilities.[15]

In spite of the Universal Declaration's limited social vision, the women delegates and activists of the Commission on the Status of Women (CSW) found ways of employing it as a "major tool to combat laws that discriminated against women."[16] At the same time as the UN Commission on Human Rights struggled to make headway on the general human rights treaty that was meant to follow the non-binding human rights declaration, the CSW used the 1950s to successfully push for new international standards on women's human rights. The most prominent example of such efforts was arguably the 1952 Convention on the Political Rights of Women. However, as Rebecca Adami and Roland Burke show in their contributions to this volume, this work also involved projects that were of direct relevance to children and adolescents. For instance, in 1954, the General Assembly adopted a declaration denouncing traditional customs and practices, including bride price and child marriage, which later influenced the 1962 Convention on Consent to Marriage, Minimum Age for Marriage and Registration of Marriages.[17] In the same period, the CSW took on questions of gender equality in access to education and joined forces with the International Labour Organization and the World Health Organization to advance social and economic rights for working mothers, such as access to daycare and child care after school hours.[18]

What often united these efforts was a strong sense of pragmatism. Focusing more on mitigating existing inequalities than on securing equal treatment, the delegates of the CSW were drawn to working within a conventional view of women as mothers.[19] This approach came into sharp focus in the revised version of the UN Declaration of the Rights of the Child, which after nearly a decade of shelf-life made its way through the UN Commission on Human Rights to the UN General Assembly in the fall of 1959. One feature that distinguished this document from the 1924 Geneva Declaration was the several references to parents and especially mothers. The child, the declaration stated, "shall, wherever possible, grow up in the care and under the responsibility of his parents, and, in any case, in an atmosphere of affection and of moral and material security; a child of tender years shall not, save in exceptional circumstances, be separated from his mother."[20] The declaration further announced that the child (consistently referred to as a "he"), "shall be entitled to grow and develop in health; to this end, special care and protection shall be provided both to him and to his mother, including adequate pre-natal and post-natal care."[21] Thus, in keeping with the precedent set by the UDHR, the child rights declaration did not separate the rights of children from the rights and duties of motherhood.

There is limited research on the making of the 1959 child rights declaration and what prompted the rise of interest in children's rights during this period. One important reason why the needs of children came to the fore in this period was clearly the lack of progress in other areas of human rights. Since the early 1950s, the drafting of the main covenants on human rights had been stalled because of deepening Cold War tensions. Children's rights and women's rights were among the few areas where states nonetheless managed to find common ground. There were also other reasons. For instance, historian Zoe Moody notes how the archival records include frequent references to trends in development psychology, including a report that the influential attachment theorist John Bowlby penned for WHO in 1952 that stressed "maternal deprivation" in the child's earliest years as a key predictor of later "mental disturbances."[22]

Such maternalist discourses on child development provided space for women's activism. In the fall of 1959, Paul Hofmann, *The New York Times* reporter to the United Nations, commented that the work to finalize the UN's "children's charter" had been spearheaded by "women delegates, many of them mothers."[23] The sessions of the Third Committee were chaired by the Belgian lawyer and liberal politician Georgette Ciselet, who had been one of Europe's most prominent champions of the rights of women and motherhood. In 1946, Ciselet had been the first woman elected into the Belgian parliament and had initiated progressive national legislation on marriage equality and the rights of children born out of wedlock. As part of the Belgian UN delegation, she had monitored the development of international standards on women's political rights and the registration of marriages, and had served as her country's representative to the CSW.[24] While Ciselet helped to ensure that the child rights declaration was unanimously approved in the UN General Assembly, some delegates quibbled over aspects of the document's design. Zoya V. Mironova, the USSR ambassador and founding member of the Women's International Democratic Federation, lamented that the declaration lacked adequate mechanisms of enforcement and contained no reference to the rights of working mothers. The problem in Mironova's view was not that the document tied children's rights to the plights of mothers, but that it did not imagine women as active citizens and economic agents.[25]

Gender and the UN convention on the rights of the Child

In hindsight, what is most striking about the 1959 UN Declaration on the Rights of the Child was how quickly it became obsolete. Moody, who has studied the document's drafting and early reception, claims that within only a few years, the document had been virtually forgotten, including by international and non-governmental bodies working in the fields of child welfare and child development. In light of the geopolitical, social, and cultural transformation of the 1960s, the declaration seemed to be a statement of principles belonging to an increasingly distant postwar moment.[26] This was not just because it reflected stereotyped ideas about motherhood and the division of domestic labor. The text was completed just before states of the Global South breathed new life into the international human rights project, effectively paving the way for the completion of the UN's core human rights covenants in 1966, documents which contained only scattered references to child protection again in the context of parental rights.[27] While the language of children's rights still featured in international human rights resolutions of this era (e.g., in the final communiqué of the 1968 World Conference on Human Rights in Teheran), it was subordinated to the increasingly dominant causes of decolonization and non-discrimination.[28] There was, as of yet, no talk of a binding treaty directly concerned with children's specific needs and interests.

In the 1970s, UN human rights politics took a structural turn. Influenced by the launch of the New International Economic Order, it became a field that was increasingly occupied with global economic inequalities and domestic patterns of racial and gender discrimination.[29] At the same time, structural interpretations of human rights project were countered by other, predominantly Western, readings focusing on individual liberties and equality of opportunity. These differences came into full view during the World Conference for the International Women's Year in Mexico City in June 1975. While this served as a crucial event in forging new international alliances among women's rights activists and established the UN Decade for Women, it also revealed deep divides among feminists, including the conflict over the relationship between the struggle for equal human rights and economic justice.[30]

Some of these tensions were built into the 1979 UN Convention Against All Forms of Discrimination Against Women (CEDAW), which oscillated between an emphasis on liberation from stereotyped gender roles and protection within such roles. In some respects, then, the treaty was of direct relevance to the rights of children. More specifically, Article 5 on family education mentioned the need to promote awareness of "maternity as a social function" as well as the "common responsibility of men and women in the upbringing and development of their children," and suggested that such education must carry out with respect for the child's best interests. Article 16(2) addressed the question of child marriage, although it evaded the question of who counts as a child.[31] Still, CEDAW was not a child rights treaty. As Cynthia Price-Cohen argues, its shape and content reflect how the international movement for women's human rights was principally occupied with correcting inequalities between adult men and women. It did not address the needs of the girl-child, effectively ignoring what Price-Cohen saw as the "importance of preparing girls to become women."[32]

Still, the advances in women's rights and feminist theory were crucial for reviving the question of children's rights during this period. Some of the most outspoken proponents of the radical but short-lived movement for child liberation, like Richard Farsons and John Holt, sought to transfer some of the energy and arguments of the civil and women's rights movements to a project of challenging the ingrained assumptions of childhood.[33] Partly inspired by the works of historian Phillippe Ariès, these child liberationists claimed that "childhood" was a recently innovated category, which served only to justify the adult oppression of young beings, and which therefore could and should be dismantled.[34] In her influential 1970 pamphlet *The Dialectics of Sex,* Shulamith Firestone included a full chapter on childhood, where she claimed that discrimination on the basis of age was akin to that of gender, and that women had to "include the oppressio of children in any program for feminist revolution."[35]

The proponents of child liberation were met with strong suspicion, not just among conservatives who saw their views as an attack on family values, but also among child rights advocates, who maintained that they denied the natural vulnerabilities of young age. At the international level, the discourse of children's rights was still dominated by its ties to child protection.[36]

In the UN context, the protectionist view of children's rights was reinforced in the context of the International Year of the Child (1979). The initiative for a child year was first put forward by Canon Joseph Moerman, the International Catholic Child Bureau's representative in Geneva. Moerman was disheartened by the ideological battles that had dominated the recent international years on women (1975) and population (1976), and he suggested that the international community now needed to engage in a more reconciliatory project. In 1975, he began lobbying other non-governmental organizations and international agencies and eventually secured the backing of both UNICEF and UN Secretary General Kurt Waldheim. The basic condition set up by UNICEF Executive Director Henri Labouisse was that there would be no international conference like the one on women in Mexico, and that the year would be geared towards actions at the national level. The international side of things would mainly be about scaling up international aid to developing countries and boosting awareness of UNICEF's work in securing children's basic needs. Once the project had been scheduled for 1979, it was decided that it would also be labelled as a year for children's rights, since it would coincide with the twentieth anniversary of the 1959 Declaration. Nevertheless, the underlying premise of the International Year of the Child was that children's rights, unlike general human rights, was a non-political, non-disruptive concept that was principally about securing basic needs and protections from the worst forms of abuse and neglect.[37]

It was in this context that the Polish government unexpectedly tabled a draft Convention on the Rights of Child. This in and of itself was not a novel idea. Already in the 1950s, the Communist states had called for a binding international instrument that would emphasize the importance of national legislation and the effective use of state power in safeguarding children's rights to protection and welfare. The advent of a child year seemed like a fortuitous moment to give it another try. Besides, the Polish government was weary that "progress in legislation on the rights of the child should not lag behind that made in other spheres of international law."[38] However, the Polish draft was not well received outside of the Warsaw Pact. The few states who cared to respond to the initial draft were unenthusiastic about the way it largely reproduced the content of the 1959 UN Declaration of the Rights of Child, merely changing its form into a binding treaty. The Netherlands and the Nordic countries pointed directly to the ways in which the draft failed to recognize the transformations in social values and the structures of modern welfare states that had taken place during the intervening decades; not only was there an increasing awareness of the dangers of child abuse, but the realities of working parents were also more apparent. Further, the text was criticized as flotsam from a pre-decolonization era in UN human rights politics.[39]

Though the Polish initiative led to the creation of a designated working group under the Commission on Human Rights, it was not until the mid-1980s that the project of completing the UN Convention on the Rights of the Child gained momentum. This was partly due to the changing global landscape with the rise of Gorbachev, which eased Cold War tensions, at least in Europe. Another key factor was the finalization of the UN Convention Against Torture, which freed up space and resources for UN delegations in Geneva. Significant in this process were the concerted efforts by non-governmental organizations who participated in the drafting process. Through the creation of a designated NGO group on the UN Convention on the Rights of the Child, these groups—spearheaded by Defense for Children International, the International Catholic Child Bureau, and the Swedish Save the Children—not only influenced those states partaking in the drafting process, but they also helped to convince an initially reluctant UNICEF to get on board with the idea of formulating a binding human rights treaty for children.[40]

Some of the organizations that followed the drafting process from its earliest days were women's rights groups, including the International Federation of Women Lawyers and the Women's International Democratic Federation. Several of the most active NGO delegates were women, including Rachel Brett of the Quakers, Geraldine van Bueren of Amnesty International, and Cynthia Price-Cohen of the Human Rights Internet. In the final stages of the drafting, some of these women helped to ensure that the child rights convention was the first international human rights treaty written in completely gender-neutral language. Whereas the 1959 Declaration had spoken of the rights-bearer as a "he," the convention either used the neutral "the child" or the combined pronoun "he or she."[41]

Still, it would be an exaggeration to label the UN Convention on the Rights of the Child as a "feminist landmark." In her thorough analysis of this event, political scientist Anna Holzscheiter notes how the drafting process was characterized by a general lack of attention to issues of gender. It was generally assumed that childhood was a universal experience, and very little attention was paid to its intersection with other grounds of vulnerability and discrimination, such as class, race, and gender. Further, the term "girl-child" was absent in the text. Perhaps most striking was the fact that the convention did not include a reference to child marriage, like the one in CEDAW. This inattentiveness to gender, Holzscheiter argues, "seems all the more astonishing in view of the fact that several women's NGOs participated in the drafting," and that it "coincided with the International Decade for Women (1975-1985)."[42] This lack of attention to gender equality also explains some reluctance that women's rights organization had in becoming involved in the project. The Portuguese delegate to the drafting process and would-be UN Special Representative Marta Santos-Pais claimed that some women's rights organizations saw it as "taking away the light from them and the focus they were receiving in the previous years."[43]

A notable exception to the general lack of focus on gender was the discussion on harmful traditional practices, a phrase which was code for female genital mutilation. As is well-known, female genital mutilation was one of the main global issues around which feminists of different origins and orientations coalesced in the 1970s. While they often disagreed in their analysis of what it was—Western feminists like Fran Hosken thought of it as a cultural and religious practice, whereas southern feminists like Nawal el Saadawi framed it as but one of many instances indicative of a global patriarchal structure—they generally agreed on its detrimental effects on women. Still, the issue had not been addressed in CEDAW, and it remained highly uncertain as to where, if anywhere, in the landscape of international agencies and multilateral organizations it really belonged. Internationally, the concept of female genital mutilation was frequently linked to culture, religion and civilization, rather than patriarchy, which meant that it rekindled infected debates on Western moral imperialism, and aggravated North-South tensions between feminist activists. More still, many within the human rights community considered it as a matter that belonged to the private sphere and which therefore was beyond the reach of the emerging field of human rights law.[44]

In this context, the drafting of the UN Convention on the Rights of the Child was a significant step forward. At the back of Article 24 on the right to health, the convention calls on states to take "effective and appropriate measures with a view to abolishing traditional practices prejudicial to the health of children."[45] This was the first time that an international treaty labelled female genital mutilation as incompatible with human rights. One key to this development was that the talks on children's human rights were relatively open to interventions by non-governmental organizations and that many of these organizations were becoming increasingly committed to facilitating co-operation across North-South divides. In the mid-1980s, the Inter-African Committee on Traditional Practices Affecting the Health of Women and Children (IAC)—represented by the Ethiopian rights activist Berhane Ras-Work—and the Swedish Save the Children successfully lobbied Senegal to demand a UN report on female genital mutilation. The report, which appeared in 1986 and was penned by the Moroccan diplomat Halima Embareck Warzazi, helped to legitimate discussion on the topic in the UN Commission of Human Rights and to defuse charges of moral imperialism. In 1987, the Swedish Save the Children, acting on behalf of a wider group on NGOs tabled a draft article that became the basis the for the final version of the Convention's Article 24(3).[46] As this clause was unanimously approved, it helped to define female genital mutilation and other forms severe abuse of children in private spaces, as legitimate targets of human rights law and politics.[47]

Concluding reflections

The UN Convention on the Rights of the Child was not launched as a project aimed at challenging gender relations. Instead, the treaty grew out of the International Year of the Child of 1979, an event which had partly been launched to counterbalance the contentious international debates on gender equality that had taken place in the second half of the 1970s. Moreover, the convention's drafting unfolded with little attention to the intersections of age and gender. The point of concern was not that gender was too sensitive a topic to influence the convention. Rather, as Holzscheiter puts it, "gender did not even emerge as an issue in its own right," and if it did, it was generally neutralized in reference to the convention's general clause on non-discrimination.[48] The text reiterated some provisions of earlier international instruments on human rights and children's rights that highlighted the importance of the nuclear family in the child's physical, mental, and emotional development. It further contained a preambular clause on the child's rights to protection, both before as well as after birth, thus raising doubts about the treaty's compatibility with the right to abortion. It was, in short, a convention that affirmed rather than challenged many of the conservative elements in international human rights discourse.

Still, as this chapter has shown, some women diplomats and activists found ways of using the drafting of the UN Convention on the Rights of the Child to address issues that were of strong significance to the rights of girls, including female genital mutilation and domestic violence. While the convention's language was imprecise and open to all kinds of interpretation, it helped pave the way for a more radical transformation of human rights politics that would take place in the 1990s, especially during the Vienna Conference on Human Rights 1993[49] and the Beijing Conference of 1995,[50] where the rights of women and girls emerged as central topics of concern.

These events, and especially the Vienna Conference, are now best remembered for the slogan that "women's rights are human rights."[51] Still, what changed in this period was not strictly the understanding of to *whom* human rights applied. As many of the contributions to this volume show, women's rights, much like children's rights, had been part of the international human rights discourse since its inception. Rather, the transformation was mainly about *where* human rights norms were of relevance.[52] The developments in the 1990s struck a decisive blow to the public-private distinction in international human rights law and politics, affirming that the right to privacy is no justification for gender violence. These transformations were partly carried forward by the gains made in the UN Convention on the Rights of the Child. While this text did not emerge as a feminist treaty, some of its clauses, and especially the provisions on harmful traditional practices, became a means of casting violations of girls and women in the private sphere as affronts to their fundamental human rights and dignity.

In a broader sense, the history of children's rights reminds us of the difficulties in writing about women's agency in UN human rights politics. There is always the danger that we may be highlighting only those examples in which women were championing what we now, with the benefit of hindsight, consider as progressive projects and ideals. It is also easy to overlook that the women who participated in these processes, for the most part, were loyal representatives of their respective governments and host-organizations with limited possibility to influence policy. It is therefore worth noting how the codification of romanticized ideas of motherhood in, for instance, the 1959 UN Declaration of the Rights of the Child was spearheaded by women delegates. Also, the strong presence of women diplomats and activists in the drafting of the UN Convention on the Rights of the Child did not ensure that this treaty was crafted with special attention to the structures of gender inequalities. For the history of women's activism in the context of UN human rights politics to be a source of deepened understanding, such tensions, including those among feminists, must not be bracketed; instead, they should be framed into central objects of study.

Notes

1 See, for instance, the Universal Declaration of Human Rights (1948), Article 25; International Covenant on Economic, Social and Cultural Rights (1966), Article 10.

2 Frances Olsen, "Children's Rights: Some Feminist Approaches to the United Nations Convention on the Rights of the Child," *International Journal of Law, Policy and the Family* 6 no. 1 (1992): 192.

3 It should be noted that this chapter forms part of a much bigger undertaking of charting the history of children's rights in international politics. Thus, my general concern here lies not with the histories of female activism or women's rights, histories which are better told by others (e.g., see Valgerður Pálmádottir, "Perplexities of the Personal and the Political: How Women's Liberation became Women's Human Rights" (PhD diss., Umeå University, 2018). Instead, I am mainly interested in challenging an established and overtly linear narrative portraying the UN Convention on the Rights of the Child (1989) as a natural endpoint of moral development that was spurred by a growing appreciation of children as individual human beings. In response, I want to sketch an account that brings to light the situational and often-times conflicting uses of children's rights at the international level, an account that is attentive to the "mélange of contradictory intentions, moral dilemmas and divergent interpretations of the term itself," as human rights historian Jan Eckel puts it in *The Ambivalence of Good: Human Rights in International Politics Since the 1940s* (New York: Oxford University Press, 2019), 340.

4 Helen Swanwick of the Women's International League for Peace and Freedom, cited in Linda Mahood, *Feminism and Voluntary Action: Eglantyne Jebb and Save the Children, 1876-1928* (Basingstoke: Palgrave Macmillan, 2009), 190.

5 Bruno Cabanes, *The Great War and the Origins of Humanitarianism, 1918–1924* (New York: Cambridge University Press, 2015), 296.

6 For a notable exception pointing to the lack of discussions on gender, see Anna Holzscheiter, *Children's Rights in International Politics: The Transformative Power of Discourse* (Basingstoke: Palgrave Macmillan, 2010), 229–231.

7 Cited in Zoe Moody, "The United Nations Declaration of the Rights of the Child (1959): Genesis, Transformation and Dissemination of a Treaty (Re)constituting a Transnational Cause," *Prospects* 45 no. 1 (2015): 19.

8 The Universal Declaration of Human Rights (1948), Article 25(2).

9 UN Doc. E/CN.4/AC.2/SR.6 (1947), 2. For more on Begtrup see Kristine Midtgaard, "Bodil Begtrup and the Universal Declaration of Human Rights: Individual Agency, Transnationalism and Intergovernmentalism in early UN Human Rights," *Scandinavian Journal of History* 36 no. 4 (2011): 479–499.

10 UN Doc. A/C.3/SR.145 (1948), 576.

11 UN Doc. A/C.3/SR.143 (1948), 555.

12 UN Doc. A/C.3/SR.144 (1948), 570.

13 The French delegate René Cassin stated that while "he had voted in favour of according social protection to illegitimate children, he had not been able to vote for granting them equal civil rights." UN Doc. A/C.3/SR.146 (1948), 579.

14 Nancy Fraser, *Fortunes of Feminism: From State Managed Capitalism to Neoliberal Crisis* (London: Verso, 2017), [197].

15 Jessica Whyte, *The Morals of the Market: Human Rights and the Rise of Neoliberalism* (London: Verso, 2019), 94–95.

16 Allida Black, "Are Women 'Human'? The UN and the Struggle to Recognize Women's Rights as Human Rights," in *The Human Rights Revolution: An International History*, ed. Akira Iriye, Petra Goedde and William I. Hitchcock (New York: Oxford University Press, 2012), 141.

17 Devkai Jain, *Women, Development, and the UN: A Sixty-Year Quest for Equality and Justice* (Bloomington: Indiana University Press, 2005), 22.

18 ILO Maternity Protection Convention (Revised), 1952 (No. 103).

19 Jain, *Women, Development, and the UN*, 22.

20 UN General Assembly Resolution 1386(XIV) of 20 November 1959.

21 UN General Assembly Resolution 1386(XIV) of 20 November 1959, Principles 4 and 6.

22 Zoe Moody, *Les droits de l'enfant: genèse, institutionnalisation et diffusion, 1924–1989* (Neuchâtel: Éditions Alphil), 190–191; John Bowlby, *Maternal Care and Mental Health* (Geneva: World Health Organisation, 1952), 13.

23 Paul Hoffmann, "UN Body Backs Child Charter," *New York Times*, October 20, 1959.

24 Catherine Jacques, "Georgette Ciselet," in *Dictionnaire des femmes belges: XIXe et XXe siècles*, ed. Éliane Gubin, Catherine Jacques, Valérie Piette and Jean Puissant (Brussels: Éditions Racine, 2006), 100–103.

25 Hoffmann, "UN Body Backs Child Charter."

26 Moody, "The United Nations Declaration of the Rights of the Child (1959)," 24.

27 See, .e.g., CESCR, arts. 10 and 13; CCPR, arts. 18, 24. For more on the context of decolonization, see Steven L. B. Jensen, *The Making of International Human Rights* (New York: Cambridge University Press, 2016).

28 "The Proclamation of Teheran" (1968), in Final Act of the International Conference on Human Rights, April 22–May 13, 1968, UN Doc. A/Conf.32/41 (1968), p. 4, art. 14.

29 Julia Dehm, "Highlighting Inequalities in the Histories of Human Rights: Contestation over Justice, Needs and Rights in the 1970s," *Leiden Journal of International Law* 31 no. 4 (2018): 871–895.

30 Roland Burke, "Competing for the Last Utopia? The NIEO, Human Rights, and the World Conference for the International Women's Year, Mexico City, June 1975," *Humanity Journal* 6 no. 1 (2015): 47–61.

31 Convention on the Elimination of All Forms of Discrimination against Women New York (1979).

32 Cynthia Price-Cohen, "The United Nations Convention of the Rights of the Child: A Feminist Landmark," *William & Mary Journal of Race, Gender, and Social Justice* 3 no. 1 (1997): 36–40.

33 Jean Fortin, *Children's Rights and the Developing Law*, 3rd ed. (New York: Cambridge University Press, 2009), 5–7.

34 Phillippe Ariès, *Centuries of Childhood* (Pimlico, London, 1996).

35 Shulamith Firestone, *The Dialectic of Sex: The Case for Feminist Revolution* (New York: Morrow, 1970), 104.

36 Michael D. A. Freeman, "The Rights of Children in the International Year of the Child," *Current Legal Problems* 30 no. 1 (1980): 30.

37 This summarizes Linde Lindkvist, "1979: A Year of the Child, but Not of Children's Human Rights," *Diplomatica* 1 no. 2 (2019): 202–220.

38 UN Doc. E/CN.4/SR.1438 (1978), 10.

39 See comments by Netherlands and Sweden in UN Doc. E/CN.4/1324 (1978), w.

40 Cynthia Price Cohen, "The United Nations Convention on the Rights of the Child: Involvement of Nongovernmental Organizations" (Conference presentation, The United Nations in a Changing World: Looking to the Next Half-Century, Academic Council of the United Nations System, New York, June 19–21, 1995), in Papers of Canon Joseph Moerman, Box 5, Folder 10.

41 Cynthia Price-Cohen, "The United Nations Convention of the Rights of the Child: A Feminist Landmark," *William & Mary Journal of Race, Gender, and Social Justice* 3 no. 1 (1997): 47.

42 Holzscheiter, *Children's Rights in International Politics*, 230.

43 Cited in Ibid., 230.
44 Kelly J. Shannon, "The Right to Bodily Integrity. Women's Rights as Human Rights and the International Movement to End Female Genital Mutilation, 1970s–1990s," in Akira Iriye, Petra Goedde, and William I. Hitchcock (eds.) *The Human Rights Revolution* (New York: Oxford University Press, 2012),285–310. See also Devkai Jain, *Women, Development, and the UN: A Sixty-Year Quest for Equality and Justice* (Bloomington: Indiana University Press, 2005), 28.
45 UN Convention on the Rights of the Child (1989), Article 24.3.
46 UN Doc. E/CN.4/1987/25 (1987), para. 28.
47 Simone Ek, *Självklart barnets rättigheter* (Stockholm: Rädda Barnen, 2009).
48 Holzscheiter, *Children's Rights in International Politics*, 231.
49 Declaration on the Elimination of Violence against Women, 20 December 1993, UN Doc. A/RES/48/104 (1994).
50 Beijing Declaration and Platform for Action (1995), which was one of the first documents to provide a sustained treatment of girls' human rights.
51 Charlotte Bunch and Roxanna Carrillo, "Women's Rights are Human Rights: A Concept in the Making," in *Women and Girls Rising: Progress and Resistance Around the World*, ed. Ellen Chesler and Terry McGovern (London, Routledge, 2016), 32–49.
52 Dorothea Anthony, "The World Conference on Human Rights: Still a Guiding Light a Quarter of a Century Later," *Australian Journal of Human Rights* 25 no. 3 (2019): 411–417.

Bibliography

Anthony, Dorothea. "The World Conference on Human Rights: Still a Guiding Light a Quarter of a Century Later." *Australian Journal of Human Rights* 25 no. 3 (2019): 411–427.

Ariès, Phillippe. *Centuries of Childhood*, New Edition. London: Pimlico, 1996.

Black, Allida. "Are Women 'Human'? The UN and the Struggle to Recognize Women's Rights as Human Rights." In *The Human Rights Revolution: An International History*, ed. Akira Iriye, Petra Goedde and William I. Hitchcock. New York: Oxford University Press, 2012: 133–158.

Bowlby, John. *Maternal Care and Mental Health*. Geneva: World Health Organisation, 1952.

Bunch, Charlotte and Carrillo, Roxanna. "Women's Rights are Human Rights: A Concept in the Making."In *Women and Girls Rising: Progress and Resistance Around the World*, ed. Ellen Chesler and Terry McGovern. London: Routledge, 2016, 32–49.

Burke, Roland. "Competing for the Last Utopia? The NIEO, Human Rights, and the World Conference for the International Women's Year, Mexico City, June 1975." *Humanity Journal* 6 no. 1 (2015): 47–61.

Cabanes, Bruno. *The Great War and the Origins of Humanitarianism, 1918–1924*. New York: Cambridge University Press, 2015.

Dehm, Julia. "Highlighting Inequalities in the Histories of Human Rights: Contestation over Justice, Needs and Rights in the 1970s." *Leiden Journal of International Law* 31 no. 4 (2018): 871–895.

Eckel, Jan *The Ambivalence of Good: Human Rights in International Politics Since the 1940s*. New York: Oxford University Press, 2019.

Ek, Simone. *Självklart barnets rättigheter*. Stockholm: Rädda Barnen, 2009.

Firestone, Shulamith. *The Dialectic of Sex: The. Case for Feminist Revolution*. New York: Morrow, 1970.

Fraser, Nancy. *Fortunes of Feminism: From State Managed Capitalism to Neoliberal Crisis*. London: Verso, 2017.

Freeman, Michael D. A. "The Rights of Children in the International Year of the Child." *Current Legal Problems* 30 no. 1 (1980): 1–31.

Fortin, Jean. *Children's Rights and the Developing Law*, 3rd ed. New York: Cambridge University Press, 2009.

Holzscheiter, Anna. *Children's Rights in International Politics: The Transformative Power of Discourse*. Basingstoke: Palgrave Macmillan, 2010.

Jacques, Catherine. "Georgette Ciselet." In *Dictionnaire des femmes belges: XIXe et XXe siècles*, ed. Éliane Gubin, Catherine Jacques, Valérie Piette and Jean Puissant. Brussels: Éditions Racine, 2006: 100–103.

Jain, Devkai. *Women, Development, and the UN: A Sixty-Year Quest for Equality and Justice*. Bloomington: Indiana University Press, 2005.

Jensen, Steven L. B. *The Making of International Human Rights*. New York: Cambridge University Press, 2016.

Lindkvist, Linde. "1979: A Year of the Child, but Not of Children's Human Rights." *Diplomatica* 1 no. 2 (2019): 202–220.

Mahood, Linda. *Feminism and Voluntary Action: Eglantyne Jebb and Save the Children, 1876–1928*. Basingstoke: Palgrave Macmillan, 2009.

Midtgaard, Kristine. "Bodil Begtrup and the Universal Declaration of Human Rights: Individual Agency, Transnationalism and Intergovernmentalism in early UN Human Rights." *Scandinavian Journal of History* 36 no. 4 (2011): 479–499.

Moody, Zoe. "The United Nations Declaration of the Rights of the Child (1959): Genesis, Transformation and Dissemination of a Treaty (Re)constituting a Transnational Cause," *Prospects* 45 no. 1 (2015): 15–29.

Moody, Zoe *Les droits de l'enfant : Genèse, Institutionnalisation et Diffusion, 1924-1989*. Neuchâtel: Éditions Alphil.

Olsen, Frances. "Children's Rights: Some Feminist Approaches to the United Nations Convention on the Rights of the Child." *International Journal of Law, Policy and the Family* 6 no. 1 (1992): 192–220.

Pálmádottir, Valgerður. "Perplexities of the Personal and the Political: How Women's Liberation became Women's Human Rights." PhD diss., Umeå University, 2018.

Price-Cohen, Cynthia. "The United Nations Convention of the Rights of the Child: A Feminist Landmark." *William & Mary Journal of Race, Gender, and Social Justice* 3 no. 1 (1997): 29–78.

Shannon, Kelly J. "The Right to Bodily Integrity. Women's Rights as Human Rights and the International Movement to End Female Genital Mutilation, 1970s–1990s." In *The Human Rights Revolution: An International History*, ed. Akira Iriye, Petra Goedde and William I. Hitchcock. New York: Oxford University Press, 2012: 285–310.

Whyte, Jessica. *The Morals of the Market: Human Rights and the Rise of Neoliberalism*. London: Verso, 2019.

9 Creating UNSCR 1325

Women who served as initiators, drafters, and strategists

Cornelia Weiss

Introduction

On 31 October 2000, in the 55th year of the UN Security Council (Council), the Council, at its 4213th meeting, unanimously adopted a four-page resolution with a preamble and 18 numbered operative paragraphs.[1] That resolution was UN Security Council Resolution (UNSCR) 1325,[2] the Council's first resolution on women, peace, and security.[3] This chapter explores how, in a Council of 15 State members—five permanent and ten elected—and with only one UN Security Council State represented by a female Permanent Representative, the almost all-male Council adopted the first Council resolution addressing women, peace, and security in its over a half-century existence. This chapter highlights the women who served as initiators, drafters and strategists of UNSCR 1325. It starts with the State that sponsored UNSCR 1325—Namibia.

The Sponsor

In 2000, Namibia was in the second and final year of its two-year term as an elected member of the Council.[4] In its first term as President of the Council (August 1999), Namibia sponsored a resolution on children in armed conflict (UNSCR 1261), the "first one in history to focus exclusively on children and armed conflict."[5] The question for Namibia then was: what "first in history" resolution to sponsor for its second term as president of the Council in October 2000? Netumbo Nandi-Ndaitwah of Namibia had the answer. In 1995, Nandi-Ndaitwah was the Rapporteur-General of the Fourth World Conference on Women.[6] The resulting Beijing Declaration and Platform for Action addressed "Women and Armed Conflict."[7] In 2000, Nandi-Ndaitwah was serving as Namibia's Director-General of the Department of Women's Affairs and Minister of Women Affairs and Child Welfare.[8] In May 2000, Namibia was the first State, along with Senegal, to ratify the Optional Protocol to the UN Convention on the Elimination of All Forms of Discrimination Against Women (OP-CEDAW).[9] Thus, unlike women in States that refuse to ratify OP-CEDAW, the women of Namibia possess the power to hold Namibia accountable if it violates CEDAW.[10] Nandi-Ndaitwah, "early in the planning process" for 2000, made a "suggestion" that Namibia sponsor a Council resolution "recognizing the contribution and participation of

DOI: 10.4324/9781003036708-9

women in peace and security."[11] In 2020, twenty years later after "suggesting" a Council resolution on women and security, Nandi-Ndaitwah is the Deputy Prime Minister of Namibia and Minister of International Relations.[12] Why did Namibia choose to sponsor UNSCR 1325 during its presidency of the Council? According to Nandi-Ndaitwah, "In Namibia, we have always recognized the link between peace and gender equality. That is what we have learnt from our long years of our liberation struggle for independence."[13] She elaborated: "Before returning from exile ... our Founding President ... called on Namibian women to be on alert and not to allow the country to be messed up once independence is achieved ... the peace we are enjoying today since Namibia's independence 25 years ago, was achieved through a critical role, played by women" -- "[w]omen's meaningful participation in our post-conflict reconstruction has been pivotal to the peace and stability in our country today."[14]

A decade prior to UNSCR 1325, on 23 April 1990, Namibia became the 160th Member of the United Nations.[15] Namibia became a State after lengthy foreign rule. Germany, when it ruled Namibia in the early 1900s, marked women as "special targets" in the "first genocide of the twentieth century."[16] Later South Africa engaged in "racist ... brutal repression" against Namibians,[17] resulting in the UN General Assembly on 3 May 1978 "condemn[ing] ... South Africa for its continued illegal occupation of Namibia in defiance of repeated demands by the Assembly and the Security Council for its withdrawal."[18] South Africa did not withdraw. Instead, on 4 May 1978, the South African Army attacked the refugee camp of the current (2020) Namibian Ambassador to the U.S., Monica Ndiliawike Nashandi. Subsequent to the May 1978 attack, the Council resolved to provide "free elections [for Namibia] under the supervision and control of the United Nations"[19] through "a United Nations Transitional Assistance Group,"[20] known as "UNTAG." Yet it took 11 years for the Council to "decide to implement" its 1978 resolution to establish UNTAG.[21]

After the 1978 attack, Nashandi became "a freedom fighter alongside my fellow women combatants who served at the frontline."[22] (Today Nashandi states she is "proud to have fought for my country at the frontline because that experience made me whom I am today."[23]) By 1989, during the UN deliberations on the budget allocation for the deployment of UNTAG to Namibia, Nashandi was serving as Deputy Representative to the SWAPO Observer Mission to the UN in New York. According to Nashandi, the budget negotiations for UNTAG were "not easy" as the "size of the territory and the huge number of the South African troops in Namibia required a large UN contingent" and that "a lean budget ... would translate into the deployment of a small UNTAG ... leaving most of the country still occupied by the South African forces."[24] The resulting UNTAG budget and deployment ensured elections on 7-11 November 1989, with 97% of eligible voters voting.[25]

Was UNTAG effective because UNTAG did not exclude women? The Director of the Special Representative's Office for UNTAG explained: "Many of our most effective officers, at all levels up to the regional director, were women, often working in exacting circumstances."[26] Women comprised 40% of the professional service and "much more than 50%"of "the general service, in the regions and districts."[27] Given that "working in the field can be exhilarating," assessments of the experience by female peacekeepers included "the best year of my life."[28] UNTAG, describing itself as the "first [UN] mission to 'give women a chance,'" reported that its civilian men "were described as sometimes helpless," with women "seen by a number of women as 'more resourceful and resilient.'"[29] UNTAG reported "with its large numbers of women, Namibia may be the first mission where the conduct of [male] UN staff vis-à-vis local women was called into question."[30]

The Windhoek Declaration and the Namibian Plan of Action on mainstreaming a gender perspective in multidimensional peace support operations

In May 2000, Namibia hosted a seminar culminating a three-year effort by UN Assistant Secretary-General Angela King's UN Office of the Special Adviser on Gender Issues, the Division of the Advancement of Women (DAW) of the Department of Economic and Social Affairs, and the UN Department of Peace-keeping Operations to provide "objective and empirical findings" to answer "the skeptics" regarding the need for equal participation of women in UN missions.[31] The seminar occurred on the 10th anniversary of UNTAG,[32] and it celebrated the 10th anniversary of Namibia's independence.[33]

The participants elected Dame Margaret Anstee (1926-2016) to chair the sem-inar.[34] Anstee, in 1987, became the first female UN Under-Secretary-General.[35] Anstee was also the first woman to head a UN peacekeeping mission (1992-1993).[36] With command over military, police, and civilian components, she headed the peacekeeping mission in Angola—"a State as large as France, Spain, and Germany combined."[37] Anstee had attended the first three UN Women's Con-ferences, but refused to attend the 1995 conference (which was to have taken place in Vienna) when "out of the blue ... so soon" after Tiananmen Square, China announced it wanted to host the conference in Beijing.[38]

Anstee had a plan, recalling:

> The unlikely genesis of the groundbreaking Security Council resolution 1325 during a routine meeting that I was chairing on gender and peace-keeping, in Windhoek, Namibia, in May 2000, is a telling demonstration of how the far-reaching impact that women can have if they act in unison. During a cocktail party given by Namibian minister of women's affairs, it occurred to me that our message on women, peace and security would have more impact enshrined in a Declaration of Windhoek and a Namibia Plan of Action. In discussing this with our hostess, who had been a junior minister in her country's foreign ministry, I suddenly remembered that Namibia was a member of the Security Council. I reminded her that, when Namibia's turn came to preside over the Council, it could have a meeting on a subject of its choosing. I suggested it would be a great coup for Namibia if she could

persuade her foreign minister to use this opportunity to spearhead a high-level debate about the issues we had been discussing. She agreed and, by working through the next 24 hours, our little group of women prepared both the Declaration and the Plan of Action, something that, in the UN, normally takes several months. The minister was as good as her word and Resolution 1325 was passed on 31 October 2000 with our two documents annexed. Had it not been for that serendipitous cocktail party, and the coming together of a group of like-minded and determined women, that resolution would never have seen the light of day.[39]

Jelena Grčić Polić (b. 1955), the Vice-Chair of the UN General Assembly's Fourth Committee and on the Sub-Committee on Peacekeeping Operations (and the Croatian Deputy Permanent Representative at the UN), recalls: "We worked late, all women, and had only one man, an officer from the Croatian MOD [Ministry of Defense], help with photocopying and errands."[40] Grčić Polić had grown up in Dubrovnik, which was "brutally shelled and kept under siege for months in the winter of 1991/1992" when Croatia declared independence after multiparty elections in spring 1991 and "the Serb-led Yugoslav National Army attempted to avert the dissolution of the former communist-led federation by force."[41] Grčić Polić later served as Croatia's Assistant Minister of Defense for Policy.[42]

According to Judith Hicks Stiehm, an academic, the "little group of women" that "drafted the resolution" did not include all "official" women; it did not include her.[43] The DPKO LLU had hired Stiehm to present a report to the seminar.[44] Stiehm learned "something 'bigger' was in the works," and after "consult[ing] with the representatives from the Peacekeeping Unit, they agreed her report should just be filed."[45] Stiehm today recalls being "physically present" in the room when the Declaration and Plan of Action were put on the table, that it was "a thrilling moment."[46]

Another academic at the conference, Peter Wallensteen, contends "there was also a fair number of men in the group," explaining: "In the afternoon of May 29" Anstee "suggested" that the product of the seminar be the Declaration and Plan of Action, rather than "reporting on the studies that had been made" and that he "was concerned about the possible attitude of the funder, the Swedish Ministry for Foreign Affairs."[47] Wallensteen explained: "What happened is that the second day, May 30, two working groups were formed. These groups presented their reports on May 31, when the texts were brought together into the action plan."[48]

The Windhoek Declaration castigated international and national actors for denying women a "full role" in peace support operations and for failing to "adequately address" the "gender dimension in peace processes" and maintained, that for peace support operations to be effective, "gender equity and equality must permeate the entire mission" to create conditions of "political stability in which women and men play an equal part in the political, economic and social development of their country."[49] The Namibia Plan of Action addressed "practical ways" to realize the gender equity and equality goals of the Windhoek Declaration.[50]

Beijing +5

In 2000, Namibia sat not only on the Council, it served as president of the UN General Assembly. Just days after the 31 May 2000 Windhoek Declaration and Namibia Plan of Action, Namibia chaired Beijing +5 (5-9 June 2000).[51] Beijing +5 included panels on "Mainstreaming a Gender Perspective in Peacekeeping Operations," which included issues of "peacekeeping, peace building and conflict prevention."[52] The outcome document of the Beijing +5 addressed 50/50 gender balance in peacekeeping missions and peace negotiations[53] as well as obstacles to women's equal participation in peace-building efforts.[54]

The delegates at Beijing +5 included two Indian Parliamentarians of different castes and experiences: Phoolan Devi (1963-assassinated 2001) and Krishna Bose (1930-2020). Phoolan Devi, a member of the low-caste and illiterate 85% of India,[55] had served years in prison (without trial) for extra-judicial actions she took against unprosecuted rapists who pried on low-caste and illiterate females.[56] Her extra-judicial actions: Damaging or dismembering penises of unprosecuted rapists.[57] Krishna Bose, a member of a prominent political family, sought change through legislation. For example, she introduced legislation in the Indian Parliament in February 2000 (Bill No. 62 of 2000, dated 28 February 2000) "to cancel the registration of a political party if that party does not field candidates at elections ... from both genders proportionately."[58] As of January 2020, Bose's bill, despite being reintroduced in 2016-2017 by one of her sons, is not law.[59]

For Bose, Devi "brought out [to Beijing +5] the stark reality of the situation while we were discussing women's issues only theoretically."[60]

Advocating to the security council

As of mid-2020, the dates of Nandi-Ndaitwah's "suggestion" and Namibia's decision to sponsor what became UNSCR 1325 are unknown. Whether, and to what extent, others influenced Namibia's decision remains to be deciphered. What is known is that individuals and entities were advocating to the Council for what became UNSCR 1325.

Patricia Flor of Germany held the UN Commission on the Status of Women (CSW) Chair from March 1998[61] until March 2000 and served as the Vice-Chair of the CSW acting as Preparatory Committee for Beijing +5.[62] Earlier than April 2000,[63] as Chair of the CSW, Flor "did meet with the President and Members of the Security Council and asked for inclusion of gender-related questions in the deliberations of the [Council] with reference to the women in armed conflict elements of the Beijing Platform for Action."[64] Today Flor is the EU Ambassador to Japan.[65]

While recognizing that "civil society alone ... could not have secured a resolution in the Security Council," Sanam Anderlini contends UNSCR 1325 "was driven by civil society."[66] According to Ambassador Wensley, civil society holds "certain advantages," to include:

1 "not [being] limited by the processes of government of constraints of party politics,"

2 "great freedom to lobby, to mount campaigns for particular causes and to concentrate on these," and

3 for some, "well-established networks of contacts and of support structures … stretching across countries and continents, increasing significantly the opportunities for exchanging information (because it is vital to be well-informed) and for developing effective strategies."[67]

In March 2000, "at the CSW meeting, an NGO network formalized,"[68] consisting of Felicity Hill, Isha Dyfan, Cora Weiss, Florence Martin, Maha Muna, Ramine Johal, and Betty Reardon.[69] Hill served as "the coordinator … during the build up phase."[70] They obtained a $180,000 grant from the Ford Foundation (with Mahnaz Isfahani "as a key force")[71] "for a campaign specifically for a UN Security Council resolution."[72] In addition to funding, they also needed access to individuals and entities within the UN. Anderlini credits Cora Weiss for opening doors through her contacts.[73] Cora Weiss had been an activist since the 1960s, starting with Women Strike for Peace.[74] And they needed for their work to have impact. Concerned that instead of a "resolution," the outcome would be limited to a "declaration" or a "statement,"[75] International Alert and African women's groups had approached UNIFEM to strategize on how to obtain a legally binding document.[76] The NGO network (NGO) assumed the name "Coalition on Women and International Peace and Security."[77]

According to Hill, the NGO "form[ed] an alliance with sympathetic states (Namibia, Bangladesh, Jamaica and Canada) to first secure support for an Open Debate" and then met "with each remaining member of the Security Council, utilizing different arguments with each to advocate for a thematic debate and resolution on Women, Peace and Security."[78] The NGO met with the Namibian ambassador, Martin Andjaba, on 20 July 2000, during which they "discussed the possibility of Namibia—during its Presidency of the Security Council in October 2000—holding an open debate on women and international peace and security and presenting a resolution on this subject."[79] In August 2000, the NGO informed Ambassador Andjaba that they were "working with relevant agencies … on this project," offered to provide the Namibian delegation with "information, assistance, and consultations wherever necessary … to help it in carrying out this task," and expressed their willingness to meet again in early September.[80]

UNIFEM, as a technical advisor, could be "the bridge between the real experiences of women and the high level decision-making processes of the Member States in the Security Council at the time when there was insufficient understanding and literature on women, peace and security."[81] The Foreign Minister of Namibia (Theo-Ben Gurirab) wrote to the UN Secretary-General (Kofi Annan) requesting UNIFEM to be the technical advisor to the Council.[82] (UNIFEM and civil society actors had been working with Namibia "secretly because of fear that it would be stopped if known."[83]) Yet, as technical advisor, UNIFEM had to be "visible and invisible at the same time" and had to "hide their handiwork in drafting UNSCR 1325."[84] Further, the NGO "did not seek to make [their actions] public," believing "if their interactions with delegates became publicly known the likelihood of the ... resolution would be greatly diminished"[85]; that "[i]n order for [Namibia] to succeed, it was vital that Namibia did not appear to be NGO led."[86]

Socializing and drafting

On 1 October 2000, Namibia assumed the presidency of the Council. Before October, the Namibian delegation started socializing the idea of a resolution on women, peace, and security with member States of the Council.[87] In August 2000, the socializing not only intensified, but Aina Iiyambo, the First Secretary at the Namibian Mission to the UN, started "putting the language together" as the "penholder in a team effort."[88] While a proposed resolution usually is the result of recommendations by the Secretary-General, no Secretary-General report on women, peace, and security existed.[89] Therefore, Namibia requested that the Windhoek Declaration and Namibian Plan of Action be issued as official documents of the UN Security Council and the UN General Assembly.[90]

The UNIFEM Executive Director, Noleen Heyzer, recalls assertions from States that "first research on the ground was necessary to establish evidence."[91] In response, the NGO "quickly collected copies of 10-15 recent publications for each of the fifteen Security Council delegations" and "summarized the facts and arguments in each."[92] Given the absence of UN literature on women, peace, and security, Iiyambo was "in touch with many actors, to include civil society actors," finding Graça Machel's report on children in armed conflict "invaluable in helping [her] to situate the resolution, as well as opening [her] eyes."[93] Assistant Secretary-General Angela King provided "invaluable materials" for the drafting of the resolution, with the "main source of material" from UNIFEM, "especially from Jennifer Klot."[94] Heyzer had appointed Klot as the UNIFEM point person to work with Iiyambo throughout the drafting of the resolution, with Klot "consult[ing]" Heyzer "every step of the way," aided by "a small team of staff and civil society partners, including Hill, to provide ... ideas."[95] Klot previously "led UNICEF's strategy for advancing the first Security Council resolution on children"[96] (which Namibia had sponsored during its Presidency in 1999 and which, as UNSCR 1261, is the first resolution that UNSCR 1325 references). Iiyambo also consulted frequently with Hazel de Wet, the Namibian expert on women's human rights covering the UN General Assembly's Third Committee (Social, Humanitarian, and Cultural).[97] De Wet today serves as part of the UN Mission in South Sudan.[98]

By the beginning of October, an initial draft of UNSCR 1325 was completed.[99]

Hill contends the NGO had "provided Namibia with language for a draft resolution as soon as they agreed to host the Open Session during their Presidency of the Council,"[100] and that UNSCR 1325 "resembles" the draft the NGO provided Namibia "with the preambular language virtually identical."[101] In 2004-2005, the "draft resolution [was] available on request."[102] Alas, by 2020, Hill's copy was not locatable.[103]

According to Klot, "Namibia's delegates in New York, including two exception women leaders, Selma Ndeyapo Ashipala-Musavyi [the Deputy Permanent

Representative of Namibia] and First Secretary Aina Iiyambo, enthusiastically and skillfully shepherded the negotiations."[104] Iiyambo facilitated the negotiations of the draft resolution with the participation of experts from the other 14 council members.[105] The final drafting occurred between 25 and 30 October 2000.[106] While "a UN official cannot unilaterally change what Member States have agreed to in negotiations," given that "[a]s is the practice with Security Council and other intergovernmental processes, experts negotiated the entire text, word for word" with approval of the language a process of consensus, and if a consensus was not reached, approval did not happen,[107] hauntingly misleading assertions, such as by a "UN bureaucrat who very proudly stated that the night before the debate he had edited the resolution down to 1.5 pages," are remembered.[108]

Arria formula meeting

On 23 October 2000 (the day before the Open Debate in the Council), Ambassador Patricia Durrant of Jamaica chaired the Arria Formula meeting on women and peace and security.[109] In 2000, Durrant also served as chair of the UNIFEM Consultative Committee and therefore was "informed by the work of UNIFEM on women in conflicted affected countries world-wide" and "fully briefed" throughout the process of creating UNSCR 1325.[110]

The "purpose of the Arria Formula meeting [on women and peace and security] was to convince the Security Council of the urgency of a strong resolution instead of a presidential statement."[111] Members of the Council informed Iiyambo after the Arria meeting "that they benefited from hearing from those affected, that it makes a difference, to hear about women's role in peacebuilding."[112] According to Heyzer, it was at the Arria meeting that members of the Council realized the urgent need for a Council resolution, as opposed to a declaration or statement.[113]

UNIFEM helped speakers to prepare, to include preparing statements.[114] UNIFEM hosted rehearsals, with Klot in charge, several days prior to the Arria Formula meeting, with "little recommendations on how to convey better their messages."[115]

The main speakers at the Arria Formula meeting included Inonge Mbikusita-Lewanika of the Organization of African Women's Committee on Peace and Democratization and Federation of African Women's Peace Movements, Isha Dyfan of the NGO Coalition/Women's International League for Peace and Freedom (WILPF)—Sierra Leone, Faiza Jama Mohamed of the Africa Office of Equality Now, and Luz Méndez of the National Union of Guatemalan Women.[116] Inonge Mbikusita-Lewanika, in addition to her work for peace in conflict areas, had lit the Peace Torch at the official opening of the Beijing conference and was part of the Zanzibar African Women's Peace Declaration, which Angela King attended.[117] Isha Dyfan addressed sexual violence by male peacekeepers, providing the ECOMOG Mission in Sierra Leone as an example, about which "[i]t was reported [at their departure] that women with their babies lined the runway at the airport calling attention to sexual violence that had occurred."[118] Luz Méndez, the sole woman on the negotiating team of the URNG (Unidad Revolucionaria

Nacional Guatemalteca) at the start of the negotiations in 1991 to end Guatemala's decades-long internal war,[119] succeeded in ensuring that the Guatemalan peace accords addressed the rights of indigenous women,[120] participation by women,[121] the role of women in strengthening civilian power,[122] and equitable participation by women (as a sector requiring specific priority attention).[123] When incorporating "women" provisions into the peace accords, Méndez informed detractors "they needed Guatemalan women to support the accords after signature, and that it would send a very bad message if only the proposals made by women [of the Civil Society Assembly] were excluded."[124] Her recommendations at the Arria Formula meeting included (1) the need for women's participation—"that what they achieved in Guatemala would not have been possible without women at the table" and (2) the need for equal representation of women at the table—"that the UN could ask members of the parties to include women (equally)."[125]

NGO representatives also attended. They included Eugenia Piza Lopes of the NGO Coalition/International Alert, Mary Diaz of the Women's Commission for Refugee Women and Children, Anne Burke of Amnesty International, Cora Weiss of the Hague Appeal for Peace, and Betty Reardon of the International Peace Research Association.[126] Reardon, a peace education scholar, served in 1994 as the Rapporteur of the "Gender and the Agenda for Peace" (GAP) report.[127] Missouri Sherman-Peter of the Bahamas was the Vice-Chair.[128] Today, Ambassador Missouri Sherman-Peter serves as the Permanent Representative of CARICOM (Caribbean Community and Common Market) to the UN.[129]

Maj Britt Theorin, the Chair of the GAP report, opines the GAP report "is the real starting creation of UNSCR 1325" as it contained recommendations and strategies to "increase the participation of women in all aspects related to conflict resolution and peace."[130] GAP recommendations included:

> Gender balance in all UN peace-related activities and the adequate representation of women's perspectives should be assured by including at least 40% women in all peace-keeping, peace making, peace building, preventative diplomacy, and preventative activities including fact-finding and observer missions and in all stages of peace negotiations.[131]

Six years later, on 20 October 2000, EU Committee on Women's Rights and Equal Opportunities, under the leadership of Theorin, then a Member of the EU Parliament and Chair of the EU Committee on Women's Rights and Equal Opportunities, provided the EU with a proposed 12 page resolution on women, peace and security titled "European Parliament resolution on the participation of women in peaceful conflict resolution."[132] Unlike the UN Security Council, the EU Commission put the proposed resolution "in the drawer," rather than sending it on to Parliament.[133] As such, the EU not only failed to lead, but instead blocked, women, peace, and security. However, the EU Committee's proposed resolution may have influenced the drafting of UNSCR 1325. A two-page summary of the proposed EU resolution was part of the summaries of documents compiled by the NGO.[134]

Open debate

At 1030 AM on October 24, 2000, the UN Security Council Open Debate on "women and peace and security" began.[135]

At the table sat the five Permanent Members and the ten Non-permanent Members of the Council, with Namibia sitting as President. All were men except for two: Patricia Durrant (1943-2019) and Nancy Soderberg.

Durrant served as the Permanent Representative of Jamaica to the UN starting in 1995. Jamaica was a Non-permanent member of the Council in the years 2000 and 2001. Durrant was the sole female Permanent Representative to the Council in 2000. Subsequently the UN Secretary-General appointed Durrant at the rank of Assistant Secretary General to serve as the UN Ombudsman (2002-2007).

Soderberg was the Alternative Representative of the US and regularly "was in the seat [in the Council] because [the US Permanent Representative to the UN, Richard Holbrooke] knew there should be a woman at the table."[136] Holbrooke was "a major ally and driving force" for a thematic debate on women and peace and security,[137] a change from the Dayton Peace negotiations, which had failed to include women.[138] Holbrooke's boss was Madeleine Albright, the Secretary of State for the US 2000. Soderberg met Madeleine Albright when Soderberg was a graduate student at Georgetown.[139] When Madeleine Albright started her service as the Permanent Representative of the US to the UN (1993), out of more than 180 States, the only States that sent women as their permanent representative were Canada, Jamaica, Kazakhstan, Liechtenstein, the Philippines, and Trinidad-Tobago, and the US.[140] According to Albright:

> Being American, I naturally proposed we form a caucus, which we did, and suggested that we pledge always to take each other's phone calls. The agreement on instant access upset some male representatives, who didn't think it logical that the ambassador of Liechtenstein could get through to the U.S. ambassador more readily than they could.[141]

Albright's response: "I told them the solution was for them to give up their posts to women, which stopped them cold."[142] Prior to serving at the UN, Soderberg had a career that included being the third ranking official on the US National Security Council.[143]

At the table also sat, as invited guests, Angela King (Assistant Secretary-General and Special Adviser on Gender Issues and Advancement of Women) and Noeleen Heyzer (Executive Director of the United Nations Development Fund for Women). King had served as Chief of Mission in the United Nations Observer Mission in South Africa (UNOMSA), which appears to have had gender parity.[144]

In the seats at the side of the Council Chamber sat over two-dozen individuals representing States that were not members of the Security Council,[145] but who had requested to be on the speaker list.[146] All were men but four: Penny Wensley of Australia, Claudia Fritsche of Liechtenstein, Jelena Grčić Polić of Croatia, and Parliamentarian Krishna Bose of India.

Australia appointed Wensley in 1997 as its first female ambassador to the UN.[147] She later served as Governor of Queensland (2008-2014).[148] Wensley currently is a director of an international think tank.[149]

Liechtenstein appointed Fritsche in 1990 to serve as Liechtenstein's first ambassador to the UN, where she served until 2002.[150] Liechtenstein, like Namibia, became a member of the UN in 1990.[151] Only six years prior to Liechtenstein becoming a member of the UN did a majority of Liechtenstein's men (by a majority of 119 men) vote for suffrage for women, 2370 votes for and 2251 votes against.[152] Earlier referenda in Liechtenstein, in the years 1971 and 1973, voted against women's suffrage.[153]

Croatia appointed Grčić Polić as the Croatian Deputy Permanent Representative in 1998.[154] Grčić Polić was an author of the Windhoek Declaration and the Namibia Plan of Action.

India asked Bose, the Chairperson of the Indian Parliamentary Standing Committee on External Affairs, to deliver India's statement at the Open Debate, "in order for it to carry weight."[155] As of 2020, Bose is the only woman to have chaired the Indian Parliamentary Standing Committee of External/Foreign Affairs.[156]

At the time of the Open Debate, it appears no copy of the working draft UNSCR 1325 had been distributed to non-Members of the Council. In her statement, Wensley remarked: "I have not seen a draft of the resolution that the Council may be planning to adopt, but I hope it … will pick up the practical suggestions that have been put forward today by a number of delegations."[157] Wensley contends that her remark in 2000 about not having seen the draft "didn't mean we – the non-members of the [Council] weren't involved with the drafting/lobbying process. We were. As I recall, the remark was more a dig about the strict [Council] processes."[158] Wensley recalls that several members of the small group of women who were Permanent Representatives worked closely with King and Heyzer in the drafting process, to include her.[159] Wensley maintains that this group was:

> [A]ctively involved with the crafting and adoption of this resolution and … contributed directly to the effort to have the subject brought before the Security Council and discussed in an open meeting of the Council – which meant that countries not members of the Security Council – countries like Australia – could participate and contribute.[160]

Fritsche, while observing the resolution going through the drafting process by the members of the Security Council, tried to obtain details of the draft resolution.[161] Given that "there were no written rules or regulations prohibiting … inspiration from others, non-member States were able to 'indirectly work' with several States on the Council to 'informally' inject the drafting process of UNSCR 1325 with ideas and strong concerns as to what needed to be in the resolution."[162]

The Open Debate acknowledged the contributions of the many individuals leading to the creation of UNSCR 1325, to include: Madeleine Albright;[163] Louise Frechette, Mary Robinson, Sadako Ogata, Carol Bellamy, Catherine Bertini, and Hillary Clinton;[164] Graça Machel;[165] Rani of Jhansi, who "died fighting leading India first War of Independence in 1857," and Kaipkire of the Herero, who "led her people in battles against European slave traders;"[166] Colleen Lowe Morna, Louise Olson, Judith Hicks Stiehm, Maggie Patterson, and Colonel Festus Abo-agye;[167] and Dame Margaret Anstee and Elizabeth Rehn.[168]

A recommendation oft stated in the Open Debate concerned the need to appoint women at the highest civilian levels.[169] In October 2000, of the "61 Special and Personal Representatives and Envoys of the Secretary-General serving in peace support functions," zero were women.[170] As such, it appears that the voices against the exclusion of women from the highest civilian positions in peace operations were shaped by the lived experiences of the diplomats and politicians speaking.

In the gallery overlooking the Security Chamber sat members of civil society. The speakers appreciated these members of civil society. As stated by Soderberg:

> I also want to pay a special welcome to our guests in the gallery. I think your participation and support are very important and I think this is the first time I have ever heard applause in this Chamber. So you are enlivening it.[171]

Grčić Polić concurred: "The enthusiastic response from the gallery is proof that they [Heyzer and King] do make a difference."[172] Wensley recalls that her statement "drew applause – something quite unprecedented within the Council Chamber."[173]

Conclusion

The history of the creation of UNSCR 1325 demonstrates the power of dispa-rate actors fighting for women and peace and security. For those who hesitate to participate, the history of the creation of UNSCR 1325 may dispel the belief that agitating for women and peace and security, while it may be the "right" thing to do, ends careers. As demonstrated throughout this chapter, rather than ending careers, it may propel careers.

I write this chapter to express my gratitude to the creators of UNSCR 1325, through this attempt to crystalize the history of their work. They have given us a great gift. As this chapter concludes, another one opens. In 2019, Namibia announced that it would establish an International Women's Peace Centre,[174] and one year later, on 31 October 2020, opened the Centre.[175] I look forward to the Centre's accomplishments in 2020 and beyond.

Acknowledgement

I thank the individuals who responded to my many questions about their rec-ollections of the history of the creation of UNSCR 1325, to include via in-per-son, Skype, telephone, and/or email (which I describe as "communications"), to include Sanam Naraghi Anderlini, Krishna Bose, Hans Corell, Isha Dyfan, Patri-cia Flor, Claudia Fritsche, Jelena Grčić Polić, Noeleen Heyzer, Swanee Hunt, Aina Iiyambo, Inonge Mbikusita-Lewanika, Luz Méndez, Monica Ndiliawike Nashandi, Eugenia Piza Lopez, Betty Reardon, Judith Hicks Stiehm, Maj Britt Theorin, Peter Wallensteen, Cora Weiss, and Penny Wensley. I thank those who opened doors to individuals and documents, to include Ann Tickner, Carol Cohn, Cora Weiss, Dessislava Gereva, Isha Dyfan, Jane Bayes, Kim Kahnhauser Freeman, Lara Romano, Mavic Cabrera Balleza, Noeleen Heyzer, Selma T.P. Silveira, Sheri Gibbings, Sugata Bose, and Wendy Chmielewski. I thank the UN library and the US Library of Congress for their help and access to materials.

Notes

1   UN Security Council, S/PV.4213 (31 October 2000, 2.10 pm).
2   UN Security Council, S/RES/1325 (31 October 2000).
3   Hans Corell, the Legal Counsel of the United Nations at the time of the adoption of UNSCR 1325, confirms that Council resolutions are enforceable (author communications with Corell, 2019/2020).
4   UN Security Council, "Countries Elected," https://www.un.org/securitycouncil/content/countries-elected-members, accessed 10 January 2020.
5   Martin Andjaba, "Assessment of the Work of the Security Council, The Namibian Presidency," *Global Policy Forum*, August 1999, https://www.globalpolicy.org/component/content/article/185/41110.html, accessed 15 January 2020.
6   The Deputy Prime Minister of Republic of Namibia, Republic of Namibia Office of the Prime Minister, http://www.opm.gov.na/deputy-prime-minister, accessed 10 January 2020.
7   Beijing Declaration and Platform for Action, Strategic Objective E: Women and Armed Conflict (UN Women, 2014, reprint from United Nations, 1995), 87-100, https://www.unwomen.org/-/media/headquarters/attachments/sections/csw/pfa_e_final_web.pdf?la=en&vs=800, accessed 7 February 2020.
8   Deputy Prime Minister, fn 6 *supra*.
9   UN General Assembly, A/RES/54/4, Optional Protocol to the Convention on the Elimination of All Forms of Discrimination Against Women (6 October 1999), Status as of 7 February 2020, https://treaties.un.org/doc/Treaties/1999/10/19991006%2005-18%20AM/Ch_IV_8_bp.pdf, accessed 7 February 2020.
10   Ibid.
11   Author communications with Aina Iiyambo (2019/2020). Soumita Basu appears to write that the "suggestion" occurred around the time of the annual session of the CSW, and that it pertained to "issues relating to 'war and women,'" *see* Soumita Basu, "Security Through Transformations: The Case of the Passage of UN Security Council Resolution 1325 on Women and Peace and Security" (Ph.D. diss., Aberystwyth University, 2009), 174.
12   Deputy Prime Minister, fn 6 *supra*.
13   Statement by Hon. Netumbo Nandi-Ndaitwah, Deputy Prime Minister and Minister of International Relations and Cooperation at the Security Council High Level Debate on Resolution 1325 (13 October 2015) https://www.peacewomen.org/sites/default/files/Hon.%20Sra.%20Netumbo%20Nandi-Ndaitwah%20of%20Namibia%20at%20the%20UN%20Security%20Council%20open%20debate%20on%20WPS_0.pdf, accessed 17 December 2019.
14   Ibid.
15   Peacekeeping UN, Namibia UNTAG Background, https://peacekeeping.un.org/mission/past/untagS.htm, accessed 7 February 2020.
16   Dan Moshenberg, "Namibia: Herero women challenge German amnesia: the 1904-1908 genocide against the Herero is considered the first in the 20th century. Now the surviving descendants want their land back," *The Guardian*, 23 October 2012.
17   UN General Assembly, A/RES/S-9/2 (3 May 1978), para 4.
18   Ibid, para 4.
19   UN Security Council, S/RES/431 (27 July 1978), para 1.

20 UN Security Council, S/RES/435 (29 September 1978), para 3.

21 UN Security Council, S/RES/632 (16 February 1989), para 2.

22 Author communications with Nashandi (2019/2020).

23 Ibid.

24 Communications: Nashandi.

25 Peacekeeping UN, fn 15 *supra*.

26 Cedric Thornberry, *UNTAG experience in Namibia: First Phase* (South African Institute of International Affairs, 1990): np.

27 Ibid.

28 *UNTAG in Namibia, a new nation is born* (UN Transition Assistance Group, 1990): 134.

29 Ibid, 134–135.

30 Ibid, 135.

31 UN Security Council, S/PV.4208 (24 October 2000, 10am), 4.

32 Ibid, 3.

33 Author communications with Grčić Polić (2019/2020).

34 Author communications with Wallensteen (2020).

35 UN News, "Interview: Margaret Anstee – first woman to become UN Under-Secretary-General," 19 September 2016, https://news.un.org/en/story/2016/09/539292-interview-margaret-anstee-first-woman-become-un-under-secretary-general, accessed 18 March 2020.

36 Margaret Anstee, *Never Learn to Type: A Woman at the United Nations* (Wiley, 2003), 466, 469.

37 Ibid, 466, 469.

38 Ibid, 420.

39 Margaret Anstee, "One Woman's Experience at the UN," *UNA-UK Magazine*, 14 March 2012, https://www.una.org.uk/magazine/summer-2011/one-womans-experience-un, accessed 23 May 2019.

40 Communications: Grčić Polić. *See also* Nina Lahoud, "What Fueled the Far-Reaching Impact of the Windhoek Declaration and Namibia Plan of Action as a Milestone for Gender Mainstreaming in UN Peace Support Operations and Where Is Implementation 20 Years Later?", *Journal of International Peacekeeping* (2020): 1-52, doi: https://doi.org/10.1163/18754112-20200005, accessed 17 December 2020.

41 World Affairs Council of Western Michigan "A Conversation with a diplomat: highlights of her global career," *The Rapidian*, 9 January 2017, https://www.therapidian.org/conversation-diplomat-highlights-her-global-career, accessed 7 December 2019.

42 World Affairs Council.

43 Author communications with Steihm (2019/2020).

44 Ibid.

45 Ibid.

46 Ibid.

47 Communications: Wallensteen.

48 Ibid.

49 Letter from the Permanent Representative of Namibia to the United Nations addressed to the Secretary-General, A/55/138-S/2000/693, Annex I (12 July 2000) https://www.un.org/documents/ga/docs/55/a55138.pdf, accessed 12 May 2019.

50 A/55/138–S/2000/693, Annex II.

51 S/PV.4208: 3.

52 Five-year Review of the implementation of the Beijing Declaration and Platform for Action [Beijing + 5] held in the General Assembly, 5 - 9 June 2000, para 35, https://www.un.org/womenwatch/daw/followup/beijing%2B5.htm, accessed 13 May 2019.

53 Ibid, para 124.

54 Ibid, para 13.

55 Paul Rambali, "Introductions" in Phoolan Devi with Marie-Thérèse Cuny and P. Guilford. *The Bandit Queeen of India: an Indian Woman's Amazing Journey from Peasant to International Legend* (Lyons Press, 2003), XI.
56 Phoolan Devi with Marie-Thérèse Cuny and P. Guilford, *The Bandit Queeen of India: an Indian Woman's Amazing Journey from Peasant to International Legend* (Lyons Press, 2003), 493, 495.
57 Ibid at 397, 398, 412.
58 Krishna Bose, *An Outsider in Politics* (Penguin, Viking, 2008), 173.
59 Author communications with Bose (2020).
60 Bose, 175–176.
61 United Nations Division for the Advancement of Women, "Patricia Flor, Chair, Commission on the Status of Women," https://www.un.org/womenwatch/daw/news/flor.htm, accessed 8 February 2020.
62 Author communications with Flor (2019).
63 Ibid.
64 Ibid.
65 Delegation of the European Union to Japan, Message from the Ambassador, https://eeas.europa.eu/delegations/japan/18689/node/18689_en#Message+from+the+Ambassador, accessed 7 February 2020.
66 Sanam Naraghi Anderlini, "Civil Society's Leadership in Adopting 1325 Resolution," in *Oxford Handbook of Women, Peace and Security*, edited by Sara E. Davies and Jacqui True (Oxford University Press, 2019), 49.
67 Wensley (2009).
68 Carol Cohn, Helen Kinsella, and Sherri Gibbings, "Women, Peace and Security – Resolution 1325," *International Journal of Feminist Politics 6:1* (March 2004) 130-140, at 131, https://genderandsecurity.org/sites/default/files/women_peace_and_security_resolution_1325_-_carol_cohn.pdf.
69 Anderlini, 44.
70 Felicity Hill, *"How* and *when* has Security Council resolution 1325 (2000) on Women, Peace and Security impacted negotiations outside the Security Council" (master's thesis, Uppsala, 2005), 29, fn 101.
71 Anderlini, 43.
72 Author communications with Anderlini (2020).
73 Ibid.
74 Cora Weiss, "Cascading Movements for Peace: From Women Strike for Peace to UNSCR 1325," in *Unsettling Debates: Women and Peacemaking*, ed. Suzy Kim, Gwyn Kirk, and M. Brinton Lykes, Social Justice Vol 46 No 1 (2019).
75 Author communications with Heyzer (2019/2020).
76 Ibid.
77 "Coalition on Women and International Peace and Security" to Ambassador Martin Andjaba, Fax dated 18 August 2000, provided to the author by Sheri Gibbings, 2020.
78 Hill: 29–30.
79 NGO Coalition Fax.
80 Ibid.
81 Communications: Heyzer.
82 Ibid.
83 Ibid.
84 Communications: Heyzer.
85 Hill, 30.
86 Ibid, 29.
87 Author communications with Iiyambo (2019/2020).
88 Ibid.
89 Ibid.
90 Ibid.

91 Ibid.

92 Hill, 30.

93 Communications: Iiyambo; *see* UN General Assembly, A/51/306, "Impact of Armed Conflict on Children: Report of the expert of the Secretary-General, Ms. Graça Machel, submitted pursuant to General Assembly resolution 48/157," 26 August 1996, 3-96; *see also* Graça Machel, "The Impact of Armed Conflict on Children: A critical review of progress made and obstacles encountered in increasing protection for war-affected children," September 2000, chapter 15 addresses "Women and the Peace Process."

94 Communications: Iiyambo.

95 Communications: Heyzer.

96 Jennifer Klot, "The United Nations Security Council's agenda on 'Women, Peace and Security': bureaucratic pathologies and unrealised potential" (Ph.D. diss., The London School of Economics and Political Science, 2016), 33.

97 Communications: Iiyambo.

98 Janet Adongo, "Time for Action: Upper Nile Region Governors and Military Commanders Bring Peace to the Table in Malakal Conference," UNMISS, 5 April 2019, https://unmiss.unmissions.org/time-action-upper-nile-region-governors-and-military-commanders-bring-peace-table-malakal-conference, accessed 8 February 2020.

99 Communications: Iiyambo.

100 Hill, 30.

101 Ibid, 30.

102 Ibid, 30, fn 104.

103 Author communications with Hill (2020). Efforts by the author to locate the NGO's draft have included requests to individual members of the NGO, as well as to academics and archives that have engaged with the NGO. At the time of this writing (during COVID-19), a request is pending with the Rockefeller archives, which houses the Ford Foundation records of the NGO.

104 Klot, 92. According to Ambassador Selma Ashipala-Musavyi, "Following the introduction of the theme [on women, peace and security], what followed then was a minute of silence, followed by a mix of laughter, plain astonishment accompanied by sophisticated ridicule." Nekwaya Jileka and Julia Imene-Chanduru, "How Namibia Helped Birth UN Resolution on Women, Peace and Security," *Africa Renewal*, 27 October 2020, https://www.un.org/africarenewal/magazine/october-2020/how-namibia-helped-birth-un-resolution-1325-women-peace-and-security, accessed 17 December 2020.

105 Communications: Iiyambo.

106 Ibid.

107 Ibid.

108 Anderlini, 48.

109 Global Policy Forum, "Arria Formula and Other Proceedings," at 23 October 2000, https://www.globalpolicy.org/security-council/ngos-and-the-council/arria-formula-and-other-un-proceedings.html, accessed 2 December 2019.

110 Communications: Heyzer.

111 Communications: Heyzer. Bangladesh had issued a presidential statement on 8 March 2000. UN, Press Release SC/6816, "Peace Inextricably Linked With Equality Between Women And Men Says Security Council, In International Women's Day Statement," 8 March 2000, https://www.un.org/press/en/2000/20000308.sc6816.doc.html. The Bangladesh Mission, due to internal and external constraints, was unable to provide records, to include "official correspondence," for this chapter. Communication from the Bangladesh Mission to the author (2020).

112 Communications: Iiyambo.

113 Communications: Heyzer.

114 As a result, Heyzer was told she "broke UN rules," that she was "going to be punished." A UN Under-Secretary-General alerted Heyzer she would receive a phone

call posing one question: "Did you 'participate' in the Arria Formula?" and that her response should not employ the word "participate." When Heyzer received the call, Heyzer stated: "I 'introduced' the issue and the women who were going to speak." After the call, push-back, through allegations of "[w]e have evidence and we saw her participate," arose. Heyzer again was alerted that a telephone call was coming. The caller this time stated: "I was told you participated." Heyzer's response: "I introduced." As a result of the pushback from internal actors in the UN, UNIFEM abstained from taking any credit for the creation of UNSCR 1325 (and did not take credit for almost 20 years, until being interviewed for this chapter). Communication: Heyzer.

115 Author communications with Méndez (2020).
116 "Arria Formula," October 23, 2000, fn 109 *supra*.
117 Author communications with Mbikusita-Lewanika (2020).
118 Author communications with Dyfan (2020).
119 Mendez 2008: 224
120 Guatemala, "Agreement on identity and rights of Indigenous Peoples," 31 March 1995, Section II B, para 1.
121 Guatemala, "Agreement on Social and Economic Aspects and Agrarian Situation," 6 May 1996, Section I B, paras 11–13.
122 Guatemala, "Agreement on the Strengthening of Civilian Power and on the Role of the Armed Forces in a Democratic Society," 19 September 1996, Section IV.
123 Guatemala, "Agreement on the Basis for the Legal Integration of the Unidad Revolucionaria Nacional Guatemalteca," 12 December 1996, Section II, para 12.
124 Communications: Méndez.
125 Ibid.
126 "Arria Formula," October 23, 2000, fn 109 *supra*.
127 Division for the Advancement of Women/Secretariat for the Fourth World Conference on Women, Department for Policy Coordination and Sustainable Development, Expert Group Meeting: Gender and the Agenda For Peace, GAP/1994/1 (5–9 December 1994) para 40.
128 Ibid, para 40.
129 CARICOM, "$1.5 Billion in recovery funding and in-kind services pledged at Hurricane Dorian conference," 14 January 2020, https://today.caricom.org/2020/01/14/1-5-billion-in-recovery-funding-and-in-kind-services-pledged-at-hurricane-dorian-conference, accessed 21 January 2020.
130 Author communications with Theorin (2019).
131 GAP/1994/1, para 29.1.2.1.
132 EU Parliament, A5-0308/2000, Committee on Women's Rights and Equal Opportunities, Report on participation of women in peaceful conflict resolution (2000/2025(INI)): 5-12, http://www.europarl.europa.eu/sides/getDoc.do?pubRef=-//EP//NONSGML+REPORT+A5-2000-0308+0+DOC+PDF+V0//EN&language=EN (accessed 13 May 2019).
133 Communications: Theorin.
134 Copy of summaries provided to author by Sheri Gibbings. Gibbings wrote a history of the creation of UNSCR 1325 in 2004. Gibbings used pseudonyms stating, "Most individuals I interviewed consented to the use of their names in my research, but, at my discretion, the names of individuals have either been changed, or, in some cases, comments have not been attributed to any specific person." Sheri Gibbings, "Governing Women, Governing Security: Governmentality, Gender Mainstreaming and Women's Activism at the UN" (master's thesis, York University, Toronto, Canada, September 2004), fn 27, https://central.bac-lac.gc.ca/.item?id=mq99312&op=pdf&app=Library, accessed 14 March 2020.
135 S/PV.4208.
136 Author communications with Soderberg (2020).
137 Wensley (2009).
138 Author communications with Hunt (2020).

139   Nancy Soderberg, *The Superpower Myth: The Use And Misuse Of American Might* (John Wiley, 2005), 15.

140   Madeleine Albright, *Madame Secretary: A Memoir* (Hyperion, 2003), 195.

141   Ibid, 195.

142   Ibid, 195.

143   Soderberg, *Superpower Myth*, 16.

144   Judith Stiehm, "Peacekeeping: A New Role for Women Seeking Peace" in *Towards A Women's Agenda For A Culture of Peace*, ed. Ingeborg Breines, Dorota Gierycz and Betty A. Reardon (UNESCO Publishing, 1999), 136.

145   S/PV.4208: 2 and 4; S/PV.4208 (Resumption 1): 4.

146   UN Security Council, Provisional Rules of Procedure, Rule 37 of the Council's Rules of Procedure.

147   Women's Museum of Australia, "Penelope Ann Wensley," https://wmoa.com.au/her-story2017/woman/wensley-penelope-anne, accessed 21 August 2020.

148   Lowy Institute, "Penny Wensley," https://www.lowyinstitute.org/people/executive-directors/bio/penny-wensley, accessed 17 January 2020.

149   Lowy.

150   Author communications with Fritche (2019/2020).

151   United Nations, "Growth in United Nations membership, 1945-present," https://www.un.org/en/sections/member-states/growth-united-nations-membership-1945-present/index.html, accessed 17 January 2020.

152   "AROUND THE WORLD; Liechtenstein Women Win Right to Vote," *The New York Times*, 2 July 1984, https://www.nytimes.com/1984/07/02/world/around-the-world-liechtenstein-women-win-right-to-vote.html, accessed 17 January 2020.

153   Ibid.

154   Communications: Grčić Polić.

155   Communications: Bose.

156   Ibid.

157   S/PV.4208 (Resumption 1): 29.

158   Author communications with Wensley (2020).

159   Ibid.

160   Penelope Wensley speech, Women's International League for Peace and Freedom Triennial Conference on "Women, Peace and Sustainable Futures," 23 May 2009, https://webarchive.nla.gov.au/wayback/20140728225141/http:/pandora.nla.gov.au/pan/32459/20140729-0004/www.govhouse.qld.gov.au/the_governor/090523_wilpf.aspx (accessed 11 February 2020).

161   Communications: Fritsche.

162   Ibid.

163   S/PV.4208: 12.

164   Ibid, 13.

165   Ibid at 9 and 10.

166   S/PV.4208 (Resumption 1): 19.

167   Ibid, 30.

168   Ibid, 31.

169   King, Durrant, and Soderberg at S/PV.4208: 6, 11, and 13; Bose and Wensley at S/PV.4208 Resumption 1: 20 and 28.

170   S/PV.4208: 8.

171   S/PV.4208: 12.

172   S/PV.4208 (Resumption 1): 29.

173   Wensley 2009.

174   Republic of Namibia, Ministry of International Relations and Cooperation, *Concept Note: Establishment of the International Women's Peace Centre in Namibia* (2019).

175   "Namibia: Welcoming Remarks at the Launch of the International Women's Peace Centre," *All Africa*, 31 October 2020, https://allafrica.com/stories/202011040983.html, accessed 17 December 2020.

Bibliography

Adongo, Janet. "Time for Action: Upper Nile Region Governors and Military Commanders Bring Peace to the Table in Malakal Conference." *UNMISS*, 5 April 2019. https://unmiss. unmissions.org/time-action-upper-nile-region-governors-and-military-commanders-bring-peace-table-malakal-conference

Albright, Madeleine. *Madame Secretary: A Memoir*. Miramax/Hyperion, New York, 2003.

Anderlini, Sanam Naraghi. "Civil Society's Leadership in Adopting 1325 Resolution." In *Oxford Handbook of Women, Peace and Security*, edited by Sara E. Davies and Jacqui True. Oxford University Press, Oxford, 2019.

Andjaba, Martin. "Assessment of the Work of the Security Council, The Namibian Presidency." *Global Policy Forum*, August 1999. https://www.globalpolicy.org/component/content/article/185/41110.html.

Anstee, Margaret. *Never Learn to Type: A Woman at the United Nations*. Wiley, Chichester, West Sussex, 2003.

Anstee, Margaret. "One Woman's Experience at the UN." *UNA-UK Magazine*, 14 March 2012. https://www.una.org.uk/magazine/summer-2011/one-womans-experience-un.

AROUND THE WORLD. "AROUND THE WORLD; Liechtenstein Women Win Right to Vote." *The New York Times*, 2 July 1984. https://www.nytimes.com/1984/07/02/world/around-the-world-liechtenstein-women-win-right-to-vote.html.

Basu, Soumita. "Security Through Transformations: The Case of the Passage of UN Security Council Resolution 1325 on Women and Peace and Security." Ph.D. diss., Aberystwyth University, 2009.

Beijing Declaration and Platform for Action. Strategic Objective E: Women and Armed Conflict (UN Women, 2014, reprint from United Nations, 1995) 87–100. https://www.unwomen.org/-/media/headquarters/attachments/sections/csw/pfa_e_final_web.pdf?la=en&vs=800.

Bose, Krisha. *An Outsider in Politics*. Penguin, Viking, 2008.

CARICOM. "$1.5 Billion in recovery funding and in-kind services pledged at Hurricane Dorian conference," 14 January 2020. https://today.caricom.org/2020/01/14/1-5-billion-in-recovery-funding-and-in-kind-services-pledged-at-hurricane-dorian-conference.

Coalition on Women and International Peace and Security to Namibia Ambassador Martin Andjaba. Fax (18 August 2000). Provided to the author by Sheri Gibbings, 2020.

Cohn, Carol, Helen Kinsella, and Sherri Gibbings, "Women, Peace and Security – Resolution 1325," *International Journal of Feminist Politics* 6:1 (March 2004) 130–140. https://genderandsecurity.org/sites/default/files/women_peace_and_security_resolution_1325_-_carol_cohn.pdf.

Delegation of the European Union to Japan, Message from the Ambassador, https://eeas.europa.eu/delegations/japan/18689/node/18689_en#Message+from+the+Ambassador.

Deputy Prime Minister of Republic of Nambia. *Republic of Namibia Office of the Prime Minister*. 2020. http://www.opm.gov.na/deputy-prime-minister, accessed January 10 2020.

Devi, Phoolan with Marie-Thérèse Cuny and P. Guilford, *The Bandit Queeen of India: an Indian Woman's Amazing Journey from Peasant to International Legend*. Lyons Press, Guilford, Conneticut, 2003.

Division for the Advancement of Women/Secretariat for the Fourth World Conference on Women, Department for Policy Coordination and Sustainable Development. Expert Group Meeting: Gender and the Agenda For Peace, GAP/1994/1 (5–9 December 1994).

EU Parliament, A5-0308/2000, Committee on Women's Rights and Equal Opportunities, Report on participation of women in peaceful conflict resolution (2000/2025(INI)). (n.d.) http://www.europarl.europa.eu/sides/getDoc.do?pubRef=-//EP//NONSGML+REPORT+A5-2000-0308+0+DOC+PDF+V0//EN&language=EN.

Five-year Review of the implementation of the Beijing Declaration and Platform for Action [Beijing + 5] held in the General Assembly, 5–9 June 2000. https://www.un.org/womenwatch/daw/followup/beijing%2B5.htm.

Gibbings, Sheri. "Governing Women, Governing Security: Governmentality, Gender Mainstreaming and Women's Activism at the UN." *Master's thesis*, York University, Toronto, Canada, September 2004.

Global Policy Forum. "*Arria Formula and Other Proceedings*," 23 October 2000. https://www.globalpolicy.org/security-council/ngos-and-the-council/arria-formula-and-other-un-proceedings.html.

Guatemala. "Agreement on identity and rights of Indigenous Peoples, 31 March 1995.

Guatemala. "Agreement on Social and Economic Aspects and Agrarian Situation," 6 May 1996a.

Guatemala. "Agreement on the Strengthening of Civilian Power and on the Role of the Armed Forces in a Democratic Society," 19 September 1996b.

Guatemala. "Agreement on the Basis for the Legal Integration of the Unidad Revolucionaria Nacional Guatemalteca," 12 December 1996c.

Hill, Felicity. "*How* and *when* has Security Council resolution 1325 (2000) on Women, Peace and Security impacted negotiations outside the Security Council." Master's thesis, Uppsala, 2005.

Jileka, Nekwaya and Julia Imene-Chanduru. "How Namibia Helped Birth UN Resolution on Women, Peace and Security." *Africa Renewal*, 27 October 2020. https://www.un.org/africarenewal/magazine/october-2020/how-namibia-helped-birth-un-resolution-1325-women-peace-and-security, accessed December 17 2020.

Klot, Jennifer. "The United Nations Security Council's agenda on 'Women, Peace and Security': Bureaucratic pathologies and unrealised potential." Ph.D. diss., The London School of Economics and Political Science, 2015.

Lahoud, Nina. "What Fueled the Far-Reaching Impact of the Windhoek Declaration and Namibia Plan of Action as a Milestone for Gender Mainstreaming in UN Peace Support Operations and Where Is Implementation 20 Years Later?" *Journal of International Peacekeeping* (2020): 1–52, doi: 10.116./18754112-20200005.

Letter from the Permanent Representative of Namibia to the United Nations addressed to the Secretary-General, A/55/138-S/2000/693, Annex I (12 July 2000). https://www.un.org/documents/ga/docs/55/a55138.pdf.

Lowy Institute, "Penny Wensley." https://www.lowyinstitute.org/people/executive-directors/bio/penny-wensley.

Machel, Graça. "The Impact of Armed Conflict on Children: A critical review of progress made and obstacles encountered in increasing protection for war-affected children," September 2000.

Moshenberg, Dan. "Namibia: Herero women challenge German amnesia: the 1904-1908 genocide against the Herero is considered the first in the 20th century. Now the surviving descendants want their land back." *The Guardian*, 23 October 2012.

"Namibia: Welcoming Remarks at the Launch of the International Women's Peace Centre." *All Africa*, 31 October 2020. https://allafrica.com/stories/202011040983.html, accessed December 17 2020.

Nandi-Ndaitwah, Hon. Netumbo (Statement). Deputy Prime Minister and Minister of International Relations and Cooperation at the Security Council High Level Debate on Resolution 1325 (13 October 2015). https://www.peacewomen.org/sites/default/ files/Hon.%20Sra.%20Netumbo%20Nandi-Ndaitwah%20of%20Namibia%20at%20 the%20UN%20Security%20Council%20open%20debate%20on%20WPS_0.pdf.

Rambali, Paul. "Introductions" in Phoolan Devi with Marie-Thérèse Cuny and P. Guilford. *The Bandit Queeen of India: an Indian Woman's Amazing Journey from Peasant to International Legend*. Lyons Press, 2003.

Republic of Nambia. Ministry of International Relations and Cooperation, *Concept Note: Establishment of the International Women's Peace Centre in Namibia* (2019).

Soderberg, Nancy. *The Superpower Myth: The Use and Misuse of American Might*. John Wiley & Sons, Hoboken, N.J, 2005.

Stiehm, Judith. "Peacekeeping: A New Role for Women Seeking Peace" in *Towards A Women's Agenda For A Culture of Peace*, ed. Ingeborg Breines, Dorota Gierycz and Betty A. UNESCO Publishing, Reardon, 1999.

Thornberry, Cedric. *UNTAG experience in Namibia: First Phase*. South African Institute of International Affairs, 1990.

UN. *"Growth in United Nations membership, 1945-present."* (n.d.). https://www.un.org/ en/sections/member-states/growth-united-nations-membership-1945-present/index. html.

UN Division for the Advancement of Women. *"Patricia Flor, Chair, Commission on the Status of Women."* https://www.un.org/womenwatch/daw/news/flor.htm.

UN General Assembly. A/RES/S-9/2 (3 May 1978).

UN General Assembly. A/RES/54/4, Optional Protocol to the Convention on the Elimination of All Forms of Discrimination Against Women (6 October 1999). Status as of 7 February 2020. https://treaties.un.org/doc/Treaties/1999/10/19991006%20 05-18%20AM/Ch_IV_8_bp.pdf.

UN General Assembly. A/51/306, "Impact of Armed Conflict on Children: Report of the expert of the Secretary-General, Ms. Graça Machel, submitted pursuant to General Assembly resolution 48/157" (26 August 1996).

UN News. *"Interview: Margaret Anstee – first woman to become UN Under-Secretary-General"* (19 September 2016). https://news.un.org/en/story/2016/09/539292-interview-margaret-anstee-first-woman-become-un-under-secretary-general.

UN Peacekeeping. *Namibia UNTAG Background*. (n.d.). https://peacekeeping.un.org/ mission/past/untagS.htm.

UN, Press Release SC/6816, *"Peace Inextricably Linked With Equality Between Women And Men Says Security Council, In International Women's Day Statement"* (8 March 2000). https://www.un.org/press/en/2000/20000308.sc6816.doc.html.

UN Security Council. *"Countries Elected."* (n.d.-a). https://www.un.org/securitycouncil/ content/countries-elected-members.

UN Security Council. Provisional Rules of Procedure, Rule 37 of the Council's Rules of Procedure. (n.d.-b).

UN Security Council, S/RES/431 (27 July 1978a).

UN Security Council, S/RES/435 (29 September 1978b).

UN Security Council, S/RES/632 (16 February 1989).

UN Security Council, S/PV.4208 (24 October 2000a, 10 am).

UN Security Council, S/PV.4208 (Resumption 1) (24 October 2000b, 3.15 pm)

UN Security Council, S/PV.4213 (31 October 2000c, 2.10 pm).

UN Security Council. S/RES/1325 (31 October 2000d).

UN Transition Assistance Group. *UNTAG in Namibia, a New Nation is Born*. 1990.

World Affairs Council of Western Michigan. "A Conversation with a diplomat: highlights of her global career." *The Rapidian*, 9 January 2017. https://www.therapidian.org/conversation-diplomat-highlights-her-global-career.

Weiss, Cora. "Cascading Movements for Peace: From Women Strike for Peace to UNSCR 1325." In *Unsettling Debates: Women and Peacemaking*, ed. Suzy Kim, Gwyn Kirk, and M. Brinton Lykes, Social Justice 46 no 1 (2019).

Wensley, Penelope. *Women's International League for Peace and Freedom Triennial Conference on "Women, Peace and Sustainable Futures"* (23 May 2009). https://webarchive.nla.gov.au/wayback/20140728225141/http:/pandora.nla.gov.au/pan/32459/20140729-0004/www.govhouse.qld.gov.au/the_governor/090523_wilpf.aspx (accessed February 11 2020).

10 Commentary

The restorative archeology of knowledge about the role of women in the history of the UN – Theoretical implications for international relations

Rebecca Adami, Dan Plesch and Amitav Acharya

The role of women in the history of the United Nations should be seen in the context of emerging and re-emerging debates in International History and International Relations. A cartoon of the problem characterizes international history as lacking in theoretical self-consciousness and fearful of the contamination of contemporary relevance to policy and social practice. International Relations on the other hand is beset by increasingly reified theories distant from empiricism.[1] The original term of Michel Foucault, Archeology, is a form of discourse analysis to analyze continuities and discontinuities of thought.[2] The term also creates thoughts of the historical school of study rather than of political science. Thus, the term bridges disciplines. The word restorative carries both the archaeological meaning of an object for study and appreciation, but also a sense of buried treasure to illuminate and empower the contemporary world. At the present time politics contains both efforts to advance human rights—not least women's rights and the development of organized global humanity and also a profound reaction towards patriarchal tribalism. The works in this volume revisit the foundational period of global organizations—specifically the United Nations. They demonstrate empirically and theorize a far richer reality of global feminisms in this foundational period than has previously been recognized either by feminist scholarship or by traditional historical and international relations discourses.

By unearthing the hidden history of women in shaping human rights internationally through the UN, we gain important insights into how women from the Global South—although in minority in UN bodies and in their own delegations—not only historically sat "at the table" but were architects of "the table" at which Member States now sit in the United Nations today. The inclusion of gender equality in the UN Charter, of women's rights in the UDHR, the adoption of the first two international conventions on the rights in marriage and of political rights of women, the adoption of the CEDAW, and more recently of the Resolution 1325 in the Security Council on the participation of women in peace constitute a hegemonic norm on gender equality for international relations and broader global society. The evidence in this volume fills the absence of recognition of the intellectual thought of women of colour in international politics and

DOI: 10.4324/9781003036708-10

in the making of world politics through the United Nations, countering the false impression in the history of IR that Patricia Owens has argued against, namely that women in the history of world politics did not think seriously about international politics.[3] The hegemonic norm on gender equality that exists today was made possible through the work of non-Western feminists at the founding of the UN in the post-war years.[4] Torild Skard, a pioneer in addressing the gap in earlier research on the role of women from Latin America at the founding of the UN, recalls that while her own mother Åse Gruda Skard took an "intermediate" position on advancing women's rights in 1945 together with the Chinese delegate Wu Yi-fang, the Latin American women delegates headed by Bertha Lutz made sure that gender equality was included in the Charter.[5] The Latin American feminists had experience of international politics and negotiations from the Pan-American conferences, and they were disappointed in the Dumbarton Oaks agreement for not having included women's human rights and anti-racism.[6] The women from India and Pakistan who took part in deliberations concerning human rights in the UDHR were prominent political leaders active in anti-colonial struggles and the UN, as Khushi notes, was not their first appearance internationally. The role of international feminism during the early Cold War period has been simplified in earlier accounts as mired in dichotomies obscuring links between welfarism and feminism on the one hand and internationalism and feminism on the other.[7] By advancing the concept of "international welfare feminism" Adami argues that the role of Southern women delegates in the UN who advanced women's economic rights should not be conceptualized as caught in East-West ideologies but rather connected to a feminist international agency against patriarchal and colonial structures that limited women's rights. Nationalist ideologies have come to overshadow these vital narratives on women's rights and freedoms. The conceptualization of "international welfare feminism" further questions the assumption that Western feminism was internationalized through the UN; the push for economic and social rights by Southern feminists, as through the Indian National Trade Union Congress and elsewhere, speak about agency in international relations in a new inspiring way. The scope of agency in International Relations, as Amitav Acharya eloquently demonstrates in earlier work, needs to continue to be recast; and this is where the hidden historical narrative of feminist agency from the Global South in the UN provide us with contestations of the dominant narrative which opens space for analyzing the diverse foundations of the global order.[8] These women delegates were not, as we have seen, passive recipients of Western values and norms but rather had the agency to bring about change.[9]

The historical accounts of non-Western women in the UN provide a case for expanding Amitav's earlier conception of agency as not only including male agency from the Global South in the post-war period who used the UN to strengthen the voice of newly independent states but non-Western women politicians as well. Roland Burke[10] discloses that among the earliest travelling advisory seminars on human rights of the UN, assembling in Bangkok, Bogotá Addis Ababa, and Lomé, were those devoted to questions of women's freedoms and welfare. International feminism in the Cold War years was, as noticeable from the angles studied in this volume, marked by anti-colonialism and anti-patriarchal intellectual thought of women. The Peruvian feminist Carmela Aguilar with her Incan heritage argued for the supremacy of the UDHR over prejudice and tradition in order not to deprive women of their fundamental rights.[11] Aoife O'Donoghue and Adam Rowe in this volume demonstrate how the post-colonial context in the 1970s (the New International Economic Order, the Non-Alignment Movement, and the Group 77) meant an increasingly significant voice in international conferences[12] in their exploration of the first inter-governmental global conference to focus on women; the Mexico Conference in 1975. This shift in power led to a heightened concern in the mid-1980s regarding Western moral imperialism when Ethiopian rights activist Berhane Ras-Work—representing the Inter-African Committee on Traditional Practices Affecting the Health of Women and Children—crafted with Save the Children a proposal to eradicate harmful traditional practices that she refused to conflate with cultural or religious practices but as indicative of a global patriarchal structure.[13] This volume hence sets the last 70 decades of the UN in a different, and inspiring light, by giving long-sought after kudos to the women architects of gender equality in key UN resolutions, declarations, and conventions. Ellen Chesler provides historical context to the drafting of DEDAW and CEDAW crediting two women as principal architects of the declaration and the convention respectively, Annie Jiagge (Ghana) and Leticia Shahani (the Philippines). As Chesler notes in her conclusion; "the all too common characterization of women's rights as a western invention, imposed on innocents elsewhere in the world, is not only wrong but also insulting."[14] One would not but agree as the history of focal UN documents, treaties, and conventions on women's human rights in this volume unfold as fundamentally other than western imperialism. Cornelia Weiss continues this unfolding of UN history into a new millennium as she unearths the role of Namibia behind the first draft for the Security Council Resolution 1325 and the role of women leaders Selma Ndeyapo Ashipala-Musavyi, the Deputy Permanent Representative of Namibia, and First Secretary Aina Liyambo.[15]

The agency of women in International Relations, explored in this volume, in how they brought about change in key UN documents, was possible through the representation of feminists from the Global South at the table. As the authors of these chapters remind us, women have constituted a minority in International Relations and had to form a caucus to achieve change (see intro note on the Charter, chap 1 and 2 on the women and the Charter, chap 4 on the CSW, chap 9 on female Permanent Representatives in 1990s).[16]

Varieties of agency

Agency refers to the will and capacity to create or contribute. One of the important insights of the emerging literature on global governance and multilateralism is what Acharya has called the "pluralization of agency". Agency should not be equated with states, or organized non-state actors, but also individual women and men. While these individuals may be working for, or associated with governments, inter-governmental organizations or NGOs, they do leave their own distinctive mark on international agreements and institutions which may not necessarily reflect the positions of the organizations they work for. In this volume, a number of outstanding examples of such acts of agency by women have been discussed.

In addition, agency is pluralized in a variety of ways: broadly stated, these include (1) Agency through dissent and resistance to mainstream ideas and rules of the day, championed by influential figures or governments they represent, and the offering of alternative ideas and norms; (2) Agency of weak states and their representatives, as opposed to the agency of powerful nations and their represent-atives; (3) Agency by proposing new ideas and norms even if their backers may not have the power to propagate and enforce them; and (4) Agency that focuses not on location of the agent when they create or modify the norm, but the location of their origins or where their ideas were initially formed.

This volume offers multiple illustrations of such agency by women in the building of the UN system. One example of the first form of agency is the chal-lenge made by Indian representative to the UN Commission on Human Rights, Hansa Mehta, to the Chair of the UDHR drafting Committee, Eleanor Roosevelt, which led to the language of the UDHR being changed from "all men are created equal" to "all humans".[17] Another case is how Bertha Lutz (Brazil) argued for the importance of women to be able to hold the same positions as men in the UN-sys-tem, through Article 8 in the UN Charter in opposition to Virginia Gildersleeve (US) who thought women should not "ask for too much."[18]

The second form of agency is exemplified by how Annie Jiagge (Ghana) and Leticia Shahani (the Philippines) wrote key drafts of the initial articles on wom-en's rights in the DEDAW and the CEDAW while representing weaker states in comparison to other Member States represented in the CSW.[19] Other foundational role models are Selma Ndeyapo Ashipala-Musavyi (Namibia) and Aina Liyambo (Namibia) who played pivotal roles in international legislation and norm-setting on gender equality through UN Resolution 1235 while Namibia was UN Security Council member only 1999–2000 in contrast to the much more powerful five permanent members to the Council (China, US, Russia, France, and the UK) and to the rather better publicized work of US funded NGOs.[20]

The third form of agency can be illustrated through the articulation of gender equality and substantive rights by the first women representatives of independent India; Vijaya Lakshmi Pandit, Hansa Mehta, Shareefah Hamid Ali, and Lakshmi Menon who advocated human rights without discrimination based on their per-sonal convictions that the UN should develop international legal machinery to uphold respect for human rights in newly independent Member States and for-mer colonial powers alike.[21] Another example of the third form of agency can be found in the work against traditional abuses of women by Begum Rana Liaquat Ali Khan (Pakistan), Badia Afnan (Iraq) and Aziza Hussein (Egypt) who ques-tioned dominant patriarchal narratives that denied women rights in the countries they represented while advocating for progressive feminism in the UN as a way to influence national policies and legislation through international pressure.[22]

Lastly, the fourth form of agency is epitomized by the international advocacy for gender equality that Minerva Bernardino (the Dominican Republic) accomplished with the first international Convention on the Political Rights of Women approved in 1952 by the UN General Assembly under her leadership as chair of CSW (preceding the CEDAW by 27 years). Bernardino was born in the Dominican Republic but lived in Washington and shifted in her UN engagement between acting in the capacity of delegate representative and as Chair to the Inter American Commission on Women, to avoid the limitations and constraints that came from representing an autocracy at the UN.[23] Leticia Shahani (the Philippines) by her crucial influence on the CEDAW is another example of the fourth form of agency. Shahani had moved to and was living in the US with her husband, a Karachi born intellectual, while still representing the Philippines which was also part of the powerful alliance of the Group of 77 non-aligned Nations (G77) at the UN.[24]

The women named in this volume may be seen as not representative of women around the globe while they constituted a rather privileged section of societies through their official capacity, and others through their affiliation with international NGOs. The ambition of international diplomacy work through the UN that this volume speaks of, nevertheless, is to generate local change through international norm-setting on women's human rights. Re-thinking IR not only distinguishes these important forms of agency newly restored; but conceptualizes political space beyond a global/local divide in how people act for change. "[A] political space does not emerge solely between individuals who are equal in formal and legal terms, but (…) equal in dignity though lacking in rights."[25] The limitations with interpreting the actions of individual's in the history of the UN through solely their formal representation, their country of origin, their gender, and other social categorizations concern the ways in which identity politics obscures more relational, contextual and complex reasons for igniting change. More research is needed on the many local actors and individuals who have advocated human rights on occasion at a global level through their personal commitments based on their rooted experiences.

Acharya engages in his work on agency with individual actors outside the UN system who bring together all four types of agency, for example Wangari Maathai (1940–2011). She was the winner of the 2004 Noble Peace Prize for her work in sustainable development that led to the Greenbelt movement that she had founded in 1977. Maathi was born in poverty and became a dissenter against her own government. Her advocacy of reforestation led to threats from the Kenyan government to send her to prison. She lacked material resources to launch her movement but found support from Kenyan people and some members of the international community.

Some Western analysts think that while the ideas coming from scholars and practitioners in the Global South such as Maathai which lead to the creation of new norms and institutions are possible only because they were trained in Western academic institutions, and/or worked for international institutions based in the West and led by Westerners.

Such denial of Global South agency is based on flawed logic. Maathai was trained in the US (University of Pittsburg) and did receive political backing and financial resources from countries such as Canada. Nonetheless, her ideas and campaigns were deeply rooted in her childhood experience in Kenya. Maathai developed the ideas of planting millions of trees to rejuvenate the forests around Nairobi lost to urbanization as a solution to Kenyan women's lack of rights. These women were facing severe financial and social hardship because of their inability to find supplies of firewood due to deforestation. Hence Maathai reasoned that bringing the trees back would improve women's livelihood and the society as a whole:

> The trees would provide a supply of wood that would allow women to cook nutritious foods. They would also have the wood for fencing and fodder for cattle and goats. The trees would offer shade for humans and animals, protect watersheds and bind the soil, and, if they were food trees, provide food. They would also heal the land by bringing back birds and small animals and regenerate the vitality of the earth.[26]

This Maathai's work demonstrated "how traditional survival techniques such as intercropping and agroforestry can be inexpensively resurrected through women's special skills."[27]

Notwithstanding their Western training or workplace, multilateralists as Maathai from the Global South act from the script that was originally developed in the place of their upbringing. The ideas of human development and human security were proposed by Mahbub ul Haq and Amartya Sen, with Haq's wife, Dr Khadija Haq, a noted development economist in her own right. While these ideas were articulated through their association with the United Nations Development Program (UNDP), there is no question that they were rooted in their place of origins, South Asia, and the experience of famines and violence of the partition of the sub-continent.

The authors' skillful archaeological work restores to glory the work of women of prior generations from the Global South that may be inspirational to countless of their descendents still experiencing the world in a manner that Sator describes with such telling precision.

Notes

1 see Amitav Acharya and Dan Plesch, "The United Nations: Managing and Reshaping a Changing World Order" (2020 Annual Meeting - UN @75: The Future of Partnership and Multilaterism, London Metropolitan University, UK, 2020).
2 Michael Foucault, *The Archeology of Knowledge*, trans. A.M. Sheridan Smith (London : New York: Routledge, 2002).
3 See Singh Rathore, 'Excavating Hidden Histories', this volume, ch. 3.
4 See Dietrichson and Sator 'The Latin American Women', this volume, ch. 2.
5 See Skard 'Learning journey for a feminist', this volume, Introductory note.
6 See Marino 'From Women's Rights to Human Rights', this volume, ch. 1.
7 See Adami 'International Welfare Feminism', this volume, ch. 4.

8 Amitav Acharya, *Constructing Global Order: Agency and Change in World Politics* (New York: Cambridge University Press, 2018).

9 Acharya.

10 See Burke 'Universal Human Rights for Women', this volume, ch. 5.

11 Ibid.

12 See O'Donoghue and Rowe 'Feminism, Global Inequality and the 1975 Mexico City Conference', this volume, ch. 6.

13 See Lindkvist 'Where Children's Rights Ever a Feminist Project?', this volume, ch. 8.

14 Chesler 'Who Wrote CEDAW?', this volume, ch. 7, p.

15 See Weiss 'Creating UNSCR 1325', this volume, ch. 9.

16 See Skard 'Learning journey for a feminist', this volume, Introductory note; Marino 'From Women's Rights to Human Rights', this volume, ch. 1; Dietrichson and Sator 'The Latin American Women', this volume, ch. 2; Adami 'International Welfare Feminism', this volume, ch. 4; and Weiss 'Creating the UNSCR 1325', this volume, ch. 9.

17 Rebecca Adami, *Women and the Universal Declaration of Human Rights* (New York & London: Routledge, 2019). See also Khushi Rathore, 'Excavating Hidden Histories', this volume, ch. 3.

18 Adami; Katherine Marino, *Feminism for the Americas: The Making of an International Human Rights Movement* (Chapel Hill & London: The University of North Carolina Press, 2019). See also Dietrich Luhr and Sator 'The Latin American Women', this volume, ch. 2.

19 See Chesler 'Who Wrote CEDAW', this volume, ch. 7.

20 See Weiss 'Creating the UNSCR 1325', this volume, ch. 9.

21 See Khushi Rathore 'Excavating Hidden Histories', this volume, ch. 3.

22 See Burke 'Universal Human Rights for Women', this volume, ch. 5.

23 Adami, *Women and the Universal Declaration of Human Rights*; Marino, *Feminism for the Americas: The Making of an International Human Rights Movement*; Ellen DuBois and Lauren Derby, "The Strange Case of Minerva Bernardino: Pan American and United Nations Women's Right Activist," *Women's Studies International Forum* 32, no. 1 (January 2009): 43–50, https://doi.org/10.1016/j.wsif.2009.01.005. See Skard 'Learning journey for a feminist', this volume, introductory note; Marino 'From Women's Rights to Human Rights', this volume, ch. 1; Dietrich Luhr and Sator 'The Latin American Women', this volume, ch. 2; Burke 'Universal Human Rights for Women', this volume, ch. 5.

24 See Chesler 'Who Wrote CEDAW?', this volume, ch. 7.

25 Rebecca Adami, "Human Rights For More Than One Voice: Re-Thinking Political Space Beyond the Local/Global Divide," *Ethics & Global Politics* 7, no. 4 (2014): 176.

26 Wangari Maathai, cited in Amitav Acharya, "'Idea-shift': How Ideas From the Rest are Reshaping Global Order," *Third World Quarterly*, vol. 37, no. 7 (2016), p. 1166.

27 Wangari Maathai, cited in Acharya, "'Idea-shift'". p. 1166.

Bibliography

Acharya, Amitav. *Constructing Global Order: Agency and Change in World Politics.* New York: Cambridge University Press, 2018.

Acharya, Amitav, and Dan Plesch. *"The United Nations: Managing and Reshaping a Changing World Order."* UK: London Metropolitan University, 2020.

Adami, Rebecca. "Human Rights For More Than One Voice: Re-Thinking Political Space Beyond the Local/Global Divide." *Ethics & Global Politics* 7, no. 4 (2014): 163–180.

Adami, Rebecca. *Women and the Universal Declaration of Human Rights.* New York & London: Routledge, 2019.

DuBois, Ellen, and Lauren Derby. "The Strange Case of Minerva Bernardino: Pan American and United Nations Women's Right Activist." *Women's Studies International Forum* 32, no. 1 (January 2009): 43–50. https://doi.org/10.1016/j.wsif.2009.01.005.

Foucault, Michael. *The Archeoslogy of Knowledge*. Translated by A.M. Sheridan Smith. London: New York: Routledge, 2002.

Marino, Katherine. *Feminism for the Americas: The Making of an International Human Rights Movement*. Chapel Hill & London: The University of North Carolina Press, 2019.

Index

Page numbers in n indicate notes.

Advisory Committee on Traffic in Women and Children 90
Aduke Moore, Jaiyeola (Nigeria) 71–87
Afnan, Badia (Iraq) 71–87, 164
Africa Office of Equality Now 146
Aguilar, Carmela (Peru) 71–87, 163
Albright, Madeleine (US) 148, 149, 156n140, 157
Alekseevna Popova, Elizavieta (USSR) 60–64
All India Women's Conference (AIWC) 48, 73, 83n16
All Women's Association of Pakistan (AWPA) 73
Amrit Kaur, Rajkumari (India) 47
Anstee, Dame Margaret (UK) 139–160
Arria Formula meeting 139–160
Asiatic Land Tenure and Indian Representation Act ('Ghetto Act') 40, 50n7
Atlantic Charter 7
Ávila Camacho, Manuel (Mexico) 7
Azikiwe, Nnamdi (Nigeria) 79

Balmaceda, Esperanza (Mexico) 6
Bandaranaike Prime Minister Sirimave (Sri Lanka) 93
Bandung Conference 91
Barrios de Chungara, Domitila (Bolivia) 94
Begtrup, Bodil (Denmark) 60, 62, 90, 127, 135n9, 138
Beijing Conference, 1995, 12, 98, 134, 146
Bernardino, Minerva (the Dominican Republic) xiii–xxv, 1–16, 17–38, 49, 58, 60, 127, 165, 167n23, 168
Bose, Indira (India) 57
Bose, Krishna (India) 139–160

Boutros-Ghali, UN Secretary General Boutros 111, 121n28
Bravo, Marcia-Ximena (Ecuador) 92
'Brazilian Declaration' 10
Brett, Rachel (the Quakers) 132
Bretton Woods Conference 1–16
Bruce, Margaret (UK) 113

Cano, Gabirela (Mexico) 7, 14n28
Casselman, Cora (Canada) 8
Cassin, René (France) 75, 135n13
Chapman Catt, Carrie (US) 2, 32n43, 37
Charter on the Economic Rights and Duties of States 92
Chase Smith, Margaret (US Senate) 65
Ciselet, Georgette (Belgium) 129, 136n24, 138
Coalition of Latin American Women 95
Committee on Women in World Affairs 59
Conference of Independent African States, 1958 104–124
Congreso Inter-Americano de Mujeres, Panama City, 1926 1–16
Convention Against Torture 132
Convention for the Suppression of the Traffic in Persons and of the Exploitation of the Prostitution of Others, 1950 71–87
Convention of Belém do Para, 1994 12
Convention on Consent to Marriage, Minimum Age for Marriage, and Registration of Marriages 1962 71–87, 128
Convention on the Elimination of All Forms of Discrimination Against Women (CEDAW), 1979 104–124
Convention on the Political Rights of Women (CPW), 1952 55–70, 71–87, 125–138, 165

Convention on the Rights of the Child 72, 125–138
Convention on the Suppression of and Circulation of Obscene Publications 90
Convention on the Traffic of Women and Children 90
Corbett Ashby, Margery (UK) 17–38
Couette, Marie (U.S, WFTU) 55–70
Council on Women in Development (Ghana) 111
Covenant of the League of Nations 22, 90, 103

Dahlitz, Julie (Australia) 91
Dayton Peace negotiations 148
de Castillo Ledón, Amalia (Mexico) xiii–xvii, 1–16, 17–38, 49, 55–70
Declaration of Fundamental rights (India) 47
Declaration of Mexico on the Equality of Women and Their Contribution to Development and Peace 96
Declaration of the Rights of the Child 126–138
Declaration on the Elimination of All forms of Discrimination Against Women (DEDAW), 1967 163–164, 104–124
Defense for Children International 132
Dembinska, Zofia (Poland) 106, 120n10
Department of Economic and Social Affairs 141
Department of Women's Affairs 139
de Pérez Diaz, Lucila L. (Venezuela) 21
Devi, Phoolan (India) 143, 153n55, 153n56, 159
Division of the Advancement of Women (DAW) 141
Domínguez Navarro, Ofelia (Cuba) 3, 13n8, 15n58, 16
DuBois, W.E.B 109
Dumbarton Oaks Conference xix–xxv, 1–16, 162
Durrant, Patricia (Jamaica) 139–160

Echeverría, President Luis (Mexico) 92–93
ECOMOG Mission in Sierra Leone 146
Economic and Social Council (ECOSOC) 10, 58, 60–62, 92, 120n12
Embareck Warzazi, Halima (Morocco) 133
Encuentros feministass Latinamericanos y del Caribe 12
Equal Rights Amendment (ERA) 1–16, 55–70

Equal Rights Treaty 1–16
Estado Novo 5
EU Committee on Women's Rights and Equal Opportunities 147

Falcon, Minerva (the Philippines) 104–124
Fares Ibrahim, Emelie (Lebanon, WIDF) 55–70
Federação Brasiliera pelo Profresso Feminino (FBPF) 13n1, 21
Federation of African Women's Peace Movements 146
Figueroa, Ana (Chile) 49
Flor, Patricia (Germany) 139–160
Formoso de Obregón Santacilia, Adela (Mexico) 8, 21
Four Freedoms 7
Fraser, Arvonne (US) 104–124
Frente Único Pro-Derechos de la Mujer (FUPDM) 6
Friedan, Betty (US) 94, 110
Fritsche, Claudia (Lichtenstein) 139–160

Ghana Organization of Women 109
Gildersleeve, Virginia (US) xix–xxv, 1–16, 17–38, 55–70, 164
Ginsburg, Ruth Bader 110
González, Clara (Panama) 3–4, 13n7
Grčić Polić, Jelena (Crotia) 139–160
Great Depression 5
Greenbelt movement 165–166
Group of 77, 104–124, 165
Gruda Skard, Åse (Norway) xiii–xvii, 17–38, 162

Hague Appeal for Peace 147
Hamid Ali, Shareefah (India) 164, 39–54
Heyzer, Noeleen (Singapore) 139–160
Hicks Stiehm, Judith (academic) 139–160
Hofmann, Paul (NYT reporter to the UN) 129
Horbal, Koryne (US) 117
Hosbrugh, Frances (UK) 9
Humphrey, John (Canada) 71–87
Hussein, Aziza (Egypt) 76, 120n10, 164
Hutar, Patricia (US) 91

Iiyambo, Aina 139–160
Indian Parliamentary Standing Committee on External Affairs 149
Inter-African Committee on Traditional Practices Affecting the Health of Women and Children (IAC) 139, 163

Inter-Allied Suffrage Conference 89
Inter-American Commission of Women
  (CIM) xix–xxv, 1–16, 17–38
International Alliance of Women 17–38
International Catholic Child Bureau
  131–132
International Commission of Jurists in Rio
  de Janeiro, 1927, 3
International Convention on the
  Elimination of All Forms of Racial
  Discrimination (ICERD), 1965
  114–117
International Covenant on Civil and
  Political Rights (ICCPR) 106,
  120n11
International Covenant on Economic, Social
  and Cultural Rights (ICESCR) 106
International Day against Violence against
  Women 12
International Federation of Women
  Lawyers 132
International Labor Organization (ILO)
  55–70, 128
International Tribunal on Crimes against
  Women 98
International welfare feminism 55–70,
  161–168
International Women's Conference in
  Istanbul, 1935 47
International Women's Congress (in
  Buenos Aires, 1910) 2, 89
International Women's Council 71–87, 126
International Women's Peace Centre 150,
  156n175, 158–159
International Women's Year Conference
  in Mexico City, 1975 xvi, 12, 16,
  74, 88–103, 104–124, 130,
  136n30, 137
International Year of the Child, 1979
  125–138

Jebb, Eglantyne (UK) Save the Children
  Fund 125, 135n4, 138
Jiagge, Annie (Ghana) 104–124, 163–164
Joint Select Committee on Indian
  Constitutional Reforms of the
  British Parliament 47
Jurdak, Angela (Lebanon) 71–87

Kenyon, Dorothy (US) 39–54, 55–70
King, Angela (Jamaica) 139–160
Klompé, Marga (the Netherlands) 127
Kollontai, Alexandra (USSR) 6, 94

Labouisse, Henri (Executive Director,
  UNICEF) 131
Lakshmi Pandit, Vijaya (India) xi,
  39–54, 164
Lavelle Urbino, Marina (Mexico) 106
League of Nations 1–16, 17–38, 39–54,
  57, 67n14, 69, 82n3, 86, 90,
  103, 126
League of Nations General Assembly 6
League of United Latin American Citizens
  (LULAC) 9
Liaquat Ali Khan, Ra'ana (Pakistan)
  71–87, 164
Lima Declaration 6
London Committee of the Women's India
  Association 47
Lutz, Bertha (Brazil) x–xi, xiii–xvii,
  xix–xxv, 1–16, 17–38, 58, 90,
  162, 164

Maathai, Wangari (Kenya) 165–166
Madoe Sivomey, Marie (Togo) 74,
  84n22
Malik, Kenan (Lebanon) 60
Martin Cissé, Jean (Guinea) 71–87
Marzuki, Artati (Indonesia) 76, 82
Mbikusita-Lewanika, Inonge (Zambia)
  139–160
Mehta, Hansa (India) 11, 39–54, 55, 73,
  82, 83n16, 84n20, 164
Méndez, Luz (Guatemala) 139–160
Menon, Lakshmi (India) 39–54, 55–70,
  71–87, 164
Mironova, Zoya V. (USSR) 73, 129
Moerman, Canon Joseph 131, 136n40
*Movimiento pro la Emancipación de la
  Mujer Chilena* (MEMCh) 6
Mukherjee, Sharita (ILO, India) 53, 62
Murray, Pauli 104–124
Mya Sein, Daw (Burma) 81
Myrdal, Alva, (Sweden) 66,
  69n66–69n67

Namibia Plan of Action 139–160
Nandi-Ndaitwah, Netumbo (Namibia)
  139–160
Nardi, Shulamit (Israel) 78
Natal Indian Congress 39–54
Natarajan, Mr. (India) 44
National Association for the
  Advancement of Colored People
  (NAACP) 9, 41, 110
National Union of Guatemalan
  Women 146

Ndeyapo Ashipala-Musavyi, Selma
        (Namibia) 139–160, 161–168
Ndiliawike Nashandi, Monica (Namibia)
        139–160
New International Economic Order
        88–103, 115, 130, 163
Nikolaeva, Tatiana (Russia) 114
Nkrumah, Kwame (Ghana) 108–111
Non-Aligned Movement 91–96

Ocloo, Esther Afua (Ghana) 111
Ojeda Paullada, Attorney General Pedro
        (Mexico) 93–94
Optional Protocol to the UN
        Convention on the Elimination of
        All Forms of Discrimination
        Against Women (OP-CEDAW)
        139, 151n9, 159
Organization of African Women's
        Committee on Peace and
        Democratization 146
Organization of American States 12

Pahlavi, Princess Ashraf 105–106, 115,
        120n10, 122n50
Pan-American Chapultepec Conference on
        War and Peace, 1945 7
Pan-American Conference in Bogota,
        1948 9, 11, 162
Pan-American Conference in Rio de
        Janeiro, 1942 7, 9, 162
Pan-American Conference in Santiago,
        1923 9, 162
Pan-American Feminism 1–16, 31n1,
        32n34, 37
Pan-American Women's Congress
        (in Baltimore), 1922 8
Paris Peace Conference, 1919 92
Paul, Alice (US) 3, 13n9, 90
Pavlov, Alexei (USSR) 127
Persinger, Mildred (US) 92, 121n26
Philadelphia Declaration on women's
        rights, 1944 58
Piedad Castillo de Leví, María (Ecuador) 8
Pinto de Vidal, Isabel (Uruguay) 8
Pleic, Ratko (Yugoslavia) 127
Popular-Front Pan-American Feminism 1–16
Price-Cohen, Cynthia (the Human Rights
        Internet) 130–138

Ramaswami Mudaliar, Arcot (India) 10
Ramos Shahani, Leticia (the Philippines)
        104–124, 161–168

Ras-Work, Berhane (Ethiopia) 133, 163
Reddy, Muthulakshmi (India) 47
Reid, Elizabeth (Australia) 91
Resolution 843, 71, 82n1
Romulo, Carlos P. (the Philippines) 114,
        123n54
Roosevelt, Eleonor (US) 11, 25, 43–44,
        55, 57, 73, 83n16, 110, 164
Roosevelt, Franklin D. (US) 7
Royal Commission on Human
        Relationships, 1974 81, 85n72, 86
Rustin, Bayard 109

Sánchez de Urdaneta, Isabel (Venezuela)
        8, 21
Santos-Pais, Marta (UN Special
        Representative) 132
Seventh International Conference of
        American States in Montevideo,
        1933 5
Sherman-Peter, Missouri (Bahamas) 147
Sieu-Ling Zung, Cecilia (China) 61
Sipila, Helvi (Finland) 115, 117, 120n10
Sivomey, Marie (Togo) 71–87
Smuts, Marschall Jan xv, 22
Spanish Civil War 5
Stevens, Doris (US) 4, 13n9, 13n15
Street, Jessie (Australia) xxv, 1–16, 17–38
Sundaram, Lankan (India) 44
Supplemental Convention Slavery, 1956
        77, 85n47
Sutherland, Mary (UK) 55–70
SWAPO Observer Mission to the UN 140
Swedish Ministry for Foreign Affairs 142

Third International Conference for India,
        1993 47, 52n63
Third World Conference on Women in
        Nairobi 117
Tillett, Gladys (US) 78
Tomlinson, Ruth (UK) 49

*Unidad Revolucionaria Nacional
        Guatemalteca* (URNG) 146–147,
        155n123, 158
Union of Togolese Women (UFEMTO) 74
United Nations International Research and
        Training Institute for the
        Advancement of Women
        (INSTRAW) 115, 122n44
United Nations Secretariat's Division
        on the Advancement of
        Women 115

United Nations Security Council Resolution
on women, peace and security
(UNSCR 1325) 139–160, 161–168
United Nations Transitional Assistance
Group (UNTAG) 139–160
United Women of the Tribune 95

Valdez-Ramos, Angela (the Philippines) 112
van Bueren, Geraldine (Amnesty
International) 132
Vienna Conference on Human Rights,
1993 134

Wachuku, Prince Jaja (Nigeria) 79
Waldheim, UN Secretary General Kurt
(Austria) 93, 115, 117, 123n54, 131
Wensley, Penny (Australia) 139–160
Wilkinson, Ellen (UK) 9
Windhoek Declaration and Plan of Action,
May 2000 139–160
Women Against Imperialism 95
Women's Bureau Coalition 59
Women's Commission for Refugee
Women and Children 147
Women's International Democratic
Federation (WIDF) 55–70

Women's International League for Peace
and Freedom (WILPF) 146,
156n160, 160
Women's World Banking 111,
121n26, 124
Wood, McKinnon (UK) 90
World Committee of Women against War
and Fascism, 1934 6
World Conference on Human Rights in
Teheran, 1968 130
World Conference on Human Rights in
Vienna, 1993 72
World Federation of Trade Unions
(WFTU) 55–70
World Health Organization (WHO)
55–70, 128
World Plan of Action 88–103
WTO Ministerial Conference, 1999 88

Yi-Fang, Wu (China) xv, 8, 162
Young Women's Christian Association
(YWCA) 108

Zanzibar African Women's Peace
Declaration 146